144165

# THE TANGLED WEB THEY WEAVE

# THE
# TANGLED WEB
# THEY WEAVE

## TRUTH, FALSITY,
## AND ADVERTISERS

*Ivan L. Preston*

The University of Wisconsin Press

The University of Wisconsin Press
114 North Murray Street
Madison, Wisconsin 53715

3 Henrietta Street
London WC2E 8LU, England

2    4    6    8    10    9    7    5    3    1

Printed in the United States of America


Library of Congress Cataloging-in-Publication Data
Preston, Ivan L., 1931–
The tangled web they weave: truth, falsity, and advertisers /
Ivan L. Preston.
236 p.        cm.
Includes bibliographical references and index.
ISBN 0-299-14190-X (cloth)
1. Advertising, Fraudulent—United States.   2. Advertising laws—
United States.   3. Advertising—United States.   I. Title.
KF1614.P74        1994
343.73'082—dc20
[347.30382]        93-39166

# CONTENTS

# ACKNOWLEDGMENTS

A number of people have helped with useful comments at various stages of my writing. In particular Vincent Norris offered extensive advice based on his background in advertising's role in society. Many additional observations came from Kim Rotzoll, Gerald Thain, Connie Pechmann, Keri Shotola, and Debbie Friedman. When I distributed drafts of this work in my University of Wisconsin course on advertising law, I was rewarded by my students with very fruitful discussions on what to keep and what to change. A statement by one of them, Nick Davis, was so pertinent and well expressed that I quote it in Chapter 38. Finally, my wife Robbie served many times as a sounding board for ideas in progress, and I dedicate this work, as before, to her and our family.

THE TANGLED WEB THEY WEAVE

# INTRODUCTION:
# THE FALSITY IN OUR LIVES

*Oh, what a tangled web we weave,*
*When first we practice to deceive!*
—Sir Walter Scott, *Marmion*

This book is about falsity, with which our lives are flooded—primarily falsity in advertising, because that's what I'm familiar with. Advertising may contribute more to the flood than any other type of communication we encounter.

It's not my intention to inform the public that advertising can be false or at least phony—most consumers already know that. Nor do I intend to inform them that there's a law against false advertising. They know that, too. Most people, though, don't know which false claims are illegal and which others are legal. They probably don't even know that false claims *can* be legal. They don't realize that the law goes so far and no farther, stopping much falsity but also leaving a lot for the public to cope with on its own.

I will show how good the law is at eliminating *some* falsity. I will also show that it permits, and therefore encourages, much content that is either false or at least seriously deficient in truth. The law defines falsity very narrowly, allowing many claims that you and I might prefer to have disallowed. The result is harmful because it forces us to make buying decisions with bad information and with less than a full supply of good information. It causes us to distrust sellers when we need to be able to rely on them.

The tangled web of my title is the jumble of claims the advertisers create in their generally successful attempt to avoid illegal falsity while also avoiding large portions of the truth. An advertising claim that merely avoids illegal falsity has taken only one small step toward being a true claim in any meaningful sense. Many advertisers take that first step, but often it is the only step they take.

This book is as much about the truth that's missing as it is about the falsity that's present. Advertisers would love to have us think that their messages that are not illegally false must therefore be true. In a technical sense that may be so, but the degree of truth is often sadly small. We would be wiser to recognize the falsity in messages that convey a diminished form of truth, and thus carry a diminished significance for us consumers.

Having observed the many forms of falsity in our daily lives, I've

3

decided that it's quite resistant to going away. I used to think if you exposed falsity the perpetrators would feel so embarrassed that they would hang their heads and never deceive us again. That's not so, at least not in the marketplace, which has a limited capacity for embarrassment.

I suppose my expectations had to do with the shame I felt when caught lying as a child. Kids in my community couldn't get away with lying, not with my parents or with any of my friends' parents. We'd be punished. But that doesn't seem to apply to sellers. Too bad their parents aren't lurking around.

That lack of restraint seems to apply to many people these days, such as politicians and other public figures. They seem to think it's okay to lie. I'm tempted to comment on the matter broadly, but I'm also limited by having been professionally involved only with advertising—I worked in the field, and now I teach the subject at a university. I'll have to leave the bulk of falsity to the social scientists, philosophers, and others who examine society at large. I'll concentrate on describing what happens when sellers communicate with buyers.

The law supports advertisers in defending a great deal of falsity as legally acceptable. For that reason, the level of truthfulness is controlled primarily by the law rather than by the sellers themselves. The government regulators apparently interpret all of us as tolerating a lot of falsity. That makes things very hard for advertising's critics, who have to take on not just the marketplace but also its regulators, two powerful forces rather than just one. Those who have tried have found the combination so difficult to fight that it makes me fear that most of the falsity will be around forever.

So I'll make my comments on the matter without going into a big tirade. Just treat it as a fact of life. Tell stories about it. You'll laugh and you'll groan and you'll learn some facts, and maybe some of you will feel inclined to do something about it.

Maybe we can even get the advertisers to do something about it. That's a long shot, to be sure. Still, change is a possibility because many of the stories told here will make the falsifiers seem quite ludicrous. Plain factual descriptions of their adventures might do the job. Let's see if we can heighten the embarrassment to a level they can't ignore.

If the advertisers won't budge, then perhaps the government can help us more than it has. My proposals (chap. 46) for how it could do so involve a new conception of how to identify falsity. I base the proposals on how we consumers really act rather than on the law's erroneous assumptions about how we act. The law thinks we distrust many advertising claims—that's nonsense!

If the regulators won't budge either, then we consumers will have to help ourselves. I'll show you how to recognize how far the marketers will go in making claims, and make some suggestions for what we can do about falsity in advertising on our own.

That things certainly need doing is the message I would like to have this book leave. A system that accepts falsity routinely is not one that we should tolerate routinely.

# PART 1

## HOW ADVERTISING
## IS REGULATED

*This opening part identifies the regulators and gives the elements of their operations. It describes how they define and detect advertising deceptiveness by a process that is more subtle than simply declaring a claim to be false. The regulators must collect evidence not only about ad claims and products but also about consumers' perceptions of products as shaped by those claims. Speculating about what's in consumers' heads, or looking into their heads to the extent possible, is a big part of the process.*

*Several later parts criticize the regulatory process for failing to identify all types of deceptiveness. However, to emphasize that the process is often carried out successfully, a number of classic deceptiveness cases are scattered throughout the book. They are told in self-contained chapters; in this part they are in chapters 3 and 6. Citations for these and all other cases appear in the References section.*

# 1

# THE ELEMENTS OF DECEPTIVENESS LAW

Let's look first at the process that regulates advertising claims. I have said that the law permits many falsities, but it also prohibits many. First I'll devote some time to showing how the law stops what it stops. Eventually I'll use that background to show why it allows what it allows.

I identify the regulators, who are the principal actors in our story, a bit broadly in this book. I use the term here to include all those who make decisions on deceptiveness. At the Federal Trade Commission (FTC), the U.S. government agency headquartered in Washington, D.C., the key regulators are its commissioners and judges. Comparable officials run the states' consumer protection offices, which typically follow FTC procedures.

I'm also including as regulators the federal trial judges in whose courts advertisers bring private suits against each other. The suits are called Lanham cases because they are authorized by the federal Lanham Trademark Act. The cases involve the plaintiff advertiser, who brings the complaint, and the defendant advertiser. Advertisers need not use this procedure, because they are always free to seek action from the FTC, which protects competitors as well as consumers. However, advertisers frequently volunteer to become Lanham plaintiffs at their own expense because they are not certain that the FTC or the states will pursue the precise action and speed they desire.

Included as regulators as well are the courts that hear appeals. Advertisers may have their cases reviewed if the FTC, the states, or the Lanham trial courts find violations. Appeals occasionally advance to the U.S. Supreme Court. The National Advertising Division of the Council of Better Business Bureaus is also a regulator in a sense because it carries out advertising's self-regulation program. Virtually all advertisers honor their industry's request to submit voluntarily to this program's judgments. Although its decisions have no force of law, they have resulted in stopping many questioned claims.

Asked what regulators regulate, many readers will say "false advertising." That's fine for ordinary usage, but technically it's better to use the term *deceptive advertising*. By strict definition *false* means only claims that are explicitly, literally false. However, ads also make claims that are explicitly true but produce false meanings. Suppose an ad for diet food claims the product can reduce your weight. Could it be suggesting falsely, for example, that the product alone will reduce your weight without your doing anything else?

Consumers often see an ad make such an additional claim even though the ad doesn't explicitly state it. In this case the added claim is

false because you can't accomplish weight reduction without also reducing your calorie intake. Along with eating the diet food, you must
stop eating other things. The ad is not "false on its face," yet what it
conveys to consumers is false. For that reason the law finds it necessary
to prosecute both explicit and conveyed falsity. Since the phrase *false
advertising* might imply only the first kind, we customarily use the
broader term deceptive advertising.

What the FTC may prohibit is defined by law as "deceptive acts or
practices." The commission interprets an *act* as not noticeably different
from a *practice*, in practice. The law often uses two terms where one
might do, apparently seeing differences most of us would hardly recognize. The custom is no doubt encouraged by the Ways and Means Committee. Deceptive acts or practices are sometimes called *misleading*,
which creates another set of virtual twins. The same thing happens
with *cease and desist,* which is what the regulators tell advertisers to do
with their deceptive acts or practices. I looked up *desist* in my dictionary
and found that it means "cease."

The FTC may prohibit *unfair* as well as deceptive acts or practices,
and those two terms are really different. Of course it's unfair to be
deceptive, but the former is interpreted as referring to other unfairness. Such unfairness is not often applied, however, so this book ignores it.

An act or practice is legally deceptive when it deceives people, or
when it is merely likely to do so. Regulators choose most often to show
the latter because it's easier to prove. Also, they want to stop the acts
and practices before anybody gets hurt. The need to prove only the
potential means in theory that they can open a case on the first day an
ad appears. In practice, of course, bureaucratic procedures take many
days or months, sometimes years, so in reality any ad that may deceive
has probably done so with numerous people by the time it's prohibited. Nevertheless, the law need prove only the likeliness of deception,
the potential to deceive, deceptive*ness.*

Of course a mere potential may not create harm, which happens
only after consumers believe a false claim and act on it. Sometimes, as
with slapstick jokes that are obviously false, belief by consumers seems
utterly unlikely; actual deceptiveness would be impossible. So, when
the regulators examine a false claim that they assume consumers will
disbelieve, they typically dismiss it as having no potential to deceive.

To make their case, the regulators must first show evidence of what
advertising was run. Getting print copies or tapes of ads is not a problem because legal rights to investigation require advertisers to supply
such things on request. In addition, the FTC monitors many magazines

and some newspapers and receives copies in pictureboard form of television ads run by the major networks. The states do similar monitoring in their own areas.

While national advertising is easy for the FTC to track, local advertising is less so. Car dealers and other retailers get heavy scrutiny around Washington, where it's not unusual for congressmen to call in complaints. Elsewhere local advertising will often escape federal notice. Although the FTC has offices in several major cities, large areas remain outside its ability to monitor. Furthermore a federal agency may not act unless violations affect business in more than one state. For these reasons, the consumer protection offices of the individual states play a heavy role in handling local ads.

Once they establish what the ads say, you might think the regulators need only to compare the claim to the item advertised. If they find that the claim matches the actual features, they call it true and acceptable. If they find a contradiction, the claim is false and illegal, and they may prohibit it. That would be simple indeed, but that's not what they do. Instead, they must decide what is inside consumers' heads, what consumers saw the ad to be claiming. Naive advertisers may think they're responsible for no more than what they specifically stated, their literal words. On dealing with the regulators they quickly find that what the public saw and heard them saying is what counts.

Naturally, looking for the claims that ads convey makes the job more complicated. It's much harder to see inside the head of a human being than to identify what a piece of print or tape is saying. Advertisers often exploit this difficulty by protesting that they did not convey a certain message, and occasionally they win such arguments. They can never escape the rule, however, that any message consumers get from an ad is just as much its real message as if the ad had explicitly stated it.

After the regulators determine what the ad conveyed, they sometimes also determine whether consumers believed it and relied upon it. Such information could help show whether the claim will harm consumers if false. However, the regulators need not prove actual belief and reliance, nor is evidence on such points often available anyway. Unless they see that the claim is a joke or other variety of obvious falsity, they typically assume that it has a potential to be believed and relied upon by consumers.

Such an assumption could lead to errors, because straightforward nonjoking claims can be factual but have little or no chance of being believed. Perhaps consumers have prior information from other sources that prompts them to disbelieve the claim. Although the regulators detect such a situation occasionally, they most often persist in assuming the potential for belief. Advertisers typically have not challenged the regulators to produce proof rather than presumption on this matter.

After finding what's conveyed, the regulators examine the relevant facts about the product or service. If those facts are contrary to the conveyed claim, the law may call the claim illegally deceptive and prohibit its further use. The advertiser pays no penalty for its actions up to the time of such an order. It can be punished, however, if it runs the claim later in violation of that order. Although a few such violations occur and result in fines, most advertisers permanently cease the claim.

Thus the law has eliminated a great deal of potentially harmful advertising. It has greatly reduced the cheating.

## 2

# HOW MANY CONSUMERS MUST BE DECEIVED?

The process just described sounds so simple! The ad regulators merely find what consumers see an ad to be telling them and find whether that conveyed claim is true or false. If it's true, everything's okay. If it's false, it's unlawfully deceptive and the advertiser must stop. Basically that's it, but we must absorb some additional details that make it a little less simple.

For one thing, the regulators may decide that an ad conveys a claim to consumers, though not to all consumers. Let's say an ad stated explicitly, "Our car has the new X-10 engine." While the regulators find that all consumers saw that message conveyed, they also find that 99 percent saw the ad making another claim that was not explicitly stated. The second claim, which is that the new engine has features that no other engine has, is false and the regulators want to prohibit it.

Will they have any problem, though, with the fact that 1 percent of the car-buying public did not see the ad conveying that second message? That small minority agreed with everyone else that the engine had a new name, but they did not see the ad as stating that the engine had any other new feature. What do the regulators do about these people to whom no falsity was conveyed?

The answer to that question is easy: The 1 percent won't matter. The law will rule that the claim was conveyed to consumers generally, and the regulatory process will advance predictably to the finding of a violation. But what if just 80 percent saw the false claim conveyed? The 80 percent is almost as overwhelming a number as 99 percent, but the remaining 20 percent is certainly more significant than a mere 1 percent.

Let's make the example even harder: What if only 40 percent saw the claim? That's still a lot of people, but it's no longer a majority. Can the law treat such a smaller percentage as a fair representation of the whole population of consumers? It's becoming more difficult to decide. We are being forced to recognize that consumers aren't all alike, which means we must reflect the typical or average response they make to ads. Advertising claims hardly ever seem true or false to everybody, although often they will seem to be one or the other for nearly everybody. Other times, the group seeing truth and the group seeing falsity will both be large enough to be important.

What should the rule be when the people seeing a false claim are only a minority, although a significantly large one? Should we say that a majority is necessary, as in electing candidates? Should we require a larger percentage, such as two-thirds or three-quarters? Legislatures often do the latter, to assure that decisions more closely represent the true will of the people.

The FTC, which by law must act in the public interest, follows another line of argument. It decides that it will best fulfill that mandate by recognizing quite small percentages, often in the area of 20 to 25 percent. The federal trial courts adopt an even smaller minimum for Lanham Act cases, 15 percent. The result is that the law may interpret an ad claim as conveyed for legal purposes even though it is not seen conveyed by 75 to 80 percent of the public, for the FTC, or 85 percent, for Lanham cases. Advertising people have yelled bloody murder about that, and certainly have some basis for doing so.

If only a few consumers see a claim conveyed, it might be through what could fairly be called their faulty response. It could be inattention, poor listening, carelessness, stupidity, ill will toward the advertiser, whatever. If it is the consumers who are committing such actions, why should the law hold the advertisers responsible? The FTC has a ready answer for that. It says its mandate is to prevent the possible deception of any group that is large enough, even though a minority, to represent the public interest.

The Supreme Court has validated the FTC's thumbing-of-the-nose at past precedent in this area. To explain the process, I want to tell a story that goes far back in legal lore to examine a traditional way of defining the public interest. It lies in a rule called, in all its current political incorrectness, the reasonable man standard. I will take you back in time to it, bring you up to date on it, and use another name for it.

The *reasonable person standard* of Anglo-American law has held for centuries that citizens must act sensibly and rationally. They must do what a reasonable person ought to do. If they do not, they deserve and will receive no protection from the law. It means the regulators may find consumers to see an ad conveying a claim only if it also finds them acting reasonably in doing so.

The standard suggests that the FTC should choose a high percentage figure. It would not act on a low percentage because it would not interpret a small number of consumers as acting reasonably. There should be no good reason for a legal decision that the new name "X-10" implies new engine features if only 1 or 2 percent saw that claim conveyed. On the other hand, a high percentage would mean the claim must have been conveyed not just to unreasonable consumers but to many reasonable ones as well. You can't argue that the conveyance is only to unreasonable persons if the figure is 99 or even 80 percent.

The regulators do not necessarily use precise percentage figures in stating their conclusions. However, the reasonable person standard's general drift implies the requirement of some minimum percentage, which presumably is much higher than the FTC's 20–25 percent level. Let's assume, very conservatively, that over the centuries it has implied at least 51 percent.

When the FTC was created in 1914 it had to consider this prior legal rule. If it followed the rule, it could not call a claim deceptive unless the ad conveyed it to more than half the consumers. The early commissioners decided they did not like that. The commission had been born under a congressional mandate telling it to get serious about consumer protection. Members of Congress had specifically encouraged the FTC to interpret the law in new ways rather than clinging to old precedent. Accordingly, the first commissioners decided that the public interest required action even when a fairly low percentage of consumers saw a claim being made.

I think of this new approach as the ignorant person standard. *Ignorant* may mean different things, referring in some cases to just plain stupidity. It can also refer, though, to consumers acting sensibly to the extent of their knowledge, while having quite limited knowledge. Reflecting that, ignorant as I use it here simply means uninformed. Certainly many consumers are in that category, because numerous products, such as cars and electronics items, are very complex.

The FTC switched to the ignorant standard in part because the reasonable standard may actually be unreasonable in today's marketplace. We cannot sensibly expect that consumers will always act rationally, using all relevant information and interpreting it accurately.

Most of us probably can't do that no matter how hard we try. We would need far more extensive knowledge and experience than we could possibly find the time to acquire. We may have the capacity to acquire much information, but in practice we simply won't get around to it.

Consequently, the FTC decided to judge our behavior by what we *do* do rather than what we ought to do. It recognized that requiring us to do what we ought to do, although it's an ancient legal expectation, is unrealistic in today's world. What we do accomplish, even though it might often be dumber than it could be, should be the proper modern standard for evaluating our behavior.

A Supreme court case confirmed this approach. An encyclopedia claimed that its basic set of books was free even though the consumer would have to pay for ten years' worth of annual update volumes. The Court agreed with the seller's protest that very few consumers would take the claim of "free" literally. Most consumers, the Court found, would understand that the price covered everything. Nonetheless, the Court ruled that the perception of the few was reasonable because of consumers' lack of familiarity with such offers.

As Justice Hugo Black said in that decision, "The fact that a false statement may be obviously false to those who are trained and experienced does not change its character, nor take away its power to deceive others less experienced. There is no duty resting upon a citizen to suspect the honesty of those with whom he transacts business." That was a strong step toward achieving for consumers what they so badly need. As I said in the Introduction, consumers must be able to rely on advertisers rather than being prompted to distrust them.

For a decade or so the FTC interpreted Black broadly, prohibiting claims almost no one would see an ad to be saying. When Clairol advertised that it would "color hair permanently," the commission decided that the phrase conveyed to consumers the false claim of coloring all hair to be grown for the rest of the user's entire lifetime. The available evidence was that one person—not 1 percent, just one person—testified that some consumers, although not herself, would see that message.

Such cases have not been frequent in recent times and do not accurately indicate current practice. The commission soon cut back that very ignorant person standard to what we might think of as a normally ignorant person standard. It said in effect that a certain number of ignorant persons would have to see the false claim conveyed. The regulators endorse no exact number and determine each case separately on its unique circumstances.

However, the generalization from many decisions is that the required minimum percentage lies in the range of 20 to 25 in FTC cases, and as low as 15 in Lanham Act cases. An advertisement that conveys nothing false to the great majority of its readers can get in trouble for what the rest see. The ad community may find this infuriating but it knows it must live with it.

# 3

# THE SEARS DISHWASHER CASE

This is the first of a number of chapters in which I interrupt the flow temporarily to tell a classic story of advertising deceptiveness. The cases are chosen for the way they demonstrate the depths of falsity to which advertisers can go, both in their ad claims and in their subsequent legal defenses. The cases also demonstrate the power of the regulators in identifying and stopping the falsities.

For a number of years Sears, Roebuck & Co. advertised that its Kenmore dishwasher could completely clean dishes, pots, and pans "without prior rinsing or scraping." The dishes could be taken directly from the table, the pots directly from the stove. All you needed to do was remove any bones. The dishes could be "crusty with leftover food," but even many hours later you just put them in the machine, flipped the switch, and used your new freedom to enjoy all the things in life that are much more fun.

The Federal Trade Commission found the claim to be utterly false. It also found that Sears, the largest seller of home dishwashers, knew it was false. A company home economist had long since informed her superiors that "baked or burned-on soil" would require additional handling for complete removal. The company's own surveying had shown many buyers indicating that they, too, thought the claim was false.

Earlier surveying, though, informed Sears that consumers *wanted* a dishwasher that required no prerinsing or prescraping. Don't we all! Knowing the claim would be appealing—though false—the company went ahead with it. Consumers bought the machine, put dishes into it dirty, and took them back out, dirty. The claim cheated them by prompting them to pay money for a feature they did not receive. And it taught them to distrust advertising claims when they need to be able to rely on such claims. The result hurt Sears's competitors, too, by prompting consumers to ignore other brands that may have cleaned just as well but did not make the false claim.

Upon delivery of the dishwasher, well after placing the order,

Sears' customers received an owner's manual. It told them to presoak or scour baked-on foods, directly contradicting the ad claim. Later, at the FTC hearing, the company argued that the instruction was simply a mistake it couldn't explain. When asked how the mistake could have been retained in the manuals for years, the company said the reason was simply oversight or error. The FTC called the explanation "incredible." It said the source, a Sears executive, gave "self-serving and unreliable" testimony.

In the FTC hearing Sears maintained the claim was true and offered tests to support the dishwasher's performance. Many of the tests showed that the machine did not remove all the dirt. The company protested that it did the tests under "aggravated" conditions, meaning it used foods especially prepared to stick to dishes and pans. Therefore, it said, the finding that some food remained did not prove that similar failures would occur under conditions normally found in the home.

In other words, Sears called the tests inappropriate after originally calling them appropriate. The commission, however, found that Sears had dirtied the dishes prior to testing in a way suitably reflective of what happens in normal households. Further, the Association of Home Appliance Manufacturers had identified that method as appropriate for establishing a uniform standard for dishwasher performance. The FTC thought an industry organization would not create an unreasonable standard for its members to meet. Besides, the commission added, the advertising claimed that the dishwasher could remove the most difficult foods consumers might normally encounter. Shouldn't the tests have to verify that exact claim?

In total, Sears's tests failed to support the claim even though the company greatly biased the testing conditions in favor of doing so. The tests typically did not use as wide a range of foods as consumers would normally encounter. Some tests used foods easy to clean, but even those tests didn't always show complete cleaning. Other tests used higher water temperatures than consumers would use, indeed higher than consumers can obtain safely in their homes. The tests used lighter loads than many consumers would use.

Some tests used more detergent than the owners' manual recommended. Others used a rigged wash phase, longer than available in the dishwashers actually sold to consumers. Sometimes the testers placed the dishes horizontally, an approach favorable to Sears's interests but not to consumers' because the machine can hold only a few dishes that way. Some tests used water softener, but Sears was reluctant to say so. Its silence could imply that the performance was achievable with untreated water.

In some cases Sears reported test performance by providing photographs of the dishes and pans after washing. The FTC found photos to be inadequate evidence of whether the machine removed all soil (especially for the side away from the camera!). In other cases Sears introduced the dishes themselves as evidence, but the FTC said it was impossible to assess their cleanliness after so long a time. The company also offered tests of other dishwasher brands as evidence of the performance of its own. What such tests could say about Sears's own brand is hard to imagine.

The FTC found that Sears's legal counsel improperly participated in the formulation and conduct of these biased tests. It also found inadequate retention of records of some tests. One of the requirements of legitimate research in any field is that the method should be described thoroughly enough that later researchers can do a similar study to recheck the results. Confirmation by independent researchers is a major key to acceptability. With Sears's tests, however, so much information was missing that retesting would have been impossible.

None of the tests were legitimate; they simply did not pertain to the performance that consumers would get in their homes. Nevertheless, the company insisted in court that all of its evidence showed that the dishwasher would perform as advertised. If it had succeeded, the commission may have dropped the charges and the company would have been able to continue indefinitely making its deceptive claim.

Sears Roebuck & Co. is a nationally known retail firm with a long history of being charged with false advertising and other practices. The latest incident is the recent scandal involving unnecessary car repairs in its auto shops. Although its business has fallen some recently, it is a firm for which the American public retains a generally high regard!

# 4

# FINDING THE FACTS OF DECEPTIVENESS

Let's see how the FTC and other regulators determine the facts they must establish to find deceptiveness. You recall that the explicit content of a company's advertising is easy to identify because the ads are out there in public. In contrast, learning what claims consumers see conveyed by that content is difficult. Such information is locked away inside each of our heads. Learning whether the conveyed claims are true can also be difficult, because the evidence of a product's features is also often hard to see.

So how do the regulators learn these facts? You might think the area of their expertise ought to be nothing more than the law itself. They couldn't possibly be experts on all the facts about ads and consumers and products. They should obtain the latter facts, one would think, from those who *are* experts.

That's a sensible expectation, but the law nonetheless empowers the regulators to decide what the facts are. It does so because no one can apply a rule without first identifying the events to which it will be applied—the actions people took, statements they made, impacts that resulted, and so forth. For that reason, the law *presumes* the regulators to be experts in determining such facts. Legal observers have frequently questioned that presumption because so many regulators obviously lack the needed training and experience. Appeals courts have upheld the practice, however, because government simply cannot function without it.

Meanwhile, the process that appoints people to fill regulatory positions has not been responsive to the fact-finding obligation. In 1914, a senator sponsoring the legislation to create the Federal Trade Commission said, "It is expected that the trade commission will be composed not only of eminent lawyers but of eminent economists, business men of large experience, and publicists." I take the word *publicist* to be the then-current equivalent of what we today call a marketing communication expert.

No FTC commissioner has ever been such an expert. We can see the lack reflected in the comment of one of the law-trained appointees that "[t]here is no reason to believe that commissioners of the FTC have unusual capacity or experience in coping with questions of meaning [i.e., of what claims consumers see an ad to be conveying]." But despite such cautions, the commissioners and other regulators retain the legal right to decide what ads mean to consumers by looking nowhere but at the ads, even though no one can discover a consumer's perception of an ad by depending on the ad. That perception exists only in the consumer's head.

It's true that indirect judgments made by looking only at the ad are sometimes easy to make. An ad may say prominently, "This is an alcoholic beverage." If so, we may reasonably assume that the great majority of consumers will see the claim conveyed that the advertised beverage contains alcohol. Still, looking solely at the ad is often not an adequate substitute for looking inside consumers' heads. Among other reasons, an ad's words will not always be clear and conspicuous. They might be in very small type at the bottom of a print ad, or flashed briefly on the television screen. Consumers' eyes might never fall on such words.

An even more difficult problem is that the messages getting into consumers' heads are more than just ads' explicit claims. Ads also convey claims without making them explicitly. These *implied* claims are even harder to determine by looking at the ad alone. Because an implication is by definition not present in specific words, a sensible presumption could be that the consumer won't see what's not there to be seen. Advertisers enjoy that presumption; they use it to argue that what is conveyed consists of nothing more than what is stated explicitly.

Although winning that argument would keep the advertisers out of a lot of trouble, the law does not let them win it very often. Considerable expert evidence shows that consumers see advertisements conveying many claims that aren't specifically present. The regulators, although permitted to decide conveyed content by looking at nothing but the ad, have frequently used expert evidence to identify implied claims.

As we go on, we will see more about these difficulties in identifying deceptiveness. We will examine the process of thinking that leads consumers to see certain claims conveyed. We will look at the methods consumer behavior experts use to identify those claims. Eventually we will see that for some types of advertising content the process breaks down. It doesn't identify all the implied claims. I will show how the breakdown helps explain why advertising and its regulation are the way they are today.

The law makes it possible for consumers to trust many claims. At the same time, it leaves many others that will hurt those who trust them.

**5**

**LOOKING HORSES IN THEIR MOUTHS,
AND CONSUMERS IN THEIR HEADS**

Why do we see messages sent to us that are different from the messages actually sent? If they typically tell us much more than they actually state to us, it's because we do more with them than just see them. We also interpret their words and pictures; we take them to mean certain additional things because of the overall context.

In a recent television spot, a beer bottle as huge as a ship was floating in the ocean. A tugboat took it in tow to the delight of thirsty drinkers gathered on shore. The depiction defied reality; it was an impossible event in the context of the world as we know it. Presumably virtually all viewers disbelieved that such a bottle actually existed. We see the words and pictures of such a message, but we also see the total ad telling us it's only a joke. Most of us would take a dim view of anyone who thought a real event was being reported.

While that example involves taking a meaning away from the message, it's more common for our interpretations to create added meanings. Remember the claim, "Our car now has the X-10 engine." We may see that as saying the engine has features the previous model didn't have. Maybe it does, or maybe it has only one new feature, the name "X-10." The ad doesn't explicitly say that the claim means anything more than that.

Another ad discussed a feature of a new computer. Consumers might reasonably have seen such an ad to be claiming that the feature was for sale and they could buy the computer having it. Usually that would be true, but the FTC found that this particular computer had not yet been manufactured. The computer industry has a term for hardware or software items that exist only in the advertising—*vaporware.*

How does the FTC decide that an advertisement conveys a certain unstated claim? In the computer example we probably would not object if the FTC found the implied claim by looking only at the ad. Certainly the advertising of an item should ordinarily mean it's for sale— why else would it be advertised? The number of consumers who would see such a claim conveyed is surely many more than the minimum of 20–25 percent that the FTC requires.

However, not all cases are so easy. Suppose a brand of a product is claimed to be superior on one attribute; for example, a car's brakes are said to stop more quickly than those of any competitor. Does that imply the car is better overall? Does it convey the message that the car is better on some other attribute, such as giving a more comfortable ride? Does it imply that the car is better on all other attributes? These questions are harder to assess.

It's reasonable to expect some people would think those things. On the other hand, they aren't as obvious as the implication about the advertised item being for sale. Moreover, we must find how many people saw the claim conveyed, and then compare it to the percentage criteria specified by FTC or Lanham decisions (chap. 2). The difficulty these questions pose eventually forces us to remember that the only real way to see a meaning, a conveyed claim, is to look in the consumer's head, not in the ad.

Determining facts by looking rather than reasoning or speculating is one of the ways that distinguishes our modern life from the way people lived before. One of the foresighted persons who taught us how

to look was the philosopher Francis Bacon, who did so in part by telling
the following parable:

> In the year of our Lord 1432, there arose a grievous quarrel among the
> brethren over the number of teeth in the mouth of a horse. For 13 days the
> disputation raged without ceasing. All the ancient books and chronicles were
> fetched out, and wonderful and ponderous erudition, such as was never before
> heard of in this region, was made manifest.
>
> At the beginning of the 14th day, a youthful friar of goodly bearing asked
> his learned superiors for permission to add a word, and straightway, to the
> wonderment of the disputants, whose deep wisdom he sore vexed, he be-
> seeched them to unbend in a manner coarse and unheard of, and to look in the
> open mouth of a horse and find answer to their questionings.
>
> At this, their dignity being grievously hurt, they waxed exceedingly
> wroth; and, joining in a mighty uproar, they flew upon him and smote him hip
> and thigh, and cast him out forthwith. For, said they, surely Satan hath
> tempted this bold neophyte to declare unholy and unheard of ways of finding
> truth contrary to all the teachings of the fathers.
>
> After many days more of grievous strife the dove of peace sat on the assem-
> bly, and they as one man declared the problem to be an everlasting mystery
> because of a dearth of historical and theological evidence.

In 1965, well after the rise of scientific inquiry that Bacon fostered,
the Supreme Court ruled in an advertising case that there was no need
to survey the viewing public. Technically, the Court said only that there
was no need under certain circumstances, but later references interpreted the rule to cover all cases. To its credit, the FTC in the 1980s
realized the potential for trouble in that ruling. It decided that all parties, be they advertisers or consumers or anyone else, would be served
most satisfactorily by methods that obtain the best information.

The commission therefore decided to survey consumers often,
with results that this book will report. Nonetheless, it retains to this
day the privilege in all cases to count the horse's teeth without looking
at them.

# 6

# THE ASPERCREME
# (THOMPSON MEDICAL) CASE

What does the name Aspercreme convey to you? Your first hint is that
it's a product, although that won't help much. The "creme" portion
may indicate a creamy substance of some sort. What about the "Asper"

part? We better move on to the next hint: it's a pain relief product. Well, then, "Asper" must mean "aspirin." What else can you think when you see Aspercreme and pain relief associated! It's aspirin in the form of a creamy substance. I guess you rub it in, or rub it on, rather than swallowing it like regular aspirin.

Of course. If that's so, however, why did the Thompson Medical Company, Aspercreme's maker and inventor of its fascinating name, go to great lengths to argue before the FTC that the name and advertising do not convey to consumers that Aspercreme contains aspirin? Do you think maybe it's because Aspercreme *doesn't* contain aspirin?

Of course. Aspercreme's active ingredient was found to be triethanolamine salicylate, or trolamine salicylate, TEA/S for short. Its components are similar to those of aspirin, which chemically is acetylsalicylic acid, or acetylated salicylate. TEA/S has equal amounts of triethanolamine and salicylic acid. It's thus a salicylate with no acetyl group added—a nonacetylated salicylate. Do you think, however, that Thompson Medical saw a possible advantage in claiming that Aspercreme and aspirin, both being salicylates, were similar in their effects?

Once again: of course. Yet the FTC found no evidence that different salicylates work similarly. You simply can't claim that TEA/S does what aspirin does. Even if you could, it could be only under the assumption that both chemicals arrive in equal degrees at the muscle or other bodily component that hurts. But how else are aspirin and Aspercreme different? Ah, it's the matter of being a creamy substance. The FTC found that when people rubbed Aspercreme onto their bodies, most of the salicylate penetrated no farther than the dermis. That's the inner layer of skin, in contrast to the outer layer, the epidermis.

Thompson ran claims that Aspercreme "concentrates all the strong relief of aspirin directly at the point of pain." But Aspercreme got little or no salicylate beneath the skin and into the hurting body parts that a medicine must reach to relieve pain. It had what the scientists call a limited bioavailability. Further, it showed no sign of bioactivity, which in layman's terms means it doesn't work. Apparently any delivery that Aspercreme achieved was in quantities too small to relieve pain to a measurable degree.

Additional ad copy interpreted the reference to concentration as making a comparison that was negative to ordinary aspirin. Aspirin takes a long detour into the mouth and down the throat and into the stomach and into the bloodstream, meandering all over the body before it finally reaches your sore muscle. It's a wonder it ever gets there! Then, having dissipated its effects from all that travel, the aspirin presumably can have little impact at the one place where a person hurts. What's more, it upsets some stomachs!

The only problem with all that analysis, the FTC found, is that aspirin works and Aspercreme just plain doesn't. The faster delivery and avoidance of upset stomachs were technically true, but were being used as smoke screens, irrelevant to the main point. Aspercreme's claim to be superior to regular aspirin was false, cheating consumers and prompting them to distrust advertisers even though consumers need to be able to rely on them.

Did Thompson Medical know it was making these claims without evidence? Did it deliberately lie about them? Of course. That's a serious charge, so I'm going to quote exactly what the FTC said:

Thompson has known or should have known for some time now that its efficacy claims for Aspercreme are unsubstantiated. . . . Thompson has deliberately continued making efficacy claims despite this fact.

Likewise, it seems clear that Thompson deliberately sought to lead consumers into the belief that Aspercreme contains aspirin. . . . Thompson has known full well for some time that consumers misunderstood the identity of the principal ingredient in Aspercreme and has continued to advertise in a manner that creates more such misunderstanding.

Aspercreme was a phony product and its maker knew it. It also knew, or should have known as an expert in drugs, that the research it offered in defense of its false claims was equally phony. This research came to light in the FTC hearing in which Thompson defended against charges that it had no valid evidence of Aspercreme's effectiveness. It said it did have such evidence, consisting of clinical tests that compared drugs with each other by using them on patients and observing the results.

Thompson's tests found that users reported no difference in pain relief between Aspercreme and aspirin. That finding superficially would make Aspercreme equally as effective as aspirin, and it would support a claim that Aspercreme was superior to aspirin if it were also true that Aspercreme was delivered more quickly. However, we've already seen that the delivery claim was false, because Aspercreme didn't deliver the medicine in sufficient quantity.

The claim of being equally effective turned out to be unsupported, too. The logic Thompson offered was defective, because for a test to show no difference doesn't mean there is no difference. It was a matter of sampling in one test in which Thompson gave Aspercreme and aspirin to only twenty persons each. That's so few that equal effects are likely to result even if the two drugs really are different. The test was unable to reveal any differences.

Other Thompson research tested Aspercreme alone. Medical experts know that people are highly subjective and variable in reporting increase or decrease of pain. They also know that pain will spontaneously disappear in a short time even when people take no drug. Therefore a test is of no value if it simply measures pain both before and after use of the drug. A decrease in pain is not proof that the drug caused the decrease.

The scientific solution is to control the results by testing both the product and a placebo, the latter looking exactly like the product but lacking the active drug ingredient. Pain often disappears after people use such an item, and this "placebo effect" casts doubt on what happens when they use the active drug. If the test uses both drug and placebo, and the same pain relief occurs with both, the test shows the drug made no contribution. Only if the pain decreased with the drug and not with the placebo can the drug be proved effective.

You might suppose that in a test of two drugs, such as aspirin and Aspercreme, each could be the placebo for the other. However, the experts say that a finding of no difference between the two cannot distinguish between whether they were both equally effective or simply both ineffective. So that type of test needs a placebo, too. It can then prove one drug superior to another if that drug is superior to both the other and to the placebo.

Of course the users must be blinded so that they do not know whether they're getting the drug or the placebo. Better yet, they shouldn't even know that two versions exist. It's necessary also that the doctors who make the judgments be blinded; that's called double-blinding. The doctors should not know who gets what, and of course they should not know who is sponsoring the research and what results are sought.

The Thompson Medical tests lacked these various safeguards and thus were invalid. They did not produce legitimate evidence to support the advertising claim. The company also failed with reports it introduced about consumers indicating satisfaction with Aspercreme. The law considers such testimonial evidence worthless also, among other reasons because there is no way to eliminate the chance that the placebo effect influenced the results. Uncontrolled comments by consumers are no way to find out anything about drugs.

Thompson's tests also lacked adequate record keeping and reporting. That defect produced uncertainty about what kinds of people were involved, what drugs were given, what questions were asked or observations made, and what results really occurred. In some cases, the tested persons used or may have used other drugs that could have interacted with the test drugs and thus affected the results improperly. One research study involved two investigators in different locations, with the results later combined. Thompson, however, was unable to show that those two researchers followed the same instructions or conducted the test in the same manner.

In another Thompson test, the researcher developed a set of categories for analyzing the results only after seeing the data and determining how to manipulate them to favor Aspercreme. Fairness in testing requires the researchers to specify all aspects of their methodology in advance and to follow them without change to prevent a biased impact on the results.

In summary, the company offered no tests that were scientifically adequate. It simply had no support, and the FTC said it knew it had none, for its claims of Aspercreme's performance.

The quality of Thompson's research on the conveyed claim was equally low. It tried to show, by surveying consumers on what they see ads to be saying, that its ads had not claimed that Aspercreme contained aspirin. In two surveys conducted by the same research firm, Thompson asked consumers to name the ingredient in Aspercreme. That question was open-ended, that is, it invited people to give whatever answer they chose with no hints as to possible answers. Five percent or fewer said aspirin, probably because the ads had not mentioned aspirin explicitly. That favored Thompson's position.

The first of those two surveys also asked whether the ad said the product contained aspirin. That was a forced-choice question, making people choose from answers supplied by the surveyor—in this case Yes, No, or Don't Know. The FTC calls forced-choice questions more valid because they get people to respond specifically about the topic in question. Open-ended questions don't reliably get people to say what they know about the specific topic. Because the second question mentioned aspirin specifically, you would expect more affirmative answers than the 5 percent obtained from the first question. That was confirmed, with 22 percent answering Yes on the second question.

However, in the second survey Thompson omitted that question. Do you think maybe the higher figure had something to do with it? Of course. As the FTC decision said, "The evidence is consistent with the conclusion that the direct ingredient question was dropped because it had produced results unfavorable to Thompson." The commission thereupon accepted the 22 percent figure, which met the minimum requirement of 20–25 percent discussed in chapter 2. Thus it found that the surveying showed a significant number of persons saw the message that Aspercreme contained aspirin.

Another Thompson trick was to criticize a survey as unreliable for determining conveyed meanings. The FTC rejected the argument because Thompson had used that research for making an important business decision—picking which of a group of commercials to put on the air. The commission wouldn't allow Thompson to call research unsuitable that it had earlier treated as acceptable.

Thompson took its case to a U.S. court of appeals, claiming consumers didn't care whether Aspercreme contained aspirin, and besides, the labeling had always indicated the actual ingredient. The court said, "One wonders why Thompson is upset about being ordered to disclose that its product does not contain aspirin if no one cares and everyone has always known anyway." Thompson's argument, it said, "borders on the frivolous."

The court also had this rejoinder to Thompson's complaint that the FTC order would destroy its business: "Allowing firms to continue such advertising because to stop would hurt the firm's economic interests is obviously not part of [what] Congress intended the FTC to consider. Thompson has no right to stay in business if the only way it can do so is to engage in false and misleading advertising."

As with Sears, Thompson's cheating in the FTC hearing had a potential to further disadvantage consumers. Had the effort succeeded, Thompson would have been able to continue making claims that would prompt the public to spend money for a benefit that did not exist.

The company, with its Slim-Fast Food Cos. affiliate, was the seventy-first largest national advertiser recently, spending $137.5 million. Its major brands were Slim-Fast, Ultra Slim-Fast, and Dexatrim diet and nutrition products. It also marketed NP27, Cortizone-5, Cortizone-10, Sportscreme, Sleepinal, Aqua-Ban, Breathe Free, Tempo, Lactogest, Silk Solutions, and Arthritis Hot.

And it still sells Aspercreme. By that name. The FTC did not stop the usage because it decided that requiring an accompanying disclosure would be sufficient to dispel the falsity. The disclosure must state prominently and conspicuously that Aspercreme does not contain aspirin.

# PART 2

# DECEPTIVE IMPLICATIONS

*This part examines implications, which are a major cause of the complexities in identifying deceptiveness. Implications enable advertisers to make claims to consumers that go far beyond what their ads literally state. The literal content can be true, but the implication may be false. The chapters that follow describe the process of creating such implied claims; identify many varieties of them; assess their value to advertisers in gaining sales, as well as their harm to consumers in making purchases; and present two classic deceptive advertising cases.*

# 7

# IDENTIFYING IMPLICATIONS

Determining what claims ads convey to what percentage of consumers' minds is easy in some cases but hard in others. The difficulty depends on whether there are implied claims, which can't always be identified by looking only at the ad. The FTC has decided that in the hard cases it will insist on looking into the horse's mouth; it will look into consumers' heads to determine their perceptions of ads. That's a relief to us all. You'd feel the same way if your dentist decided not to count your cavities just by looking at your face.

The commission's exact rule is that for explicitly stated claims, and for implied claims that it can interpret with confidence, it can depend on intrinsic evidence, that is, it need look only at the ads. If it cannot decide confidently, it will insist on extrinsic evidence, or evidence apart from the ads. In the past extrinsic evidence often meant the testimony of individual consumers, but today the preferred method is the consumer survey.

A minor remaining problem is that the FTC retains the right to decide which cases are hard and which are not. If it decides wrongly that a case is not hard, it gets itself right back into the problems that occur from looking only at the ad. Despite that possibility, however, the commission's rule means that it looks into consumers' heads much more often than before.

The various states tend to follow the FTC's lead, though they are less likely to use surveys because they lack the expertise and the money. In Lanham Act cases in which advertisers sue each other, however, surveys are more likely than at the FTC because the federal courts that handle such cases have ruled that all decisions on implied claims require extrinsic evidence. They made that rule upon recognizing their own lack of the expertise that they presume the FTC to have on such questions.

The easiest implications to identify are those that ads imply logically. Suppose a headache remedy known from past consumer experience as having two active ingredients now advertises that it has two additional ingredients. The implication that it has four ingredients is easy to detect, because the meanings of the words simply require it. The same is true for logical relationships, such as the simple syllogism: if the ad claims that products with X ingredient are the best, and our brand has X, then the claim that our brand is the best cannot help being made even if not explicitly stated. Such implications are so virtually synonymous with explicit claims that the law typically will treat them as such.

Most of advertising's false implications, though, are not strictly logical in that way. Instead, they are *pragmatically* logical, that is, consumers reasonably infer the claims from the context or background of the ad. When Anacin's maker, American Home Products, argued that it was improper to charge it with implications not logically made, the FTC replied, "[T]he interpretations that AHP presses upon us rely primarily on technical readings of the advertisements. . . . AHP would have the Commission perform a 'semantic' analysis of the advertisements, whereas the Commission, consistently with settled law, is more interested in a 'pragmatic' analysis."

The same was true for the ad that implied falsely that a computer was for sale. Strict logic does not compel that implication. Yet the experience of consumers virtually demands that it be conveyed, because people do not expect an advertised item not to exist. (Well, in the computer field this ordinarily unreasonable expectation apparently occurs so often that experienced consumers now *do* expect it.)

Another pragmatic implication stems from statements on food packages that a serving of the product has so many calories or vitamins or minerals. Although we are free to feed ourselves different amounts, we generally expect the serving to be of a size that people typically use. *Consumer Reports,* though, discovered a brand of bread that identified a serving as three-quarters of a slice. Raise your hand if you've had a serving of bread lately!

A pain reliever called Efficin, from Adria Laboratories, claimed to "contain no aspirin." The claim was truthful, yet the active ingredient was chemically close to aspirin. You'll recall from chapter 6 that the active ingredient of Aspercreme, TEA/S, is too little related to aspirin. By contrast, Efficin's drug relates so closely to aspirin as to be capable of causing the same side effects. The FTC found a violation out of concern that the no-aspirin claim would make consumers think falsely, by pragmatic implication, that Efficin could have no such side effects.

Of course not all consumers will see pragmatic implications conveyed. You may have wondered about the finding that Aspercreme ads implied aspirin content to only 22 percent of those surveyed. That might seem a small number for such a suggestive name. Why wasn't it higher? The reason was that the ad contained conflicting elements that could convey different meanings. A product named Aspercreme would obviously suggest aspirin. On the other hand, the ad also had a statement that "Aspercreme contains salicyn, a strong non-aspirin pain reliever." That could have cut the number of aspirin perceptions.

On the *other* other hand, the latter statement was far less conspicuous than the product name. Also, it said only that salicyn was present while not saying that aspirin was absent. So, what parts of the total content did people see? And what additional implied content did they see? What experience or understanding might they have applied in formulating their perceptions? Given such a mess of conflicting possibilities, the FTC was wise to say that without consumer surveys it could not have decided whether the ads claimed that Aspercreme contained aspirin.

The principal defense offered by advertisers for implied claims is the simple protest "We didn't say it." Very often, though, the regulators decide they did say it in the sense that they implied it. The advertisers' next defense is that consumers must have been unreasonable in seeing the implication; they shouldn't have done so. Usually the advertisers mean that the claim wasn't logically implied, thus consumers couldn't reasonably have seen it to be implied.

Unfortunately for that position, the regulators have identified many pragmatic implications that they feel are reasonably implied. Identifying such implications, and removing them when they are false, has gone a long way in allowing consumers to trust and rely on advertisers' claims.

# 8

# THE VOLVO CASE

The Swedish firm Volvo makes automobiles that attract attention. Recently its ads attracted even more attention. "Ad industry suffers crushing blow" was how a headline in *Advertising Age* put it. That must have been some accomplishment! It must also have been some memory failure! It meant doing what virtually every other American advertiser learned years ago not to do. The law has been clear for decades—do this and get clobbered. The issue went all the way to the Supreme Court, and the justices agreed. But heck, Volvo did it anyway.

Some advertisers just perpetuate falsity. One of their group gets caught and punished, and then another goes and does the same thing. There must be an unlimited capacity for embarrassment. Or maybe there's no capacity for remembering. After all, Volvo, those other ads, such as the ones Colgate did for its shaving cream, occurred a long time ago. You could have forgotten, right? Probably your lawyers weren't in the habit of checking *Do's and Don't's in Advertising Copy,* or the *Trade Regulation Reporter,* or those other legal sources that tell you flat out not to do phony demonstrations. Dull stuff, those volumes.

Another reason for the memory lapse could be the now-popular dependence on the short-run rather than long-run outlook. Make the quick buck and let the future fend for itself. I won't be in this job tomorrow, says today's executive. Similarly, many branded goods now rely on sales promotion rather than image-building advertising. The ad people all know that twenty-five cents off demeans their brand while advertising gilds it, and yet that coupon will make some quick sales in the current fiscal year.

Volvo, you've learned about the marbles in the soup by now, haven't you? Way back in the 1960s Campbell was having trouble photographing its vegetable soup. The solid ingredients hunkered down below the broth where they wouldn't show up in those beautiful full-color smell-it-right-off-the-page magazine pictures. So they put some marbles in the bowl first, which lifted the carrots and beans so high that they poked right up like periscopes on submarines. They were just taking the public below the surface to get the truth, no? Well, no, not after Campbell's toy department tossed in so many marbles that the soup seemed to have many more solids than Heinz soups had. The Federal Trade Commission got a quick 57-page complaint from you-know-who, and the jig was up for the kid with the tomato cheeks.

Then there was the automobile window demonstration. Libbey-Owens-Ford made the windows for General Motors' cars, and they jointly decided to advertise how clear the glass was by showing theirs versus the competitors'. Fair enough, if it's fair. The true difference must not have been convincing, though, because the pictures they took didn't exactly show theirs versus the competitors'. They made one shot with the windows rolled down, and another with them rolled up with Vaseline smeared on them. One of those views out the window was superior to the other, no kidding, and Libbey wasn't unduly shy about letting people think which brand that was. Neither was the FTC shy about telling the company and the world what it thought about that.

Carter Products chimed in with a televised competition of its Rise shaving cream against a competitor. The other brand dried out and became worthless on a man's face more quickly than Rise did. What they showed on the screen, however, was not the competing cream but a specifically concocted formula that evaporated as fast as the science of chemistry could manage. Better things for better living. . . . There were similar false demonstrations for Borden's Kava coffee, Mattel's and Topper's toy cars, and Rhodes Pharmacal's cosmetics.

Meanwhile, the granddaddy of all such creative efforts had come in Colgate-Palmolive's 1950s ads for Rapid Shave shaving cream. In those early television days Colgate told us we were seeing sandpaper being shaved immediately and quickly after application of its rapid product. What it really filmed was the shaving of loose grains of sand sprinkled on clear plexiglas. The ads said, "Apply, soak, and off in a stroke." It really was, too, although not with anything you couldn't rub off with your little finger. No actual sandpaper could be shaved rapidly, "off in a stroke." It could be shaved only after long soaking, but that couldn't support the claim the ads conveyed.

In appeals that reached the Supreme Court, Colgate blamed the limitations of television. Real sandpaper would look like plain paper because the picture was not sharp enough to show the grains. Therefore, the company claimed, it was justified in using bigger grains of sand so that TV viewers could see them. The problem with that, the Supreme Court said, was that it conveyed a false claim. The demonstration claimed to be proof of something users really couldn't do; they couldn't shave sandpaper immediately after application of the shaving cream. In fact, even if that claim were true and independently verifiable, the Court said, it was still illegal deception to tell consumers they were seeing proof of that truth when they were not.

Twenty-five years after the Court's decision, and almost that many after the law apprehended anyone for such demonstrations, Volvo forgot or ignored them all. In Vermont one of its models reportedly had been the only car to avoid being crushed when a "monster truck" rolled over it at a fairground exhibition. Impressed with these results but having no pictures of them, the company decided to re-create the event on film for use in ads. The eventual ads, however, did exactly what Colgate had done—they let viewers think they were seeing the actual exhibition.

The ads showed a Volvo that workers had rigged to give the roof extra strength. Early on the day of the filming, before the cameras ran, the monster truck had crushed one Volvo wagon during a trial run. The ad producers then called in welders to doctor another Volvo by building a reinforcing steel framework on its inside. For even greater certainty, they had the welders cut the roof supports on the competing brands shown in the ad.

The re-creation took place in Austin, Texas, before hundreds of people hired to act as a crowd in the grandstand. Volvo and its ad agency, Scali, McCabe, Sloves, later claimed never to have known of the changes, but an observer named Dan White said they couldn't have not known. Many in the crowd saw the welders working, and a friend of White's took photos at the scene. White then alerted the Texas consumer protection office, which gained a settlement that included a payment of $316,250 to the state.

The state also forced company and agency to admit the event in a "corrective" ad in Texas and national newspapers. The ad claimed that the film production team made the changes to "enable the filming to be done without threatening the safety of the production crew" and "to allow the demonstration Volvo to withstand the number of runs by the 'monster truck' required for filming." White called that "preposterous." Scali soon took responsibility and quit as the company's agency. Volvo and Scali later entered voluntary settlements with the FTC that they would no longer make such claims. They also agreed to rare penalties in which they each paid the government $150,000 for disgorgement, which means giving back what you improperly obtained.

Long ago an ad agency I worked for in Pittsburgh compared its client's aluminum foil, Alcoa Wrap, to a competitor's in comparison pictures showing a ham wrapped in each. Somebody wrapped a ham in the competing foil, then unwrapped it, then wrapped it again, then unwrapped it. They crinkled it and uncrinkled it, and when it had finally fallen into tatters they draped it over the ham and photographed both foil-wrapped hams. Viewers of course saw Alcoa Wrap to be superior. Later, while teaching at Penn State, I had a chance to revisit the agency. When I mentioned the incident to a former co-worker, he said, "What about it? What's wrong with that?" He later went to law school, and last I heard he was an assistant U.S. attorney. May justice prevail!

Thirty years later, and eons later in enlightenment, press comment on Volvo was uniformly negative. The company was utterly wrong; the perpetrators were crooks; the event besmirched the ad industry. False demonstrations may or may not be eliminated forever, but the sympathy has definitely drained away.

## 9

# THE ROLE OF IMPLICATIONS IN DECEPTIVENESS

If the regulators are so good at catching implications, it's mostly because the advertisers first became so good at creating them. But why did implications became so popular with advertisers? Ironically, it's largely the FTC's fault.

What? Did I just say I'm blaming the law for encouraging advertisers to make false implications? I am, in a very important sense. It happened because the FTC, on being created by Congress in 1914, was soon very successful in attacking and eliminating deceptive claims. In the early years the ad claims made the job easy, because the advertisers used much explicit, direct, blatant falsity. It was old-fashioned lying, typified by the quackery tradition of patent medicines said to cure every ailment from cancer to body odor.

Such claims promised valuable benefits and so were extremely appealing to consumers. Yet they were also easy to prosecute, once the legal apparatus existed to do so. The claims were so evidently false that they virtually revealed themselves. There was little need to look into consumers' heads to determine the conveyed meanings. As a result, a heavy degree of regulation followed the formation of the FTC. The new agency lessened the opportunity to use blatantly false claims, and properly frustrated those advertisers who cherished their use.

No doubt some advertisers wanted to keep on using such claims. Indeed today some incidence of deliberate and gross lying remains. However, the smarter operators realized they must make a better adjustment to the new realities. To use a military analogy, when a wall blocks your ability to advance, the second strategy you think of may be superior to the one that first comes to mind. You would probably think first to attack the wall head on, but cooler analysis may well lead to a method that is less direct, more subtle. Your eventual choice may be to devise a flanking movement around the end.

We are speaking, of course, of the professional activity of communication experts for whom creativity is a hallmark, competition is a given, and winning is the reason for being. Footballers advancing toward the Super Bowl do not necessarily have a stronger sense of this. If there is a way to get around the wall, advertising experts will probably find it. So, how did they switch to the strategy of indirection? Easy—they dropped the explicit lying and began falsifying indirectly with implied content. Implied falsity has a foundation of explicit content that is unassailably true. Such messages, on their face, are untouchable by the enemy regulators. Meanwhile, the falsity that lurks in the implication is difficult to detect.

Let's see the difference it can make. You recall from the previous chapter that Colgate explicitly falsified its Rapid Shave demonstration by filming loose sand rather than sandpaper. The timing, late 1950s, was long after the law gave direct falsity its bad odor. The company, therefore, used a subtle twist—a flanking movement—to carry the ads into what it thought would be a safe zone. It falsified not about the product directly, but rather about the demonstration of the product. Technically, indeed, a demonstration can be false without the related product claim also being false. Therefore, Colgate argued, the falsity of the demonstration was of no consequence to consumers because it did not misrepresent the product's features.

Clever reasoning? Not really, because the eventual ruling was that the ad did misrepresent the product's features. Moreover, the Supreme Court decided that even if the claimed features were true, consumers would make their buying decisions on the basis of the false demonstration. The demonstration would harm both consumers and competitors, so it should be called illegal. The result was even stronger support for the established principle that explicit falsity relating to a product is not acceptable. The flanking movement had not worked.

So what did Colgate, possessed of abundant flexibility in its creative overachieving, do next? It did an explicitly true demonstration. The product this time was Baggies, the sandwich bags. Two women were standing at a kitchen counter, chatting and wrapping sandwiches, one in Baggies, the other in a competitor. (In the jargon of the pre-comparative era, the ad called the latter "another leading brand." It seems funny now, but at one time ad people never mentioned competitors by name for fear of giving them free publicity.)

On the counter happened to be two containers that looked like small aquariums, so of course the Baggies lady challenged her friend to dip their bags under water. The Baggies' sandwich remained dry while the other got soaked. It turned out that Colgate had developed a new and effective seal for the top of the bag. It was truly innovative, keeping out water as other bags could not. In contrast to the sandpaper ad, this demonstration was perfectly true.

Nevertheless, the FTC charged that consumers would see an implication that the demonstration proved Baggies to be superior for protecting food under ordinary and typical storage conditions. The principal foe of freshness under such conditions is not water, of course, because most folks put their sandwich in the refrigerator or lunchbox. The problem is that air might get into the bags, and for that problem the role of the seal was illusory. True, the new design prevented air from entering through the top. So far, so good for Baggies. However, air could also enter through the pores in the plastic, anywhere on the bag's surface. It turned out that Baggies' pores were just as porous as those of its competitors, and so the implied claims of superiority in keeping out air, and of the demonstration proving that superiority, were false.

I call that the Demonstration Implication, because of the raw material that creates it. There are many more types of false implications, all representing creative efforts by advertisers to convey messages directly that they are no longer willing to state explicitly. Such efforts have not been very successful. Although implications are harder to detect than explicit claims, the regulators have caught many of them anyway.

# 10

# HOW IMPLICATIONS WORK

Making a false implication begins with making an explicit claim—E. We are discussing true E's here because the law can prohibit a false E directly, giving regulators or competitors no incentive to investigate what it might also imply. Assuming a true E, then, consumers often see an ad to convey E plus an additional claim, I, that E implies. An I may be either true or false, although when it's true advertisers will most likely state it explicitly. Professionals don't waste their efforts saying things indirectly when they can legitimately say them directly. So we'll assume that I's typically are false.

When challenged about their I's, advertisers usually do not insist they are true, but rather that they are not conveyed to consumers, or at least not to the required number. That number is the percentage criterion seen in chapter 2—20 to 25 at the FTC, 15 in Lanham cases. The typical failure of I's to derive from E's by strict logic encourages advertisers to deny that consumers see the I's conveyed. However, in numerous cases the regulators have decided from argument or evidence that I's are conveyed as pragmatically logical implications of E's. That means (from chap. 7) that the context in which consumers see the ad saying E prompts them reasonably to see it also saying I.

The value of the implication process to advertisers is that I is a stronger claim than E. I is more likely to appeal to consumers and thus create sales. E may be utterly unappealing or it may have a modest appeal, but E is not as attractive to consumers as I. The result is an interesting pair of claims. One is true and the other is strongly appealing, but neither has both of those positive qualities. E is true but weak, while I is strong but false. Although advertisers will be reluctant to state the stronger claim directly because of its falsity, they have shown a greater willingness to use such claims when they can convey them by implication.

You can see from this that the value of E to the advertiser is as a vehicle to produce I. Recalling the sandwich bags ad, what was E and what was I? E was Baggies' superiority in the water demonstration. That has no real appeal to consumers, because how many of them store their sandwiches under water overnight? E's only role was to establish a truthful claim that would in turn establish an additional claim. The additional claim, I, was Baggies' superiority for storing food under ordinary conditions—in air. That's something people care about. However, it wasn't true, so the advertiser didn't say it directly. Instead, the ad writers found a way to say it indirectly, and that's what implications are all about.

I may have been implying that Colgate was found guilty of making that false claim. Technically the company avoided any legal finding by agreeing to settle out of court. However, in doing so it agreed not to describe demonstrations in the future as being proof of a claim when they were not proof. It never admitted that its E produced an I, but it nonetheless voluntarily accepted an FTC order not to produce such I's in any future ads.

My comments may also have implied that Colgate and other advertisers produce false implications on purpose. That's because I think they usually do. I think they know exactly how the process of implication works. It's proper, however, to point out that the regulators typically do not obtain evidence of such knowledge by the advertisers, and thus there is no actual legal finding that implications occur other than by accident. Of course they occur again and again, which seems like evidence to me.

No doubt the advertisers create implications so frequently because they know the regulators come down hard on explicit falsity. Given their communication expertise, it's no surprise that they have discovered the cleverness of the process and will use it often. What's a little harder to understand is that they've continued to use the trick after being caught dozens of times, as FTC and Lanham records clearly show. Is it possible that many other implications are not being caught? Are the odds of escaping good enough to encourage advertisers to think they can get away with it?

That's impossible to check, because legal records don't contain lists of the cases that never happened. My own conclusion from examining ads, however, is that not many of the types already identified are escaping. As we will see later in this book, however, additional types of implications remain to be identified by the regulators. The advertisers are getting away with many of these, which may very well encourage ad writers to continue using implications generally.

Another encouragement to the advertisers is that they have so little to lose from running implications. When they get caught, they typically must do no more than stop the claim. There usually are no fines, no jail, no return of the profits they made from the sales the claim produced. So, although they know the law is there and it can catch them, they also know that any "penalty" won't matter very much. That could also be a reason for continuing with explicitly false claims, too. However, recent FTC activity has made it more likely that explicit falsity will result in fines and return of profits. The key is whether the falsity seems obvious and deliberate, and implications are more likely to avoid such a finding—at least for now.

I interpret the conditions I have just described as showing that advertisers display a great disrespect for the law. Another indication of disrespect is that when they get hauled into court, most of them offer incredibly lame defenses. They rarely provide any valid defense against the charge that consumers see an implication. They make loud arguments, but they have poor evidence or often no evidence about what claims, legal or illegal, they are making. Any of them who truly want to know what messages they are conveying can easily find out, because ad people are superbly prepared in such matters. Part of their preparation is that implications have the common structure described at the beginning of this chapter. That structure should be quite easily detectable by people who offer themselves as experts in communication.

Moreover, implications come in specific categories, which leads to even greater predictability. The Baggies implication, for example, illustrates the Demonstration Implication. In that type the explicit claim, E, is a demonstration that is true although weak in selling power. The record of numerous such cases easily puts advertisers on notice that the next true-but-trivial demonstration may be similarly interpreted as implying a false I.

The record includes, for example, the case of the ad in which Black Flag roach killer killed roaches while "the other leading brand" failed. The hidden explanation was that Black Flag's tests used roaches bred to be resistant to the poison used by the competitor. Automobiles fueled with Sunoco were shown pulling loads up steep inclines, or pulling railroad cars, implying falsely that they could do so with no other gasoline. Ford showed a crane lifting a car by its doors, implying proof that the doors would fend off impacts from the type of lateral force that occurs in collisions.

Chevron gasoline tied balloons to exhaust pipes to show us on television the color of a car's exhaust. The exhaust was clear for Chevron but the competing brand gave off a black sooty look, implying that it failed to remove pollutants. Chevron's clearness was legitimate to a point, because the demonstration could show legitimately that any sooty pollutants were removed. However, other gasoline pollutants are clear, and a picture of clear exhaust can't prove whether they too are gone. Besides, the cars said to have used the competing brand were actually given a fuel deliberately formulated to produce very black exhaust. The resulting contrast to Chevron was false because it wrongly implied that viewers were seeing the competitor's actual performance.

Do these examples give you any clue, Mr. or Ms. Advertiser, that maybe the regulators will examine *your* demonstration for what it implies? They should. You should also know that the Demonstration Implication is only one of a number of types of implications that the regulators are watching out for.

# 11
# THE MANY TYPES OF IMPLICATIONS

I'll introduce a number of additional implications here. All those mentioned here and previously are summarized in a list at the end of this chapter to make later reference easier.

What would you guess the Endorsement Implication involves? If the endorser gets a benefit from the product, it implies that you will too! The explicit claim, E, is that some persons, either ordinary people or celebrities, use the product and like it. The additional implied claim, I, is that you'll like it just as much—you'll get the same benefit. That's been a very popular and false implication with weight loss products. Several companies, such as Porter & Dietsch, are under orders forbidding them from using it.

You might suspect that the endorsements, the explicit E's, were themselves false despite my saying earlier that E's typically are true. The E's might indeed be false in this case, but it's not likely that the regulators will try to prove that. They would have to go back to the endorsers, who would be unlikely to admit their statements weren't true. Faced with that, the regulators will find it easier to let the explicit claims go unchallenged but attack the implication, which is often provably false.

The Expertise Implication is a variation in which the endorser is an expert in some field. The explicit E is that an expert endorses the product. That implies the additional claim I that the person's expertise is the basis for the endorsement. Suppose one of the original astronauts, Gordon Cooper, made the claim—would you imagine him to be an expert? Sure, everybody knows how well trained those Right Stuffers had to be. Cooper, however, made a claim that an auto engine attachment would save fuel. Rocket ships have engines too, so he ought to know, right? No, the implication was false because his expertise did not extend to automobiles. He accepted an FTC order that he should cease claiming to have expertise in a given field unless he had "the education, training, and knowledge necessary to be qualified as an expert in that field."

In the Significance Implication, the ad states any true fact, E, and produces a false I that E should matter to consumers. Consumers are likely to accept the old cliche that "they wouldn't be saying this if it isn't important," and so are likely to be fooled when the claim turns out to be insignificant. For example, advertising that called the pain reliever Tronolane "new" falsely implied that it was a new product. It was new only in the sense of being a new brand of an old product. The latter was not objectively significant to consumers because the product was already available to the public in existing brands. Tronolane was not new in a way that mattered.

In the Contrast Implication, the explicit E is a true difference of a brand from its competitors. The claim it implies, I, is that the brand has an additional contrast. The E contrast may or may not be valuable to consumers, but I is of definite value. The E that "only Anacin has this formula" was technically true because no other headache reliever combined aspirin and caffeine. The I, though, that Anacin was thereby better for relieving pain, was false because caffeine made no contribution to pain relief. By the reference to a "formula," the FTC found the I to include the claim that the ingredients were something other, and better, than aspirin—a valuable contrast if it had been true.

The Halo Implication occurs when superiority claimed in one way implies the product to be superior in other ways or superior overall. Sun Oil truthfully sold "the world's highest octane," but it did not give the world's greatest power. That's because octane higher than the level a car needs gives no additional power, and it costs more. In the related Uniqueness Implication the brand stresses a feature in such way as to imply that no other brand has it.

We've already seen the Confusing Resemblance Implication with the name Aspercreme implying aspirin. The explicit E is an unfamiliar term that resembles and thus through confusion implies a familiar term. The familiar term is much more valuable than the unfamiliar one, but the implication is false and consumers get only the lesser value of E. They get only Aspercreme and do not get aspirin.

To illustrate the related Ordinary Meaning Implication, the FTC found the name "National Commission on Egg Nutrition" to imply the usage of words in their ordinary ways. On that basis you would expect the words to indicate a group appointed on a national basis, for example by the federal government. That meaning would indicate to consumers that the claims the group made about eggs were valid and impartial. The true meaning, though, would not give that impression, and indeed would probably produce a negative effect. The group's members were far from impartial—they were egg industry operators.

The Ineffective Qualification Implication occurs when the qualification is so obscured that consumers either will not see it or will see it but not get it. For example, an ad may have a headline that is qualified by additional wording that is small in size, complex, or unreadable. While the explicit E includes both claim and qualification, the implied claim I includes only the claim. When Beneficial advertised its "Instant Tax Refund," it added an obscure qualification saying the offer was for nothing more than one of its ordinary loans. People saw the headline but didn't see the qualification. Advertisers in such cases will argue that the qualification counts because it is present. The rule is clear, though, that if it's not conveyed it's just as if it wasn't there at all.

A related way of advertising is to make a claim with no qualification at all, which implies falsely that there is none. That's the No Qualification Implication. It happens frequently with over-the-counter drugs or medical devices that may be suitable for many consumers but dangerous for some. The law frequently allows such a claim to continue, but only if accompanied by a disclosure that warns of the problems. In that way the claim will serve many consumers usefully, and will no longer harm others. The disclosure of course must be large or otherwise conspicuous enough that consumers will see it conveyed.

The Proof Implication involves an explicit performance or benefit claim plus an explicit claim that testing or surveying has been done. The combination implies that the latter E proves the former. It resembles the Demonstration Implication, but the ad merely cites the test or survey rather than showing a performance. Often this presumably scientific evidence is of the caliber of the tests we saw earlier by Sears and Thompson Medical, proving nothing. As the FTC has said in such cases, it is especially inappropriate for a test or survey to fail to support a claim because consumers give more credibility to claims implied to be backed up by such evidence. If the ad gives a promise of good evidence, it must keep that promise.

The related Reasonable Basis Implication involves a privilege of the FTC to prohibit a claim not for being false but merely for being unsubstantiated, which means the evidence doesn't show whether the claim is true or false. The commission says any factual E implies to consumers that the speaker has a reasonable belief that the claim is true. That is pragmatically logical because it's normal, in the marketplace or any-where else, to assume that a speaker wouldn't state a fact without hav-ing a suitable reason for doing so.

Owing to the importance of that to consumers, the false implica-tion of a reasonable basis can be prohibited even if evidence obtained later shows the claim to have been true when it was first run. Although there could be no consumer harm if the claim really was true, the FTC reasons that the advertiser acted deceptively in claiming to know some-thing it really didn't know. Doing so subjects consumers to the risk of suffering the consequences if the claim wasn't true, so the commission declares a violation in order to keep advertisers from imposing that risk.

While all the above implications may apply to numerous adver-tised items, some are specific to certain products. Hollywood Bread, for example, claimed to have only 46 calories per slice, which the FTC said implied the bread was lower in calories. The total loaf was not lower in calories, so how could the slices be lower? That's easy—just make them thinner. However, such a manipulation works only with a product that's divided into units. It can't happen with, say, automobile tires or a computer. For that reason I refer to such events as Product-Specific Implications. In previous work I have described such implications ex-tensively (see references for this chapter). Although I won't repeat all that here, another example of a Product-Specific Implication is in the next chapter, involving Kraft cheese.

In summary, advertisers are tricky, aren't they, in the way they ar-range for consumers to see ads making claims! If you know how to look for implications, though, you'll find the tricks easier to see. You'll know how far you can trust the claims, and beyond what point you should not trust them.

## Types of Implications

In all of the following, E is an explicit claim, true but insufficiently ap-pealing to consumers to satisfy the advertiser's needs. I is a claim prag-matically implied by E, considerably more appealing to consumers, but false.

• *Demonstration*—E is a demonstration of a product claim; it is not relevant or important to consumers. I is a claim suggested by the dem-onstration; it is much more relevant and important.

- *Endorsement*—E is an endorsement of the product by a celebrity or ordinary consumer. I is the claim that those seeing the ad will find the facts about the product to be as the endorser found them, or will otherwise prefer the product as much as the endorser does.
- *Expertise*—E is an endorsement of the product by a person called an expert in the product field. I is the same as for the Endorsement Implication, but with the additional claim that the endorser's expertise is relevant to the product field and serves as an adequate basis for the endorsement.
- *Significance*—E is any factual claim about the product. I is the claim that E is significant to consumers and should matter to them in deciding to purchase the product.
- *Contrast*—E is a claim that contrasts the advertised brand with its competitors. I is an additional contrast.
- *Halo*—E is a claim of superiority of the product in a specific way. I is a claim that the product is superior in another way or superior overall.
- *Uniqueness*—E is a factual claim about a brand of a product. I is a claim that E is true for this brand alone.
- *Confusing Resemblance*—E is an unfamiliar name, description, or other term. I is a familiar term that resembles E.
- *Ordinary Meaning*—E is a name, description, or other term that has a certain meaning ordinarily, but that meaning is not applicable in its present usage. I is the ordinary meaning.
- *Ineffective Qualification*—E is any claim accompanied by a qualification that is not stated clearly or conspicuously. I is the claim not including the qualification.
- *No Qualification*—E is any claim that is generally true, but is less true or untrue for some consumers under some conditions. I is the implication that the claim is true generally for all consumers under all conditions; it has no qualification.
- *Proof*—Following any product claim, a second explicit E is that evidence such as testing or surveying has been done in support. I is a claim that the second E proves the first; the evidence proves the product claim.
- *Reasonable Basis*—E is any product claim. I is a claim that the advertiser has a reasonable basis for believing that the product claim is true.
- *Product-Specific*—Because these implications depend on the specific context, no general statement can be made. The context varies because of the way the product appears or performs. For example, bread comes in a unit that is divided into smaller units. Most products

do not come that way, but other products have characteristics that produce implications in other ways specific to their nature.

## 12

# THE KRAFT CHEESE CASE

When it comes to established brand names, one of the best is Kraft, which sells more than 40 percent of the nation's cheese. Although now merged into Kraft General Foods, which is part of the Philip Morris conglomerate, it remains in itself one of the nation's largest food companies. Kraft's Singles are individually wrapped slices of what the Food and Drug Administration calls process cheese food. The category must by law include at least 51 percent natural cheese. At the time of the case described here Kraft was using 68 percent, which is probably why Singles became the largest seller in the single slice category.

Some competing cheese slices offer imitation cheese food, which is any ingredient combination that resembles process cheese food but may have as little as zero actual cheese. Vegetable oil, fortifiers, flavoring agents, and water typically create the illusion. The FDA defines the result by law as "nutritionally inferior" to process cheese food, which means technically that the imitation has a lesser amount of one or more of process cheese's essential ingredients. Strangely, however, the definition calls a product nutritionally inferior for that reason even though it may also have greater amounts of one or more other ingredients. The imitation cheese actually could be more nutritious overall than natural cheese, yet by having less of one item it must remain inferior in the eyes of the law.

The comparison would seem to favor Kraft, but Singles was losing some sales to the imitation slices. The company thought that consumers had noticed the brand's higher price but not its superior ingredients. Wanting to correct that perception, Kraft launched a claim that Singles' slices are made from five ounces of milk compared with "hardly any" for the imitators. The ads emphasized the calcium provided by that milk.

That sounds suitable on its face. And it was true—on its face. However, the FTC formally charged Kraft with claiming falsely that each Singles slice gives the same amount of calcium found in the five ounces of milk, and more calcium than most imitation slices. These claims were false because not all the milk used in cheesemaking gets into the cheese. Something most of us don't understand about the process—having to do with the curds and whey—produces a loss of 30 percent of the milk. Thus not all the calcium from the original five ounces gets into the cheese.

Kraft acknowledged the claims were false if made, but said its ads didn't make them. The ads had been saying explicitly only that the cheese "has" five ounces of milk. On getting complaints about the claim, Kraft changed the wording to read that its cheese "is made from" five ounces of milk. The change did not impress the FTC, which said that both old and new wordings implied a false claim that Singles contained the same amount of calcium as five ounces of milk, largely because the ad linked the references to calcium so closely to the references to the milk. The ads showed milk poured into a glass up to a five-ounce mark, with the glass then transferred by animation onto the cover of a Singles package. Because of the explicit linkage, the FTC felt it could easily conclude that the claim was implied after looking only at the ad. However, it also had extrinsic evidence, a consumer survey and expert testimony, which it said supported the same conclusion.

The commission also found false the claim of having more calcium than most imitation slices because some imitation brands have calcium added. The calcium doesn't come from milk, but it's there all the same, and it means the imitation slices are not inferior in amount of calcium. Kraft conceded that point, but argued it didn't convey the claim of more calcium; it only said more milk. The FTC, though, found an implied claim conveyed that Kraft's slices had more calcium than imitation ones. As before, it decided by examining the supporting extrinsic evidence as well as the ads.

Kraft's overall defense strategy tended to suggest it was unconfident of winning on the matter of what claims its ads conveyed. I say that because the company mounted a serious effort to persuade the FTC to call the claims nondeceptive even if found conveyed. Kraft based its hope on an additional requirement for deceptiveness that I haven't mentioned yet. The requirement is that a claim cannot be prosecuted unless it is *material*, that is, it must affect consumers' purchasing decisions. A material claim that is also false presumably would affect such decisions harmfully.

A false claim that is not material cannot be harmful in that way. Not everything said in ads is about the product or service that's for sale. Obviously much will be, since the advertiser would otherwise be wasting its money. Some things, though, play a role merely of getting attention, and are not really about the product. They may be quite peripheral, part of the background. If so, they will not be material.

Earlier I described the FTC's prosecution of Chevron for falsely claiming that its demonstrations proved its gasoline would reduce pollutants (chap. 10). The television screen showed in the background a building with a sign saying Chevron Research Center. The building was really a county courthouse, but the commission called that misrepresentation immaterial to consumers' decisions. The claim presumably would not deceive people into purchases they would otherwise not make.

I personally have some mixed feelings about that ruling, because the false substitution certainly suggests that we take a dim view toward Chevron and its other claims. Nevertheless, I do not mean to suggest that materiality is an improper loophole or technicality. As distasteful as the lie about the courthouse seems, there is merit in restricting the prosecution of falsity to claims that harm people in their marketplace transactions. When what people are buying is gasoline, the regulators consider it fair on balance that any claims called material should have to be about that gasoline.

Some readers might consider the depiction of the research facility to be material because it would increase consumers' confidence and so increase their chances of believing the other false claims. I am sympathetic to that possibility generally, although not regarding Chevron because the FTC found that the real research center looked more impressive than the courthouse. Any change in consumers' perceptions produced by the switch could only have been to the detriment, not benefit, of Chevron. The company had made the switch for reasons of convenience, such as poor weather in the San Francisco Bay area, the center's true location.

Elsewhere, however, advertisers may try with less justification to use the materiality requirement as a way to escape prosecution. Kraft did so when it argued before the FTC that its claims about calcium were not material to consumers. Calcium not material? Let's examine that by asking first why any advertiser would try to sell a product with claims it believed were irrelevant to why people would buy. The idea that companies will voluntarily waste their money in that way makes the suggestion preposterous. What an uphill battle for Kraft!

The building in the Chevron ad had appeared only in the background; attention was never called to it. By contrast, Kraft's calcium claims were highly prominent as a main point of the ads, and calcium is well known to be an attractive ingredient. Moreover, the FTC observed that Kraft itself had definitely thought the claims to be material. The company was found to have believed that the ad campaign increased sales. For that reason it kept the claims running even after the FTC, the state of California, and a consumer group questioned the appropriateness.

Kraft's basis for turning day into night was a consumer survey on materiality. Describing it will take us even more than before into features of research that may seem complex to some readers. You'll learn a lot about falsity from it, though, because questions of advertisers' truthfulness occur at two stages: (1) what they say in their ads, and (2) what they say in court when defending what they said in their ads.

Kraft's survey showed people ranking calcium only seventh in importance among nine factors that might affect whether they would buy Singles. That showed calcium was not material, the company said, although I can't see it as showing anything more than that it was less so than six other factors. All nine could have been material. Besides, when asked how much calcium was in Singles, most people surveyed said they didn't know. Also, over 71 percent said calcium was "extremely" or "very" important in their purchase decisions.

Kraft's surveyor informed people that each slice of Singles contained only 70 percent of the calcium in five ounces of milk. The people then stated whether knowledge of this difference would cause them to continue to buy or to stop buying Singles. Kraft thought that those who answered "continue buying" would be implying that the difference between the conveyed claim (100 percent of the calcium in the original five ounces of milk) and the truth (only 70 percent) was not material for them. Such answers would be saying that the consumers would not change their behavior. Superficially Kraft made its point—96 percent said they would continue to buy.

However, the FTC ruled the question improper because the survey restricted people to answering only "continue buying" or "stop buying." Other legitimate answers could have been that they would buy less than before, or buy the same but also drink more milk, or switch to competitors that were cheaper or that contained more calcium. If such other answers had been available, many consumers might have chosen them, and the percentage choosing "continue buying" would probably have become much lower. That in turn would have indicated calcium claims to be much more material than Kraft claimed. Aren't surveys fascinating!

Further, Kraft surveyed consumers without showing them the ads. That was a technical error, because the FTC can assess only those claims that the ads convey to consumers. The only relevant issue was whether calcium was material to consumers *as Kraft advertised it*. The very fact of advertising might itself create materiality that would otherwise be absent, because consumers might see something like calcium to be important just from the fact that a company described it to the public as such. Obviously you can't examine that effect by asking about calcium in general.

In summary, Kraft contrived its defense to find minimum materiality. Unfortunately, it was an amateurish effort that found minimum validity. Please, Kraft, keep your cheese on a higher level than your surveys!

# PART 3

## BRANDING AND THE CLAIMS IT GIVES US

*This part examines a root cause of deceptiveness: advertisers typically sell brands rather than just products. Because brands must be presented as different from other brands although they often are not, advertisers are tempted to create false differences. To work, such falsities must be immune from the law, and it turns out that the law has arranged for many to be so. Advertisers have developed a variety of claims that lie on what is here called the "slippery slope" that runs between what is fully true and what is false enough to be illegal. The claims on the slope are on a series of steps of varying degrees of falsity. The first of three general types is nearest the top, the second is farther down, and the third is closest to the bottom. The first two types are discussed in this part, and the third is the topic of Part 4. This part also has two chapters devoted to individual cases.*

# 13

# THE REASON FOR DECEPTIVE CLAIMS: BRANDING

The main reason that falsity occurs so often in advertising is that most advertisers are trying to sell exactly the same thing other advertisers sell. Unfortunately for them all, the public's normal and natural desire for most products or services prompts purchase of fewer units than the total set of competitors has the capacity to make and sell. Would you be surprised to find that Procter and Gamble could make enough Crest to supply the entire world with 100 percent of its "toothpaste needs"? I'd assume the same for Colgate or Lever Brothers, too. Throw in the other makers and the whole gang could probably turn out 1000 percent of what actually gets sold.

With excess capacity like that, it's no wonder that each seller is anxious to make us want its particular brand. When a product or service is first offered, the originator will be the only party selling it for a time. The monopoly, though, will probably not last long. If the item creates business for its maker, other makers will soon appear. From their competition, brand differences will arise.

To say that our marketplace is based on such competition may lead observers to think the various participants like such a state. Not so. They may believe in competition, meaning they accept it as the basis of the market system, but they don't like it. They compete hard when they're forced to, but they're always aware that the better strategy would be to escape, if possible, from having to compete in the first place.

They escape by selling brands of products, not just products— Kleenex, not just paper handkerchiefs. Other people sell that product, but no others sell that brand. If consumers become attracted to the specific brand there's no more competition, because nobody but Kimberly-Clark sells Kleenex. It works because the brand achieves a distinctiveness; it differentiates itself from the rest.

Ford doesn't sell just cars; it sells Fords and Mercurys and Tauruses! Everyone else in the market sells cars, but only Ford sells Fords or Mercurys or Tauruses. That's the key to success, when the public thinks not of the product in general but of your brand. They treat it as being, in effect, an individual product in itself. The ultimate level of such success is to establish your brand's name as the one everybody habitually uses for the product. Kleenex did it. Scotch Tape did it.

So did Xerox. That company can legally prohibit other sellers from using its name. It can do so, at least, as long as it protects against having the law interpret that name as referring to all copy machines. If the latter occurred, the company would lose its exclusive rights. So it's famous for writing to ask people not to use the name uncapitalized—as in "I xeroxed this paper"—which would tend to make it stand for the product generally.

It's ironic, though, that Xerox really wants all of us to use the term generically, as standing for the entire product category. When people get in the habit of referring to "Xeroxing," they are probably biasing themselves toward picking that specific brand when it's time to buy. The company can enjoy the advantage that anyone who speaks of the general category will be using a designation that legally belongs to it alone.

Such success drives competitors up the wall. My office at the university has an old copy machine made by the A. B. Dick Company. I often give my secretary a sheet of paper and say, "Here—about Xeroxing this off for me?" She carries out the job and comes back and says, "Here—I Xeroxed this off for you." If the A. B. Dick people heard us say those things they'd go absolutely wild. They would much prefer to have me say to the secretary, "Here—how about Dicking this off for me?"

Maybe not? But it shows what a problem you face when you aren't the one that owns the generic name. There's one big winner and many losers. Fortunately for the latter, differentiating doesn't have to achieve a generic name to be successful. But it has to go far enough to create the positive appeals that prompt a sufficient number of consumers to choose your brand. An appeal in a market of brands cannot be positive unless it prompts that one choice.

Brands can have very good features that don't prompt sales of any particular one. That happens because one or more of the competitors have the feature, too. Kodak film comes in speeds such as 100 and 200. That's important in the product line, but Kodak ads won't make much of it because the competitors all have film in such speeds. It's a positive product appeal but it's not a positive brand appeal.

Sure, producers want to sell the public on the generic product category, but they emphasize the category only when it's a new product, such as the relatively new markets for laserdisc players or laptop computers. New products quickly become familiar to consumers, however, and reach a mature growth phase in which a sales volume that once rose swiftly eventually levels off. The marketing effort is then switched to brands, because now the only reliable way for Brand A to increase sales is to take sales away from Brands B and C. Get a bigger percentage share of the market. Cigarette companies have been doing it for years, and Philip Morris has been winning the share battle.

As a result of this typical underlying situation, appeals must be chosen that are positive for the brand, not just for the product. They must differentiate the brand from other brands, in a favorable way, of course. If they don't do that, they are unsuitable for the purpose of selling even though they are suitable to consumers for the purpose of buying. Sellers' wants thus are different from consumers' wants, prompting the sellers to translate their wants so that consumers will see them as their own. Sellers can't appeal to the public by bothering it with their selfish concerns. Rather, they must reinterpret such matters as involving the consumers personally. And they must do it with respect to their own brands while not doing it for competing brands.

Oscar Mayer accomplished the task marvelously when it showed a kid singing "My baloney has a first name. It's O-S-C-A-R." The company had been trying to sell nationally into a market whose players were mostly local companies. Every region had different competitors; they weren't big and well known and they didn't stress their brand names. Nor did it matter that they didn't, because consumers who never thought of buying toothpaste or detergent without brand names were unconscious of brands when buying weiners and lunch meat.

Oscar Mayer's first job, then, wasn't just to stress its own brand name; it was to get people to think of its product categories as coming in brands. If the public would only think that way, the company could easily establish its own name by flooding every local market with far more ads than the various small sellers could afford. But first it had to get that kind of thinking into the minds of people who had no natural incentive to care about any such thing. Consumers were getting along just fine buying their baloney without recourse to brand names. Why should they change? Oscar Mayer's problem was not their problem, nor could it likely be interpreted as such. There was no point in trying to tell consumers about the issue stated in that form.

The solution was to translate the company's needs into things consumers *would* find appealing. It told kids their baloney had a first name and a second name, and the kids loved it. Of course while it looked on the surface as though Oscar was addressing the kids, actually it was addressing their parents about how baloney comes in names. Nice trick!

Translating seller's needs into consumers' needs in that way, and sticking with appeals that differentiate one's brand positively, is a natural consequence of the underlying nature of the market. We certainly cannot fault such sellers for responding with so rational a solution to the vexing problems of competition. Yet we'll see that their strategy produces some odd results. Among them in some cases is falsity.

# 14

## HOW BRANDING BREEDS FALSITY: THE SLIPPERY SLOPE

We have seen that selling products or services leads to selling brands. Now we'll see how brand selling leads to falsity. It happens because brand selling and truth are difficult to combine.

Advertisers want their claims to be true but also brand significant. They want consumers to demand the brand, not just the product. A claim that is only product significant will help sell the product while favoring no brand over any other. By contrast, a brand significant claim *differentiates a brand from its competing brands, positively, to a meaningful degree.*

A negative appeal of course cannot be brand significant, but neither can a positive one that fails to differentiate by being equally true for more than one brand. The consumer must see a brand as different from the competition in a positive way and to a meaningful degree. In other words, the difference will make the brand favored more than before, and more than competing brands, in the consumer's mind so as to increase the purchasing of it noticeably.

The problem for advertisers is that it's difficult to combine truth and significance. The sellers don't want to give up truth, but significance is what's essential. It's the bottom line. Many true claims are not brand significant. Some of them are product significant, while others may not be even that. Meanwhile, many brand significant claims are unfortunately not true.

All of that means, if logic serves, that the advertisers often can't have both truth and significance. Yet they can't have just one, either. There is zero incentive to make claims that are true but insignificant. There is also little incentive to achieve significance with falsity, granting a high probability that consumers or regulators will recognize the falsity.

What would the reader do to solve such a problem? It may help to try to appreciate the position advertising people are in. Without using it to justify everything that may happen, I think it's fair to recognize what the pressures are. Advertising people are always working for somebody who insists on obtaining a result. When we understand their working conditions, we can understand why they do what they do, whether we like it or not.

What can the advertisers do? For starters, they have to do *something.* If they don't, they can't be advertisers. They don't have the choice of saying, well, nothing that's true about our brand is significant, and nothing that's significant about it is true, so we're unable to come up with any ads at the present time. They can't just go on vacation like that; they can only forge ahead. Those who can't or won't do so are free to choose another line of work, and must. Those who stay will accept the challenge that to sell a brand is often to sell an item for which all or most true claims are insignificant by being equally applicable to all competitors.

That leaves the claims that are only true or only significant. I have said that the advertisers can't use a claim with only one of those qualities, but there's a way they can, sort of. I'm not referring to just proceeding blatantly with false significance or true insignificance without regard for the outcome. In light of the possibility of getting caught by the law for the first, or by the public for the second, advertisers can make a far wiser choice. It is to create in consumers' minds the *perception* of the missing truth or significance.

In other words, when they don't have a real advantage, they can treat what they have as if it were that, and hope the audience will agree. They can use claims that involve less than the full truth although having high significance, or claims that are high in truth although diminished in significance. They can even use claims that are low in both. They can offer such claims to the public, cross their fingers, and hope consumers will not notice what is missing.

Usually they don't have to cross their fingers very hard, because consumers are famous for not noticing. If consumers see a flawed claim to be true and to differentiate a brand favorably and meaningfully, then the advertiser has succeeded. Granted, there is always the risk that consumers will respond objectively, in which case the strategy will not work. However, advertisers know people often respond subjectively instead and so may *perceive* full truth and significance to exist.

That's a terrific advantage for the advertisers, who would otherwise have to search hard for a type of claim, one with high objective truth and significance, that they are unlikely to find. It's a lot easier instead to choose claims that are objectively lower on those qualities but are easier to find. The advertisers give up the high road for the low, yet they achieve the high road anyway in terms of consumers' perceptions. From this point on, then, we must discuss truth and significance not only as they exist objectively, but also as they exist in consumers' perceptions. It's a mind game, and we must learn to play it as the advertisers do.

Of course such activity takes the advertisers on a slope leading downward from full truth and significance. I'm going to call it the "slippery slope," after Chief Justice William Rehnquist's use of the term in an advertising case. His context was different; he was discussing whether a law regulating advertising violated the Constitution's guarantee of freedom of expression. As the First Amendment says, "Congress [and the states, too] shall make no law abridging freedom of speech or of the press.

Despite that, the Constitution was long interpreted to allow any regulation, including the complete banning, of deceptive commercial speech and even of truthful commercial speech. In 1976, however, a Supreme Court majority in the case of *Virginia Pharmacy v. Virginia Citizens* reversed precedent to allow a bit of truthful commercial speech to be kept from regulation. Rehnquist objected to that, but the next year in *Bates v. Arizona* the majority did it again, extending the freedom to an even greater portion of commercial speech.

That second extension caused the Chief Justice to blow his stack—within proper judicial decorum, of course. He wrote a dissenting opinion that used the analogy of a slope because he regarded the trend as leading downhill, to a bad result. It was "slippery" because the second downhill step showed that the first such step was probably the first of many. It would lead the Court into a plunge toward what he regarded as a rock bottom disaster in terms of disallowing the regulation of commercial speech.

The slippery slope I'm describing here has similar characteristics and is also about advertising. It involves a downward trek by the advertisers away from the qualities of truth and significance, a plunge that can reach outright falsity when traveled all the way to the end. My slippery slope starts with truth and significance, more or less, but it tends in the direction of less and less. It turns quickly to hype, and then it turns worse. Each turn has consequences for consumers in causing their trust in advertisers and reliance on advertising claims to result in harm rather than benefit.

Most advertisers don't go all the way down the slope—they don't hit rock bottom. Most of them, though, slide some of the way. The first slippery step produces "selected facts."

# 15

# SELECTED FACTS: STARTING DOWN THE SLOPE

The first step down the slippery slope occurs when advertisers have at least one true claim available for use that is also objectively significant. The advertised item is a brand having one or more positive features that other brands don't have, which creates brand significance. It also has one or more features the others do have, which creates only product significance. Of course the advertisers will use the brand significant claims and not the others in their ads. They are selective, using what will sell, leaving out what won't, and giving consumers incomplete information.

A comparative ad for kitchen ranges is illustrative. Created by the American Gas Association, it showed two pots of spaghetti cooking, one over a gas burner, the other over electric. Both pots had been heated to the point of threatening to boil over, and both burners had been quickly turned down. The gas burner went down immediately and quieted the bubbly mass. Guess what happened to the poor miserable competitor. That pot spilled its contents, of course, because electric burners don't dissipate their heat so swiftly. The spaghetti was caked hard against the outside surface, devilish to clean up. Avoiding such a mess would certainly be a truthful and significant reason for using gas.

That claim, however, was not the only thing we might learn about kitchen ranges. Electricity has its good points, too. Many consumers feel that electric burners distribute the heat more widely and evenly and that an electric oven is more reliable. (Some also prefer not to have to worry about the chance of a gas explosion.) My wife Robbie agonized over choosing a new stove because she wanted gas burners and an electric oven. Many consumers have similar conflicts. The issue must divide contractors, too, because both kinds of ranges appear in significant numbers in new homes.

So advertisers who use selected facts aren't telling the whole story. They tell us good things about their brand and leave out the neutral and bad. When they mention the competitor they tell the bad and leave out the neutral and the good. The consumer gets useful information but doesn't get it all. To have selected facts means also to have selected omissions. Nothing that's said is false, yet the total ad does not tell consumers the whole truth.

Does that make the ad false and harmful? The answer is complex, because the law may or may not find a violation in such claims. An omission, even one that consumers would find significant to their buying decision, does not necessarily prompt the law to find a false claim conveyed. Omissions are deceptive only when they imply false claims, which they can do if an explicitly stated selected fact implies a false understanding about an omitted fact. The regulators then typically prohibit the future use of the claim unless the advertiser includes what had been omitted.

Firestone, for example, advertised that its automobile tires had passed all inspections. That selected fact was true, but was found to convey impliedly to consumers that the tires were free of all defects. That was very brand significant, but the FTC found it to be false. The ads had selectively declined to explain that no inspections existed that could identify all defects. Thus the conducting by any tire company of all known inspections could have only a limited meaning. The company could truthfully claim to find the defects that those inspections could find, but it could not imply that it could find all defects.

Regulators, though, do not find most omissions to produce deceptiveness. In the kitchen range ad the omission of facts favorable to electric burners probably would not imply to many consumers that no such facts exist. Consumers must be reasonable in what they see conveyed. The regulators might well decide that consumers would be unreasonable to perceive the Gas Association ad as telling them that no facts favor electric ranges. Most people, after all, know that many electric ranges are sold. They also realize that advertising doesn't emphasize unfavorable points.

Advertising is a process of selling, after all, which means putting one's best foot forward. An advertising man once said, "You must expect advertising to tell the truth and nothing but the truth, but you must not expect it to tell the whole truth." That may sound very cynical, and in terms of service to the public it suggests a lack of concern that drives consumer advocates up the wall. Even many people in the ad industry probably wish their colleague hadn't made that statement so openly. It displays an attitude that can get the business world in trouble by expressing a selfish interest rather blatantly.

Still, the man probably described consumer expectations accurately. We anticipate that a claim such as "Our amplifier gives you 100 watts of power" will not also have a disclosure that "Some users don't need more than 90 watts." We expect to see additional information of that sort in *Consumer Reports*, and we expect *not* to see it in ads.

Another reason the regulators may not be bothered about selected omissions is that consumers are likely to see advertising for more than just one company. If the gas people advertise, the electric people also advertise. Indeed, the gas people's use of selected facts will likely strengthen the resolve of the electric people to do the same in their own ads. When they do, consumers will then get information on both sides of an issue in the total body of advertising, even if not in any single message. That may sound a bit smoother in theory than it necessarily works out, but it probably does often work.

Am I concluding that selected facts pose no problems? Not entirely, because I believe they produce additional trouble for consumers in a way the law has not recognized. It happens because selected facts always invite consumers to make their decisions on a basis of less than the entire truth. The explicit content may be fully true and significant, but it omits additional information that pertains to objective truth and objective significance.

I said earlier that brand selling makes it hard to be both true and brand significant. Using selected facts is a way around that problem for those advertisers who have at least one claim that is both true and significant. They can use such claims and simply forget the others. Of course while that's understandable from their viewpoint, it means that consumers get only some of the truth and significance they need to make decisions. It also means that consumers who do not notice what is happening will perceive more truth and significance than is objectively there.

For example, from being told that Firestone tires passed all their inspections, consumers might see an implied claim conveyed that the total of all available facts shows that Firestone tires are superior to other brands. They would see a suggestion that the proper purchasing conclusion overall is the one that the selected fact suggests. After all, why else does the advertiser use only that fact!

I call that the Sufficient Facts Implication. It works a bit like the Halo Implication from chapter 11, in which one true factual claim implies that one or more other facts are true. Here one true factual claim implies itself to be representative of all the facts. It implies that the entire set of facts carries the same brand significance as the selected fact, and calls for the same favorable purchasing decision.

While all identified examples of the Halo Implication are false, all instances of the Sufficient Facts Implication are not false. The difference is in the nature of the unselected facts. Sometimes those additional facts will maintain or even increase the brand's desirability, which means the selected fact is indeed representative of the whole. For example, some consumers who learn everything that can be learned about gas and electric ranges might continue to favor gas as much as or more than they had when they considered only the "turn-down" feature.

On the other hand, the additional information may turn out to favor gas less, making the selected fact deceptive. I believe this result is more likely than the other across all advertising. Advertisers select certain facts because those facts are better than others. Given that, the best guess about the remainder is that they aren't going to be as effective as the selected ones. So, although the rap on selected facts cannot be that they always imply falsity, they do always set consumers at risk. The risk is that the perceived brand significance they produce is less than what consumers will see with greater information.

In that sense selected facts are untruthful, and reliance on them is detrimental to consumers. Consumers need to trust and rely on claims, but in this case doing so may harm them. Truth and significance will inevitably suffer diminishment when we lack the whole of either. The resulting disadvantage to consumers reflects what will be a recurring theme of this book, that the absence of legal falsity does not solve all the problems consumers face. Diminishment of truth and significance is a form of falsity, and of harm to consumers, whether or not the law recognizes it. The fate of consumers in this process deserves more recognition than it appears to get.

It matters, then, that the regulators, although recognizing some problems involving certain selected facts, have not recognized the general problem described here. Selected facts aren't very far down the slope that leads toward falsity at the bottom, yet they are capable of causing trouble. The consumer may feel satisfied and have no subjective sense of harm. Still, there is always a potential for harm, objectively, when consumers make decisions with biased and incomplete information, and when they are unaware of doing so or have no access to the missing facts.

That starts us down the first slippery step.

# 16

# THE KROGER PRICE SURVEY CASE

Figures don't lie, it's said, but liars figure. Let's do a survey and we'll prove all kinds of things. Anything we want—just ask the right kinds of questions and the answers will take care of themselves. Science is wonderful. Suppose we want to show that our grocery store's prices are lower than the competition's. Nothing to it—we just figure out in advance which of our items have lower prices. Then we do a survey of those items at several stores, and the results will "prove" that our store has the lowest prices.

How do we find out in advance what items have lower prices? We can use earlier surveying or pricing information that covers everything sold, and note the items for which we compare poorly. Then we can exclude those items from the surveys that we plan to feature in the ads. Even better, we can find out what items the store is currently getting from manufacturers on special promotions. Those promotions mean lower prices to the store, which in turn lets the store lower its prices to consumers.

We must identify the employees who arrange these promotions and set the lower prices. We then have them select the items to be included in our survey. If they happen to include the promotional items in the survey—and why wouldn't they!—we're sure to get survey results that show low prices. Our efficient operation has enabled us to get right down to the nitty gritty of how to run a grocery store. Except it's cheating, it's illegal. Companies wouldn't do a thing like that, would they? Well . . .

Kroger did. That's the Kroger Company, of Cincinnati, Ohio, the country's second largest retail food chain, with over 1,000 stores in twenty states. The company felt it could make a strong appeal by conducting and advertising frequent "Price Patrol" surveys in many of its marketing areas. Ads would then report comparative prices for several competitors. The strategy would work, of course, only if the surveys showed that Kroger had the best prices. Kroger's price checks in some sales areas showed that it indeed was lower most of the time on many grocery items.

Its meat and produce prices, though, were usually higher. One reason was that they were not included in the manufacturer promotions that produced lower costs for Kroger. So, although meat and produce accounted for 28 percent of the chain's food sales, Kroger ruled them out of the Price Patrol surveys. It also omitted most private-label (house brand) items, which were also higher priced in most cases. House brand items accounted for another 19 percent of sales.

The company manual stated that if proper procedures were followed, "Kroger will be lower on more items and higher on fewer items than any competitor checked. If this is not the case, the television is wasted and cannot be used." The company did not waste its television. It arranged for items in each survey to be selected by the employee who processed the promotional discounts from the manufacturers. One of them testified to the FTC that he made a point of placing the temporarily discounted items into the survey sample, to ensure that Kroger would perform well. Those items thus were given a far higher representation among the 150 items chosen for each Price Patrol survey than they would have received if chosen randomly from the ten to fifteen thousand items typically stocked in a Kroger store.

Kroger's internal operations separated foods into four categories: grocery, meat, produce, and delicatessen. That made the word *grocery* a category separate from the other three. When Kroger then advertised its Price Patrol surveys as involving "grocery" items, it led to an implied misrepresentation that illustrates the Ordinary Meaning Implication. That's the implication in which consumers see the ordinary meaning despite an advertiser's argument that a different meaning applies (chap. 11). Kroger argued that consumers would give grocery the special meaning it had for Kroger insiders.

The FTC rejected that argument, finding instead that the usage conflicted with the commonsense understanding by consumers that grocery means all food items in a grocery store. The commission found that Kroger had used the surveys to prove to consumers (the Proof Implication) that its prices were lower than the competition on an overall basis, for all food items. And consumers apparently believed the claims, the commission found: "The Price Patrol program had a remarkably positive effect on Kroger's sales, profits, and market share. For example, in Atlanta Kroger's market share doubled."

Kroger demonstrated its unwillingness to believe its own advertised surveys by not relying on them as a monitor of its actual prices. That didn't stop it, though, from protesting that the FTC's standards for surveys were "unjustifiably strict." Apparently the company thought the standards were good enough for information given to consumers in ads, even though not good enough for information it would itself use.

The company also protested the order to cease and desist because it had completely discontinued doing the surveys and advertising them. The decision noted, however, that the primary reason Kroger stopped this highly effective campaign was that the FTC was taking it to court. Removal of the threat by ending the case with no order, therefore, could result in a repetition of the whole process, the commission said.

Accordingly, Kroger was ordered to do no more price comparisons based on surveys unless two conditions were met: (1) The people selecting the items must not be the people who priced them, and (2) the claim must not cause consumers to think the comparisons applied to any "grocery" items that were actually excluded. The price comparisons, in short, must be claims that consumers could rely on to their benefit rather than harm.

For later reasons apparently influenced by a new Reagan appointee as commissioner and chairman, the FTC sweetened the order with a "sunset provision." That meant it would run out in two years rather than observing the usual custom of remaining in force indefinitely. Although another set of charges is always possible, Kroger is now free, as most offenders would not be, to return to its prior practices without violating the order issued against it.

# 17

# MINIMAL FACTS: THE SECOND STEP

When I was a kid I had a one-speed bike. That's now largely thought of as unacceptable, although I recently rented one in New Orleans. It worked fine on that flat terrain; the only hill in sight was the dike. But elsewhere in the market bicycles have progressed over the decades to three speeds, then five, ten, twelve, fifteen, eighteen, twenty-one, and sometimes more. The same thing has happened with kitchen blenders. One speed isn't enough for them, either, so the market has progressed similarly. Clever names have been invented for the various choices, like Crush and Grate and Puree. Eventually the makers installed rheostats and gave us infinite choice.

With both bikes and blenders the additional speeds are useful up to a point. They matter to consumers because they provide benefits not there before. You can probably guess what I'm getting at, though. At some point the multiplying of choices makes any adjacent pair so similar we can't tell them apart. My kids' bikes had ten speeds but they never used them all. The pureed carrots probably can't tell the difference, either. Professionals in either field may be able to do so, and appreciate it, too. But the typical consumer has no real use or need for a twenty-one speed bike or a thirty-speed blender.

Then why do the sellers keep going? The answer's easy—to create those brand significant claims, the ones that differentiate meaningfully and positively. No other brand matches ours, because no other has this many speeds. It's more the sellers' need than the public's, but it can be a positive appeal for those consumers who accept it. And many do; they perceive and believe and appreciate that the added speeds give added benefits.

As a result, marketing people routinely dictate such needs to the production people. Production relates to outside demand, to be sure, and originally also mirrored it—a seller would recognize existing demand and seek to satisfy it. At some point the demand would fade out—the maximum number of bicycle gears that mattered to consumers would be reached. In the early days, that would have been that!

Not so with modern procedure, in which the marketing people advise the production department to add more speeds anyway. Demand for the new feature will be created by the company's promotional efforts simultaneously as the assembly line makes the physical changes. As someone said, "Invention is the mother of necessity."

Thus a whole new category of demand is created out of producers' rather than consumers' needs. Consumers don't naturally need the new feature, but the promotion staff steps in to produce the demand unnaturally. Consumers buy the values they see, of course, but what they see has been produced subjectively and artificially. Objectively they are getting no more than a strictly minimal significance.

That brings us to the second diminishment of truth and significance, the next step down the slippery slope—the minimal fact. Minimal facts are similar to selected ones in being selected and true. But selected facts are objectively significant—alone at least, despite being less so in total context. By contrast, minimal facts are objectively just that—minimal. They are merely *promoted* as significant. They are "hyped" into meaning more than they otherwise would. To consumers they are as maximal as the seller can make them.

Just as selected facts will be used when the whole truth won't do the job, minimal facts will be used when selected ones aren't available. For selected facts to be used, the advertised brand must have at least one true and meaningfully favorable difference, objectively, from its competition. Given the way brands are created, it's almost inevitable that not all do. That prompts the makers to begin making things up. Selected facts have an existing basis for objective significance, but for the minimal kind the basis must be subjectively invented.

There are various ways to establish minimal facts. The most likely is in the manufacturing process, as with the additional bike speeds. Competing brands of given products, such as Mr. Clean and Top Job, both made by Procter and Gamble, often have such minor physical variations. Their minimalness is illustrated by consumers telling them apart more by the differences in their names and labels rather than by differences in their actual ingredients.

Cars made by the same company, such as Plymouth and Dodge, or Chevrolet and Pontiac, share many of the same engineering features and component parts. *Consumer Reports* is instructive on such matters, often discussing one brand by saying it's essentially the same as another. Many such examples involve design features, as with colors, styles, or other aspects of appearance. I was washing windows at home when I noticed the paper towels had colored embossed stripes, which appeared to add nothing to their washing ability. They may have made a contribution such as delighting the eye, but on the whole I found the feature quite minimal and wondered how much more it had cost me.

While design can be far from minimal in many areas such as cars and clothing, it can also be handled bizarrely, as with the new fat Camel cigarettes, Camel Wides, two millimeters wider than usual. They reminded me that years ago there was the cigarette with a length of 101 mm. rather than 100, touted as being "a silly millimeter longer." It *was* silly, but the maker offered it as having positive appeal.

What does *minimal* mean in terms of a physical difference? The general sense is that it's a small variation rather than a new feature. The first bicycle that could change gears had a new feature. When it got ten speeds rather than three, that was a significant variation. But going to eighteen speeds from fifteen was a minimal variation. We can't say at what exact point it changed from significant to minimal, but it happened at some point.

Another meaning of minimal involves peripheral features that do not carry out the principal function. The word-processing program I use has 288 available commands. After months of use I have yet to invoke many of them, or even learn what they do. They are all potentially valuable and I am glad for everything I'm given. But some I find extremely minimal in value compared to those I use all the time. Other products even advertise peripheral features that carry out no function at all, as with the cat food said to have all the phosphorus cats need. Cats, I'm told, need no phosphorus. Gasolines with the highest octanes are the same way; octane beyond the level your car needs gives you no extra power.

Of course we have to be careful about calling a feature minimal. Meaningfulness is in the eye of the beholder, and what's minimal to me may be quite maximal to you. Marketers will rightfully call this to our attention, and no doubt many buying experiences validate the point. For example, most electronic and appliance items have multiple features that salesmen refer to as "bells and whistles." That means they're extras—the item works acceptably without them. I'm always aware of those and will buy the ones I like and can afford. They add pleasure even if they are objectively peripheral and minimal relative to the principal function.

Recently I drove a car that gave me my first chance to use an inside switch to adjust a motorized outside mirror on the passenger side. I appreciated the advantage of that, even though its absence hadn't impeded me in all my prior years of driving. I can't say I would give that feature a major place among all the considerations involved in choosing a car. But there's no reason some buyers shouldn't find the feature fascinating enough to make it a factor in their purchasing decisions. One of the pleasures of such extras, actually, is simply knowing you have them, and knowing that the people who don't have them know they don't. You get that benefit even if you never use the feature! The first kid on the block with a ten-speed or even a three-speed bike knows what that means.

A classic marketing story is instructive about the minimalness of design features. Henry Ford insisted the public should be satisfied with one car model produced in one color, black, but he changed his mind in the 1920s after General Motors stole many of his sales with colors and annual model changes. Just because such features may be peripheral to the main function doesn't mean they aren't valued. Imagine parking your car in the midst of hundreds of others at a shopping center or a sports stadium. On returning to the lot, you realize every one of those cars is the same make, same model, same color. To find your own, you will have to spend many minutes checking license plates or peering into windows to recognize personal items.

Can you guess what people would do if cars were still like that? They'd personalize them—put ribbons on the antenna, red paint on the hood ornament, whatever it took to make the car look like theirs alone. Such a feature might be peripheral, but it certainly wouldn't be minimal. So I'm acknowledging that minimalness is in the eye of the beholder.

Nonetheless, I am staying with the point that when such features are promoted heavily they are frequently claimed to be far more significant than any objective analysis would reveal. Adjacent speeds on a many-speed bicycle, for example, are so close together that tests of riders will inevitably show an inability to tell the difference. Two paper towels, identical but for certain differences in color and design, would show little difference in tests of cleaning ability.

I saw an ad for a riding lawn mower, touting its sports car styling, sun roof, radio, and cigarette lighter. I pondered what *Consumer Reports* might say about that. Surely the magazine would stress that those features cost more while doing nothing to enhance the principal function of cutting grass. The add-ons would be called irrelevant at best, perhaps even useless—you couldn't hear the radio while the machine was running. And what should we think of the cigarette lighter? I don't know about you, but when anybody who's smoking comes near my mower, on or off, I start running as fast as I start yelling.

In short, despite what may appear subjectively to beholders' eyes, many advertised facts are objectively minimal in significance. Despite some difficulties in deciding the degree of meaningfulness in certain cases, it seems reasonable to identify minimal facts as a definite category of advertising claims, and a distinct step down the slippery slope.

# 18

# CREATING MINIMAL FACTS

The methods mentioned in the previous chapter for creating minimal facts involve *physical* differences. Such brand differences involve manufacturing steps rather than communication steps, but of course they are done for communication reasons. They are ways for advertisers to find something to say about their brand when they originally have nothing to say about it.

A second type of minimal fact involves a *performance* difference. For example, a toilet soap engages in a complexion test, or a car climbs a mountain or speeds through an obstacle course. No other brand has achieved such a thing, which allows the inference that none other could. Such a performance implies an objective brand difference, but there probably isn't one. If a brand could actually perform in a way that its competitors could not, its maker would certainly say so explicitly— why miss an opportunity!

The reality, usually, is that all the other brands could achieve the same performance; they just don't happen to have done so. The performance thus creates little or no brand significance objectively. The advertiser promotes it as though it does, of course, but such performance differences are usually even more diminished in meaningfulness than are the minimal physical differences.

The trend continues with the third type of minimal fact, the *promotional* difference, in which a claim is based on an existing feature. Although one or more competitors have the same feature, consumers are to infer from the claim that the competitors don't have it when actually the competitors just have never promoted it. Objectively, then, the brand that makes the claim is differentiated only by what its messages say.

Colgate's promoting its toothpaste's ability to sweeten breath may be the most famous example. Every toothpaste could do that but none were advertising it. The emphasis was on cleaning, apparently because of embarrassment concerning bad breath. All the brands could clean, too, but Colgate doubled the value with its famous line that it "cleans your breath while it cleans your teeth." The competition was slow to copy that claim, allowing Colgate to "preempt" it. That means that even after others advertised it, consumers continued to attribute the feature solely to Colgate. Freshening breath was exceptionally minimal in the sense that it differentiated only in the mind.

The feature was far from minimal, though, in consumers' perceptions. Wonderfully for Colgate, it sold more toothpaste than ever before. Some of the added sales may have been for other brands, to be sure, but most sales would naturally flow to the one competitor that explicitly made the claim. That's considered a classic story in marketing lore for showing how promotion can overcome the lack of features that truly differentiate. It makes advertising people very important because they do what the production department cannot do—differentiate the brand. They supply a benefit that consumers have not previously perceived.

To advertisers, of course, all the kinds of minimal facts have value. They benefit when consumers perceive such claims subjectively as creating a brand difference in a positive way. Such significance typically doesn't occur to the consumers until the advertising induces it. That is, people haven't been asking for such values, or haven't noticed they were absent or felt a need for them. But once they are pointed out, such appeals can become very meaningful. To advertisers, then, minimal facts can have maximal value.

Advertisers would probably say a company such as Colgate deserves the extra sales it gets from using an appeal that its competitors don't use. Further, they would say that to correct any deceptiveness the competitors need only to get smart and copy the claim. If the competitors are not equally insightful, they deserve to lose the race. That's hard to dispute, yet an uneasiness exists in knowing that the competitors' failure to respond leaves consumers at a disadvantage. It creates a falsity, not one of the biggest in the world, but not worth ignoring, either. There is always some potential for harm when consumers' perceptions of truth and significance are not objectively accurate.

Let's look at the problems with the various kinds of minimal facts. Minimal physical differences, the first kind, are objectively true (the bike has all twenty-one speeds, as advertised), and they can differentiate positively (no other bike has that many). Yet they distort consumer perception if they imply their significance to be greater than any available objective basis can support. From a product rather than brand viewpoint, the difference has little or no meaningfulness (other bikes have all the speeds anyone really needs). Also, such claims suppress, as do selected facts, the consumer's perception of the truth and significance of all the additional product characteristics that remain unmentioned.

Truth may also be diminished in implying that the brand differentiation created by the minimal physical difference is more permanent than is objectively predictable. Other brands usually can, and probably will, acquire the differentiating feature themselves and so eliminate the difference. That's the way the market usually goes: one bike gets ten speeds, then they all do. The opportunity to maintain a monopoly over any difference, minimal or substantial, appears to be rare. Polaroid, with its instant photomaking, is a remarkable exception.

This first category of minimal facts, physical differences, might be open to disagreement, as seen in the previous chapter, over whether a claim is objectively minimal in specific instances. However, the second and third kinds, performance and promotional differences, do not seem open to the same debate. It's hard to consider those two types anything but extremely minimal in objective significance.

A brand's maker can establish that a physical difference, however small, truly exists. For minimal performance differences, however, it can establish only that some event took place for its brand while not for the competitors'. That difference is so small that it is unlikely to be objectively meaningful. It does not mean that the competitors could not perform the same way. Probably they can, and if so, the truth about the total product category is not well served.

Minimal promotional differences are the most objectively minimal of all. Their only truth is that the claimed feature exists. Their only difference is that it appears in one brand's promotion and not in the others'. No objective brand significance exists; the advertiser can only imply it.

In summary, minimal facts run from very low to nonexistent in significance, that is, in their ability to favorably differentiate the brand from others to an objectively meaningful degree. Their truth is also diminished in varying degrees. Although the features described are explicitly true, they are so only by narrow interpretations. Subjectively, consumers are likely to see broader meanings implied, ones that some-times will be false. For example, the announcement of more bicycle speeds might imply falsely that the average cyclist would find the new choices to be noticeable or meaningful additions. It might imply that the bicycle with more speeds is a better brand overall.

As with selected facts, the problems of minimal facts generally have escaped the attention of the regulators because they don't pro-duce legal deceptiveness. They don't represent the part of the slope where the regulators feel at home, the bottom. When truth and signifi-cance are minimized, however, even in perfectly legal ways, we are on the way down. There is likely to be more harm than good for consum-ers who trust and rely on these claims.

# 19

## THE INFOMERCIAL CASES

Suppose an advertiser buys on television not thirty or sixty seconds but thirty or sixty minutes. It runs what the listings describe as a program on some fascinating topic. It's not really a program, though, but a form of advertising called an infomercial. Infomercials often falsely imply, the FTC has said, that they are independent news programs. Actually, each one is a carefully disguised program-length commercial.

We can think of the result as a brand new addition to the types of implications discussed earlier: the Independent News Program Implication. It's a bit different from the implications we've seen already. The latter all involve specific deceptive content in ads, whereas this one involves a deceptive impression about the overall communication.

In the one called "Money Money Money," Hal and Debra Morris introduced themselves on a set that television viewers would find similar to those of Jay Leno or Larry King. Hal began by saying, "Welcome to our show today. Today you're going to learn about how to get government grants. Grants mean the government gives you the money to go out and get involved in a business. We have America's foremost expert on low interest government loans and government grants . . ." He then introduced Wayne Phillips, who began by thanking Hal and Debbie "for inviting me on your program today." As the FTC complaint later stated, Phillips was "purported to be a guest of the talk show" while the Morrisses were "represented to be the hosts of a talk show."

The "guest" then launched a long presentation about the huge amounts of money the government will give people to use in starting businesses, and how to get that money. The script moved smoothly toward its actual purpose of selling his book, *How to Start Your Own Business by Doing Business with the Government*. It also offered follow-up information called the "Grant Alert Service." The charge for both was $49.95 plus $4.00 for shipping. The ad highlighted an 800 number and mailing address, and invited credit card usage.

The FTC felt that a number of the reasons Phillips gave for buying his book were open to question. Its complaint contradicted them by saying the truth was that:

• government sources do not provide $33 billion in grants for starting businesses;

• it is not easy for the average consumer to obtain such a grant;

• the book did not contain primarily information on how grants can be obtained easily;

- the federal Small Business Innovation Research Program does not provide $25,000 grants easily and does not provide grants to start virtually any kind of small business;
- grants are not provided without regard to the applicant's financial history and resources; and
- not all purchasers of the book received the additional "Grant Alert Service."

The program featured endorsements from satisfied consumers. One appeared personally to say that three months after he quit driving a taxi and started an import-export company he got a contract to handle over $4 million worth of business annually. He gave credit to Wayne Phillips for teaching him how to do it. The FTC, though, saw a false Endorsement Implication in that. It charged that "the claimed success stories are not true and do not illustrate or substantiate that the information provided in the government grants book has been used successfully by average consumers to start small businesses."

"Money Money Money" was not the only program-length commercial the FTC attacked. Another began, "Hello, my name is Vince Inneo, your inside information investigator. Welcome to this very special edition of TV Insiders. It's no secret that having inside information keeps you steps ahead of the others. That's why we're here." He continued, "This installment is critically important. Many of you have written possibly the most valuable inside information we have yet uncovered. Here are some of the hundreds of letters telling us about a seventy-three-year-old Phoenix, Arizona, man who many have claimed has rediscovered nature's formula for youth. Listen to some of these amazing stories."

Later he concluded, "It's your cards and your letters alerting 'TV Insiders' to new discoveries and inside information. We need inside information. You tell me what you've heard; we will research it, investigate it, and then we will share our findings with everyone. If we use your information, we will send you a 'TV Insider' investigator's card. So until next mission, this is your inside investigator, Vince Inneo, wishing you good health and God's blessings."

Much effort was taken in that format to convince viewers that "TV Insiders" would investigate a wide range of topics. It would not. The only topic the program cared about was the formula for youth, made of bee pollen. The producer, TV Inc., and the marketer, C C Pollen Company, eventually agreed to make no future unsubstantiated claims for bee pollen's effects on people's health or physical condition.

Another program, "Consumer Challenge," falsely implied an independent assessment of BluBlockers sunglasses. The true sponsor was the product's seller, JS&A Group. A company called Twin Star Productions produced several program length commercials: "The Michael Reagan Show," "Breakthrough '88," and "Let's Talk with Lyle Waggoner," touting nostrums that the FTC said didn't work.

Along with stopping the false product claims, the FTC made a specific point of stopping the phony representations about being news programs. The order against Wayne Phillips was typical, forbidding any future message "that misrepresents, directly or by implication, that it is an independent program and not a paid advertisement." Further, any such program must state the following from now on: "The program you are watching is a paid advertisement for [name or product or service]." The script must include that disclosure visually within thirty seconds of the program's beginning, and again before each reiteration of instructions for ordering the advertised product.

Infomercials are still permitted as long as they follow those rules. There's no law against long commercials, although the audience may be a lot smaller when viewers realize what's going on. Lately I have noticed that television listings in newspapers indicate "Paid Programming" for some half hour slots.

The information is now revealed candidly, and we can assess it accordingly.

# PART 4

## THE BOTTOM OF THE SLOPE: NONFACT CLAIMS

*The third and lowest type of claims on the slippery slope is treated separately here, because it is the farthest from the truth and the closest to falsity. It comes in two forms, nonbrand facts (that is, facts about something other than the item for sale) and opinions. Although nonfact claims are widely used, the regulators have barely recognized their capacity for deceptiveness. Nor have the regulators recognized the potential for these claims to cause, in addition to deceptiveness, some of the most serious social problems of which advertising is capable.*

## 20

# NONFACTS: THE THIRD STEP

In contemplation of a third step down the slippery slope, let's recall the advertisers' goals. They want to achieve a perception by consumers of a brand truthfully differentiated from its competitors, positively, to a meaningful degree. They must avoid a perception of insignificance at all costs, because the brand must sell. A perception of falsity must be avoided, too, for along with inviting the wrath of the regulators, falsity would suggest insignificance to consumers.

The advertisers may avoid consumers' perceptions of falsity and insignificance, however, without fully embracing truth and significance. As selected facts and minimal facts have already shown us, advertisers often do not give consumers truth and significance in full flower. Rather, they give varying degrees of diminishment of those qualities, objectively. That reflects the amount of truth and significance that the sellers need, which is no more than what it takes to make the sale.

Consumers' subjective perceptions may provide the needed amount quite adequately. Objectively false claims could do the job, too, although only under the threat of regulator intervention. Thus some minimum avoidance of falsity is preferable. But once the regulators are neutralized, the amount of additional truth needed to make the sale is only that needed to create the necessary minimum of perceived significance.

From the buyers' quite different view, truth and significance should be maximized—in reality, not just in perception. We shouldn't want merely to perceive that something is meaningful; we should want it to be really so. And we should care about that not just for brands, but for overall product categories.

It isn't natural for consumers to think about individual brands. What we care about is the product. We care about its variations, to be sure, but we care about all of them, not just some, certainly not just one. We should feel disadvantaged when advertisements give us the degree of truth and significance associated with one and only one brand. We should regard such information as being too small a portion of the facts associated with the entire product category.

With that background, we move to a development that further diminishes what consumers want and need. Thus far we've seen that selected facts are true, even though they leave out additional truth and much significance. Minimal facts are also true, but they leave out even more truth and significance. What follows in logical progression is to have truth and objective significance be missing altogether—we have arrived at *nonfacts*.

We have not arrived at falsity, which lies at the bottom of the slope. There is no falsity about the advertised item in nonfact claims, even though there is no truth either. While a fact is capable of being true or false, a nonfact is capable of neither. "Coke is it" is a nonfact, as are Mr. Bartles and Mr. Jaymes, as are countless claims that a brand is the best, superior to all others. An advertiser uses such claims when it finds no facts, not even selected or minimal ones, worth conveying about its brand.

That can happen for various reasons. First, the brands may simply not physically differ from each other. For example, drugs such as aspirin are prohibited by law from varying. Second, actual physical differences may be irrelevant to consumers. For example, one brand of instant coffee may be slightly darker than another, or grainier or whatever, but many consumers will choose by taste alone. (For those who do choose on appearance, the color or whatever will probably be a minimal fact objectively.)

Third, and most often, physical differences may be too small to matter. While what I have called minimal facts are perceivable, nonfacts may involve differences so much more minimal that consumers just don't notice them. For example, many competing brands of food or drink vary slightly in ingredients. The differences exist technically but are nonexistent for purposes of selling because consumers do not perceive or respond to them. Such facts cannot be brand significant.

Services such as long distance telephoning, life insurance, express mail, grocery stores, and banks have definite differences. So do electronic products such as television sets and VCRs, and appliances such as washers and microwave ovens. The differences in these categories are often so small that consumers don't see them, and thus see no meaningfully positive differentiation in them. If a fact cannot affect a purchasing decision, then it does not exist for purposes of promotion.

When differences are so minor, perceiving them takes training and expertise that consumers typically lack. They are of the sort that, say, a brewmaster could detect in beer, or a dairyman in milk, or an electronics engineer in television screens. If there is an actual physical difference between Kodak and Fuji film, an expert may see it. What counts to me as a consumer, though, is that I cannot or at least will not see it, and therefore I will not choose on the basis of it.

Thus by literal absence or more often by lack of consumer interest or sheer lack of recognition the advertiser often has no facts to use in creating true and favorable differentiations. It's no accident that these

are the product categories that generally get heavy advertising sched-
ules. The less there is to say factually about an item, the more it must be
advertised in order to make up for that deficiency.

It's the case with numerous beverages—milk, orange juice, colas,
lemon-limes, beer, whiskey, gin. It's so for many other food items, such
as fruits and vegetables, white bread, corn flakes, margarine, cheese,
popcorn, pet food. It's true of household items, such as paper towels,
bleach, detergents, hand soaps and other cleaners, or personal items
such as shampoos and cosmetics. Some products come in categories
that do differ in ways that matter to consumers: for example, beer, cigarettes, and peanut butter (light, menthol, chunky). Still, within those
categories the brands don't differ in consumers' perceptions.

Readers may feel they recognize and care about physical differences in some of the examples I've given. If so, they will be operating in
the selected or minimal fact categories. Many other consumers will not
make such recognitions. A useful insight is that many physical distinc-
tions people say they make are actually very hard or even impossible to
discern when brand identification is missing. The ability to identify
brands of beer, margarine, bananas, or perfume can fall to zero when
consumers take "blind" tests. When they are not shown the package or
told the brand name, they are unable to see the differences they once
saw. What they had seen or tasted or smelled must have been the
nonfacts, such as the names and claims.

Coca-Cola's original tests of New Coke were blind tests that found
a preference for the new formulation. Yet when people were later
tested with full knowledge of what they were tasting, they preferred
the old formula. Once the nonfacts came into play, the small physical
difference made no difference because people no longer perceived it.
Since consumers do their actual purchasing with identification, the
company saw little choice but to reinstate the old Coke, which they
now call Classic.

The absense of facts, and consequent relevance of nonfact claims,
is a logical result of the process that leads to creating brands. Remember, a brand in the beginning is nothing more than a product as made
by any of two or more companies. The version made by one of them
need not differ intrinsically from that made by its competitors. The
desire to differentiate arises out of the nature of the competitive marketplace, not out of the nature of products. Thus it is entirely natural that a
brand advertiser should have no objectively true significant facts to
convey.

That is the situation in which nonfacts enter the picture. We will
soon see more about what they are and how they work.

# 21

# IDENTIFYING NONFACTS

If a claim is a nonfact, does that mean it's an opinion? You might say yes, because a standard breakdown says statements are either facts or opinions. Yet in the context of brand selling nonfacts also include something else—facts that are not about the advertised brand. They are facts about something, but are no more factual regarding the brand than are opinions. Accordingly, nonbrand facts are combined with opinions here to make up the category of nonfacts. Let's see what varieties there are.

Opinion claims give an evaluation. The brand is good, or better than one or more competitors, or the best. These can be global evaluations, summarizing the entire brand, or they can pertain to a specific attribute or performance feature. Opinions often come directly from the seller, simply by stating them in the ad or quoting a representative of the company. They may also come from outside persons, to create a perception of independence in the judgement. Outsiders may be of many sorts, such as specialists in the product field or celebrities. Sometimes the outsiders are just plain consumers, whose opinion would presumably make sense to other consumers.

Opinions and facts differ in that facts must be the same for all observers. A beer brand may or may not contain alcohol. That, as a property of the brand, cannot differ from one consumer to the next. Opinions can differ, though. They are the private property of each person, who usually varies significantly from others in background and experience. Thus while facts are true or false, opinions are neither. While a brand fact says something about the brand, a brand opinion technically says something only about the speaker. That's why objectively it's a nonfact about the brand. Of course advertisers intend for consumers to regard the opinion as being "about" the brand.

The other kind of nonfact is the nonbrand fact. It is a fact, but not about the advertised item. Nonbrand facts come in many types because they can be about anything in the world besides the brand. Make that almost anything, because the advertiser wants consumers to accept them as believable and significant about the brand. Just as with opinions, consumers must perceive nonbrand facts to be "about" the brand in order to work. They can't be claims that consumers will find obviously false or obviously unrelated to the brand.

That limitation is not great, however. Consumers tend to see many types of facts as pertaining to brands and as differentiating them positively and meaningfully from their competitors. Because such facts will most likely be present in the general buying and consuming context within which people encounter the brand, advertisers look for them there.

What kinds of things are in that context? The whole world, we might imagine, but let's narrow it down to things closest to the brand. The advertisers have recognized two sources of nonbrand facts as most useful. They are ourselves, as we play our role of consumers, and also the society in which we play that role. Translating that into claims, the things we are most likely to see as being "about" the brand, even though not really a physical part of it, are our own inner features and the features of other people. They are the psychological and social surroundings within which we encounter a brand.

That such things are not "in" the brand does not mean the advertiser cannot use them as values of it. I recall an incident from my boyhood in which my mother created a value that was simply not present in any objective way in the item she wished her family to value positively. She was raising three young sons during the Great Depression of the·1930s, when money was short in many homes. Our father was fortunate in retaining his railroad job while many in the ranks just below him joined the millions of unemployed. His salary, kept at a meager level, allowed us to live adequately although austerely. Our mother had to make the most of every penny spent, and in retrospect it appears that she learned to do so very well.

Most of this I didn't realize until much later, after which I could see the significance of certain events that had occurred. One of them involved our eating of bread, specifically the end pieces of a loaf, what we Pittsburghers called the "crusts." One day Mom said to us, "Too bad there are only two crusts and there are three of you." We looked at the crusts with initial puzzlement, and then looked at each other with increasing involvement. When she asked who wanted a crust we all said, "Me."

So, she said, what we'll do is we'll take turns. First we'll have a three-way coin flip and the two that match will get the crusts from this loaf we have now. But don't worry, those two will take subsequent turns being left out, so things will always stay even. Okay, we said, and from that day no loaf of bread was ever open long before the crusts disappeared.

The strength of that manipulation brought eventual shocks. At a summer church camp some years later I spotted the bread plate and blurted out, "Hey, anybody else want that crust?" All the guys said, "Heck, no," which started me realizing that not many others shared my view of the world. To this day, however, although I don't go out of my way to find a crust, I don't turn them down when they appear before me.

What my mother was doing was exactly what the advertisers do, making something out of nothing. The crusts had nutritive values, of course, but that was relevant only to her motivation, not to ours. Nothing about the crusts could interest us in eating them for their own sake. Of course that didn't prevent our recognizing a value, as Mom well knew.

What we were "tasting," in effect, was very real. It was our own satisfaction in coping successfully with the challenges of a complexly competitive-cooperative three-person society. Losing was bad, but while winning was good it meant someone else had to lose, so staying even was the preferred outcome. Very likely the need to hold off the threat of imbalance kept the three of us from ever noticing how Mom generously sacrificed the chance to have a crust herself. She slipped that one right by us.

The story's message is that one's role within a group, the group dynamic, can be attached, related, linked to an advertised item. It thereby creates a value for the item that exists in the consumer's mind even though not objectively existing in the item. In the case of brands it can lead to a meaningful positive differentiation that consumers will not otherwise perceive.

Advertisers have long since known where to look when they can find nothing to say about their brand that is really about their brand. In such situations they make careful examinations of consumers' personalities and the social contexts within which consumers do their buying. It's a standard way of solving a standard problem.

## 22

# HOW ADVERTISERS USE NONBRAND FACTS

The context within which people buy and use advertised items contains additional attractive things, such as contests or gift premiums. Most nonbrand facts, however, reflect consumers' psychological features or social surroundings. Many such things are relevant, or can be made relevant, to decisions about purchasing and using. Let's describe them some more by seeing one of the thousands to be found in ads. It's a claim from a 1992 newspaper ad for Vic Tanny's health club: "You don't just shape your body. You shape your life."

Is there a fact in that ad about Vic Tanny? Yes, to the extent that shaping your body means building muscles or losing weight. It is the factual promise that your membership will give you access to the health club's exercise machines, aerobics classes, and swimming pool.

Fine, but what about the other part of the claim? If you walked into Vic Tanny's and said, "I'm here to shape my life," they'd probably say, "Sure, why don't you try a shrink?" They have no machines or classes aimed specifically at addressing that goal. Except to the extent that shaping your body might play a role in shaping your life (which it might), you will get no help in that direction from Vic Tanny.

The reference to "your life" can appear very factual to those many consumers who are motivated to change their physical appearance and thus also their personal image. The statement is a fact about them, depicting a desire they have. However, it's rather less certainly a fact about Vic Tanny. Granted, consumers who use Tanny's equipment and classes may change their body shape and consequently change other people's image of them. Despite that, what you factually receive from Tanny, in exchange for the quite real money you pay, is related only intangibly and ambiguously to the social goal you may have.

What you factually receive is access to equipment and classes— that's it! If you pay your money for that and are denied the access, you have a basis for demanding a refund. But if you pay your money and don't get the psychic or social satisfaction you were seeking, what then? You will find you have no ground for an adjustment because the company will say it never offered you that in the first place. As far as Vic Tanny is concerned, the reference to such desires is not really a fact about the health club at all. In the terms used here, it's the nonbrand fact form of a nonfact.

Now, why would an advertiser want to say something about itself that is not about what it's trying to sell but only about a certain category of consumers? Obviously it's because it wants to attract those people. Often, too, it's because the product or service does not have a built-in attraction to that group. Originally exercise equipment and classes had a natural attraction mainly for body builders and other exercise freaks. The attraction was not so obvious for those who merely wanted to lose weight, and yet the latter make a much bigger potential audience. So somebody had the insight that the demand that didn't exist naturally could probably be created by clever suggestion. The explosion of health clubs shows how right they were.

Sometimes the desired demand already exists in a segment of the population. For example, the elderly are naturally targeted in ads for denture adhesives, or northerners are given more attention than southerners in promoting snow tires. The nature of the item dictates its use by certain people and not others. When that happens, the advertiser simply describes the pertinent physical facts and runs them in media that address the pertinent people. That's targeting to a segment, which does not in itself involve the problems of facts and nonfacts I'm discussing. Today, however, there's often more to the situation than just segmenting.

Today a specific type of consumer is frequently the subject of the ad rather than merely its object. The consumer's personal profile becomes the appeal that the advertiser makes to that consumer. It's happened because sellers have become well aware, as did Vic Tanny, that they are not blocked from appealing to a particular group just because their brand's features or even the product category's features do not naturally attract such folks.

When consumers don't recognize the relevance to themselves without prompting, they can be prompted. The advertisers can make sure consumers see themselves reflected in the ads. If I can link a fact about me to a brand, I'm likely to think I've just heard something very important about that item. Today brands of jeans, perfume, cologne, colas, and sneakers, among other products, are promoted largely through images of various kinds of persons that buyers are invited to copy. Dewar's Scotch tells us virtually nothing about itself while devoting its print space to detailed profiles of persons it thinks we might want to associate with or be like.

As we saw in the Vic Tanny ad, the process often helps promote a brand to a larger segment. A light beer is directed to those who drink the most beer, diet soft drinks are directed to men as well as women, complex cameras are aimed at amateur users, and so forth. It can also be the reverse. When a company already has a brand used by many consumers, it can promote a separate brand to an additional narrower segment. Cereals are addressed to adults, premium beers are addressed to upscale users. Budweiser gets a huge market of the biggest beer drinkers, but Michelob enables Anheuser-Busch to reach additional folks that Bud doesn't get.

Brands sometimes change segments. For thirty years Pepsi positioned itself for younger consumers, but its 1992 Super Bowl ads switched to claiming the drink was for everybody. That's what Coke had been doing for some time. Switching your appeal to another group is risky because you might alienate the ones who have been seeing themselves reflected in your brand for a long time. You're accepting a big challenge when you cater to a new market but also try to retain the old.

Another angle in explaining the use of psychological and social nonfacts is that they help advertisers interpret products and services as solutions to problems. If you're selling something that can be perceived as a solution, the thing you need most is a problem for it to solve. That's not always easy to do. You can't sell umbrellas in the sunshine, and you can't turn the sunshine into rain. Most days umbrella sellers don't even try.

However, if a product can be interpreted as involving psychological or social consequences for the user, then there's a way to try. To the seller's delight every day can be a rainy day in terms of pointing out some problem that needs solving. An encyclopedia doesn't just give you information; it helps eliminate your guilt about being a good parent to your kids. Deodorants keep you from smelling—things like that. An automobile doesn't give you just transportation; it helps you keep up with other people socially, or get ahead of them. McDonald's doesn't just feed your kids; it solves your need to entertain them. The phone company doesn't just give you electronic access to people; it lets you "reach out and touch" them. Hallmark cards do that, too.

Many products answer our needs to show ourselves to others: clothing, watches, jewelry. DeBeers has not typically sold diamonds by explaining that they're made of the very best carbon. Rather, they show how a necklace or ring will reflect light in other people's envious faces. For some products the solution involves hiding rather than displaying: hearing aids, hair coloring: "Does she or doesn't she?" A recent version of the latter shows two elderly women and asks, "Can you tell who's wearing the [Minitran] nitroglycerin patch?"

There are many indirect ways of indicating the consumer's psychological or social environment. Names do it: Healthy Choice or Lean Cuisine for diet foods; Viper, Explorer, Mustang for cars. Celebrities do it: Michael Jordan, Michael Jackson, Michael J. Fox, Michael Douglas. Don't forget cartoon characters: Tony the Tiger, Old Joe Camel, Bart Simpson.

Sometimes nonbrand facts play the role of attention-getting devices rather than claims. There are attractive models, small children, pets, sunsets, landscapes, jokes, Budweiser's Clydesdale horses, the Swedish Bikini Team, Oscar Mayer's Weinermobile, the Energizer bunny, the Olympics, on and on. As such, they may merely attract us so that we will pay real attention to the actual claims. However, many such items can get attention and be claims at the same time. Michael

Jordan can stop us from switching channels and can also serve as a strong reason for buying the shoes associated with him.

Remember, nonfacts are claims that are not facts about the advertised brand, although they are intended to be perceived by consumers as though they are. They consist of opinions about the brand and also nonbrand facts, facts that are not about the brand. The latter usually are either psychological statements about the consumer or social statements about the context within which the consumer buys and uses the brand.

## 23

# NONFACTS AND CONSUMERS' PERCEPTIONS OF TRUTH AND SIGNIFICANCE

We have barely touched on the great variety of nonfacts. Although I am tempted to discuss them at greater length, I think it's not necessary here. The many types of psychological and social motivations, such as the kind my mother attached to the bread crusts, are examined at great length in numerous books and articles long since published. Readers who have not yet encountered such analyses will find them exciting, but they are not news.

What hasn't been examined is the contribution of nonfacts to the problem of falsity. Although they are not legally deceptive, they are the next thing to it, the last step on the slippery slope, just before the bottom. They are a problem for us because we get nothing, and in fact because there's typically nothing to get.

Gertrude Stein said it about Oakland: there's no there there. Nonfacts objectively eliminate truth and significance, forcing consumers to make buying decisions with bad and incomplete information. Because consumers are thus forced toward distrusting rather than relying on sellers, the law might reasonably consider calling such claims legally deceptive or otherwise find a way to keep them for running wild as they do.

The trouble occurs for consumers who perceive a nonfact to be a reason for buying. They take an opinion claim not merely as a description of the seller's evaluation of the brand. They take a nonbrand fact not merely as a description of something apart from the brand. Rather, they interpret these claims as differentiating the brand, as having brand significance, and thus as affecting their purchasing decisions in favor of the brand.

A nonbrand fact, for example, relates a brand to a certain lifestyle or problem or motivation. To consumers the claim means that the brand offers that lifestyle, solves that problem, or satisfies that motivation. Indeed, in some cases such a prior relationship exists, as described in the previous chapter, and if so there is no problem. Because elderly people, for example, develop bad teeth and so have a natural need for denture adhesives, the depiction of a smiling oldster is not a nonbrand fact. The claim is used to target a further audience of similar consumers, identify them and appeal to them. It's a case of legitimate segmenting.

For many ads, however, the claim comes first and tries to create a relationship that does not already exist. The advertising is trying to create the relationship from scratch. The person shown smiling or otherwise displaying satisfaction does not reflect any significant number of persons who have already been making that response to the advertised item. The advertiser is suggesting that people should respond favorably and is hoping they will, but it hasn't happened yet. If so, we are dealing with a nonbrand fact.

Any consumer who sees nonfacts as saying nothing about the brand will be a lost cause to the advertiser. To work, the consumer must see a claim as somehow being about the brand, being a quality of the brand. Advertisers may be tempted to deny that they try to get consumers to see nonfacts that way. Yet they would be wasting their money if consumers did not. What would be the point, when the goal of an advertisement is to sell a certain item, of talking about or seeking response to something other than that item?

The advertisers might also protest that they could not, even if they tried, get consumers to see nonfacts as being literally about the brand. It would be too irrational, after all, for us to see a reference to a personal problem or motivation as being about anything other than ourselves. Sensible persons will realize that suggestions about achieving various psychic satisfactions or relieving dissastisfactions are not literally statements about the features of the item for sale.

Maybe not, but that doesn't mean we won't see the claim as being *about* the brand. Here's an example. We've seen that for a long time Pepsi was targeted primarily to youth. Now let's say I'm not exactly a spring chicken anymore; I've moved along from being a Yuppie to being a Grumpy—that's a Grown Up Mature Person. Still, I want to retain that association with youth, which I see displayed more by Pepsi than by Coke or other soft drinks. Engaged in such wishful thinking, which overcomes the objective reality, I make Pepsi my choice.

I recognize that Pepsi's claim about youthfulness can exist only subjectively; I don't see it as being literally in the Pepsi. But that claim can nonetheless be a reason for buying. It wouldn't be sensible for Pepsi to claim that those references are not offered as a reason for me to buy. If they were not, there would be no reason for Pepsi to make them. Given that they are a reason, it wouldn't be sensible for Pepsi to deny that such a claim can be material and brand significant, subjectively, to me.

Remember the idea that a claim may be material, which means it affects a purchasing decision. That is very pertinent here, because an opinion or nonbrand fact can be a statement about the brand if consumers see it as affecting their purchasing decisions for that item. If the claim is also brand significant, differentiating the brand positively to a meaningful degree, it will prompt greater purchasing.

Now how does all this create problems of truth or significance? Let's look at it by starting where we should always start—with what's factually true. Objectively, the relationship of Pepsi to my motivation toward youthfulness is nonexistent. Whether or not the claim is "about" the brand in consumers' perceptions, the relationship doesn't exist physically. What I buy is a can or bottle of liquid containing certain ingredients—nothing more. I receive nothing from Pepsi that has any natural relationship to any personal characteristics of me.

Nonetheless, I can see a relationship if I want to. I am free, as is everyone, to decide in my own perception that Pepsi *reflects* my motivations or my psychological or social needs. If I say it does, then the relationship is true as a statement about me, not about Pepsi. And from that relationship I receive a value that I appreciate and enjoy—and might not receive from any other soft drink. These benefits are real in a very important way, not as physical realities, but as the realities of my own mind.

Given that, many observers will say that nothing's been stated so far to suggest any problem with the truth or significance of nonfacts. If it's all in the mind, any consumer who doesn't like relating a nonfact to a brand can simply reject the idea of such a relationship. It's not the same as considering whether a brand of pain reliever does or doesn't contain aspirin. It either does or it doesn't, and that's that. But when I consider whether to let a drink's image of youthfulness affect my purchase decision, I am free to accept or reject such influence as I choose. Since the feature is objectively a nonfact, existing in me and not in the drink, I am free to decide for myself whether to see it as being "about" the brand.

There's reason to believe that consumers often enjoy imagining that various nonbrand facts are "about" the brand. Here's powerful support from an article in *The New Yorker*: "We take it for granted that companies will tell us that our emotional needs can be eased through purchases . . . We're used to being told that a car equals frequent sexual relations, not that it's a way to transport your body and your belongings around town. Perhaps you could even argue that this is good— that if your particular brand of beer makes you feel like a cowboy, or a tweedy professor in a bar, or a flat-bellied beach-volleyball star, that's a bonus."

I'm sure many people feel that way, and on that basis there's apparently no problem at all. Not with Pepsi, at least. But what about with PowerMaster?

## 24

# THE DARK SIDE OF NONFACTS

PowerMaster! Do you remember the short-lived malt liquor addressed to young urban blacks and Hispanics? It was short-lived because community spokesmen, such as black ministers, protested that the name created an unconscionable appeal. The federal Bureau of Alcohol, Tobacco and Firearms then forbid the brand's further promotion.

The urban poor are unquestionably seeking power and are frustrated over their lack of it. But the power they want is social and economic, not the additional alcohol content that malt liquor has over beer and that PowerMaster had over other malt liquors. Although such products may create a short-lived perception of increased physical ability, it is undisputed by any objective analysis that alcohol reduces, not increases, personal power.

With PowerMaster, not only was the perceived benefit absent, but an abusive disbenefit could occur that would be definitely harmful. The same thing happened with another name that was a claim: Rely, the Procter & Gamble tampon. The company had advertised, "Remember, they named it Rely!" Then the brand was removed from the market after being associated with toxic shock syndrome.

Nonfacts can have similar effects elsewhere, though not always so dramatically. We saw earlier, for example, that problems are what make solutions useful. It's perfectly fine to offer solutions to real problems, but it's not so helpful to invent problems or blow them out of proportion. That happens with various products, such as Listerine, which suggest to us that we have certain deficiencies.

The man who created Listerine also made up the term *halitosis*. Certainly people had bad breath before that, but it wasn't on their agenda as a problem urgently needing to be solved. Not everyone thought they had it. Not everyone who thought they had it were worried about it. And not everyone who worried about it worried very much. After the ads came along, people who hadn't thought they had bad breath now decided they did, and the worry increased tremendously. So did the consequent perceived significance of Listerine.

Do you think you might analyze the following recent television claim from Clairol the same way? It said, "Isn't it amazing that a little thing like hair coloring can change your whole outlook!"

I hope you're beginning to see that nonfacts can be harmful, despite many being quite innocent. Among many other advertised items, Pepsi seems innocent of the problems cited for PowerMaster. I may utterly reject the idea that Pepsi is youthful. Or, I may accept the image for the enjoyment it gives me even though I don't literally believe it. If I don't believe the image I won't buy the drink for that reason, and yet there are other good reasons for buying Pepsi, such as refreshment and taste. Since they make the purchase worth the money, I can buy the brand and enjoy the simple pleasure of the youthfulness image without worrying whether it has any real meaning.

Still, the dark, harmful side of nonfacts always looms. Because of the "non" in their name, they lie at the lowest level of the slippery slope. Selected facts are true and significant about the brand, and so are at the top. Minimal facts are by definition only minimally significant about the brand, and thus are farther down. Nonbrand facts and opinions are at the bottom because objectively they are not factual at all; the first is not about the brand and the second is not factual. Consumers who respond to these claims are perceiving brand significance in an entirely subjective way. They are making a decision about an item on the basis of nothing that is really about it.

The advertiser slides down the slope when it has no real facts to provide, and the fewer it has the farther it slides. When we see nonbrand facts being used, we know the advertiser has nothing physical to offer us, just something psychological. That should prompt us all to feel a bit uneasy, except perhaps when the presentation of the nonfact is so silly, intentionally or not, that we see it as a joke.

My favorite in the joke category involves the cologne Brut, whose ads say "It smells like a man." My reaction is that women don't want to smell like men, and men already do, so what's this stuff for, anyway? I had a similar laugh on learning one year that Electrolux was the official Olympic vacuum cleaner. Was it for cleaning the track, or did you race it like a wheelbarrow? In such cases the incongruity makes it unlikely that we'll accept the nonfact claim as meaning anything.

Apart from such oddities, though, shouldn't we feel uneasy about the general idea of responding on the basis of nonfacts alone? The advertisers will point out that the type of problem that occurs with PowerMaster is unlikely to occur with many brands and products. Will it occur, for example, with Pepsi? Is there a similar downside to drinking that brand in normal quantities? Surely not.

How about the Clairol example? There we may see a potential for harm a bit more readily, because psychological or social motivations will loom larger as legitimate reasons for buying hair coloring than for buying a soft drink. Along with the Listerine and Vic Tanny examples, Clairol involves enhancing in consumers' minds the fear that a problem exists. The advertisers would probably protest that there is no harm in such a mental manipulation, because we don't have to be bothered by any psychological concerns if we don't want to be. But is unnecessary worry not a harm? Or wasted money? The possibility of objective reasons against buying looms somewhat larger for Clairol than for Pepsi.

The PowerMaster example illustrates the greatest potential harm of nonfact claims. While the claim in that name offers nothing factual about the brand, the overall context contains some highly significant factual reasons for *not* buying. When such negative reasons exist alongside nonfacts, the consumer who is persuaded to purchase on the basis of the nonfacts alone is at a definite disadvantage.

Apologists for advertising suggest that consumers' own judgments give them all the help they need in dealing with something like PowerMaster. Lawyer Floyd Abrams said, "To say because a product is dangerous or contributes to problems, that this group shouldn't be targeted, is to assume that people can't make decisions for themselves." Lawyer Burt Neuborne said, "The notion that there are certain adults who are not able to make decisions for themselves can perpetuate stereotypes about those groups." Of course it's politically incorrect these days to suggest that persons from certain ethnic, educationally disadvantaged groups can't make decisions properly. However, in the case of PowerMaster it was the groups' own community leaders who suggested exactly that, and they should know.

The difference between the Pepsi and PowerMaster examples suggests a method we can use to assess the harm in nonfacts. We can ask the same question posed earlier for selected or minimal facts: What else is there to be considered about this brand? Does the claim give us sufficient facts for buying, or does it leave things missing that we might usefully take into account? Where the potential for harm lies in what's unspoken, the amount and quality of what's unspoken become critical. Sometimes there's very little more to be considered, at other times a lot. That explains why nonfacts can range so widely in the degree of harm they can cause.

Meanwhile, where does advertising law stand on all this? Its answer is simple, indeed simplistic. It says there is no violation because there is no deceptiveness, no falsity conveyed either explicitly or impliedly. Advertising law doesn't say there is no harm. However, we have to remember that the law isn't written to stop harm. It's written to stop what it recognizes as deceptive (or as unfair, although that is vaguely defined and hardly ever prosecuted). The law acts against harmful claims only when they fit into those specified categories.

It's true that the potential harm of PowerMaster's claim was recognized and eliminated. However, that was not a matter of advertising law. It was a matter of licensing alcoholic beverages, the job of a different federal agency. That agency played a role that advertising's regulators could play, but, since the latter were not involved, no precedent was created for advertising in general. Precedent would be useful, because such events will continue.

PowerMaster's would-be seller, Heileman Brewing, more recently planned to use an all-black cast of youthful actors to market its Colt 45 malt liquor as "Cool Colt." And Converse planned to market a basketball sneaker as the "Run 'N Gun" brand. That could be interpreted as a basketball phrase or, in the inner cities, as a reference to using handguns. Such recent examples suggest that nonfact claims having a potential for harm will continue to appear in the future if nothing stops them.

Before this book ends, I will show how advertising law might change its perceptions of what's deceptive so that it could take meaningful action on these matters. To show why it needs to change, I will show beginning in chapter 26 why the law sees no deception in the various slippery slope claims down which we slide from truth to falsity.

## 25

# THE HEADACHE REMEDY CASES: ANACIN, TYLENOL, BAYER, AND OTHERS

In probably no heavily advertised product category are the brands as similar objectively as they are with headache remedies. That's because drugs are carefully controlled by the federal Food and Drug Administration. Before they are marketed, the FDA must approve their ingredients and verify their functions.

For a long time only aspirin was involved. Each of its brands must give users a drug fitting the FDA's exact designation, which is acetylsalicylic acid, chemically known as $CH_3COOC_6H_4COOH$. Each brand must also give exactly the same dose. Some versions are called things like "extra strength," but within such categories the dosage must be the same. Eventually acetaminophen and ibuprofen became big competitors of aspirin, and all three differ in certain beneficial and harmful effects. On the principal feature advertised, though, which is the ability to relieve pain, the government has set dosages so that there is no difference among them. With controls like that, no brand can differ from its competitors on an objective basis.

None of that poses any problem, however, to dedicated brand promoters. It's the kind of challenge they like; it gets their adrenaline flowing. As a result, they have established perceptions of differences in millions of consumers' heads for all three drugs, and for all brands of each. The companies have accomplished the job primarily by the expert creation of ambiguous language, carefully calculated to suggest differences that aren't really there. The most famous is Anacin's claim to contain "the pain reliever doctors recommend most." That's the most complex way ever found to say a brand contains aspirin without actually saying it.

The FTC found that claim to imply falsely that Anacin's active ingredient was other than, and superior to, aspirin. It was the Contrast Implication (chap. 11), aided by additional language saying Anacin had a combination of ingredients that made its formula special. It's true that Anacin contains more than just aspirin, but also true that the extra ingredient, caffeine, is not a pain reliever. Thus for headaches, Anacin is really nothing but aspirin. The commission also found that ads for Excedrin, Midol, and Bufferin tried the same "combination of ingredients" trick (and, as we saw in chap. 6, so did Aspercreme), allowing for similar creations of confusion.

Bufferin is "buffered" aspirin, said to relieve pain faster than what its ads called "plain" or "simple" aspirin. The FTC found, against Bristol-Myers's denial, that consumers interpreted those two terms to mean all aspirin—an Ordinary Meaning Implication. That made the comparison false. Brands with "buffering," although that feature may reduce stomach upset, do not give greater pain relief than all other brands of aspirin.

Obviously it had become popular to differentiate an aspirin brand by pretending it was something else. Other such methods used by

Anacin were to claim to have more pain reliever or to get a higher level of pain relief ingredients into the bloodstream. Since that happened only because the pills were bigger than usual, the FTC found a false implication that Anacin was stronger in the sense of giving greater relief per unit of pain reliever.

Anacin also claimed to have more of its "specific pain relief ingredient" (another of its names for aspirin) than any leading headache tablet. It did; it contained more aspirin than any competitor. The FTC, however, took that to imply to consumers that Anacin contained more total pain relief ingredients of all kinds, not just more aspirin. That Halo Implication was false.

Similarly, Anacin's claim to have more than twice as much of its "ingredient" as the "other leading extra strength tablets" implied that it had that much more than any other nonprescription pain reliever. The FTC explained that if you are saying you are better than those that would otherwise be the best, you are implying that you are better than all. It was another false Halo Implication.

When Maximum Strength Anacin came along, its ads compared it favorably to a competitor described as extra strength. That was found to imply falsely that Anacin was more than extra strength (Uniqueness Implication). In truth it was no greater because maximum strength and extra strength were the same thing. The only thing truly unique was the name Maximum Strength.

Some Anacin ads spoke of relieving tension. The FTC did not dispute that tension caused by a headache could be relieved if the headache were relieved. However, the ads showed domestic situations, such as a mother finding the kids had made a mess. They were situations in which people became tense with no suggestion of having a prior headache. The commission found such scenes to imply falsely that Anacin could relieve tension entirely apart from its ability to relieve headaches.

Bayer ads claimed superiority over other aspirin brands in various aspects of manufacturing, such as greater stability, purity, freshness, and speed of disintegration. The claims were true, but they falsely implied that Bayer was better at pain relief (another Halo). You might reasonably think that those characteristics made Bayer better somehow. However, they did not do so for what the ads were claiming, which was to relieve pain.

When acetaminophen and ibuprofen entered the race, they became equally tricky. Ads comparing Tylenol to competitors on the risk of producing certain side effects omitted reference to potential liver damage. That's a good example of selected facts with an important selected omission, because Tylenol poses a greater risk than its competition for liver-related side effects. The maker, Johnson & Johnson, choosing to protect its legal liability above its public image, argued that the law doesn't make sellers disclose disadvantages along with advantages. The court retorted that where the health of consumers is at risk, advertisers must observe a higher standard.

Another claim was that hospitals dispensed ten times as much Tylenol as the next four brands combined, so shouldn't consumers trust it, too? The underlying truth was that Johnson & Johnson was distributing it to hospitals very cheaply, virtually for free. A court found this to imply that hospitals preferred Tylenol because it was safer and more effective. However, the court also found the implication wasn't false because hospitals wouldn't use an unsafe and ineffective product even if it were free. The court also observed cynically that Tylenol's competitors were free to offer the same low price. In other words, fight falsity with falsity.

That decision seemed to represent a lower standard of consideration for truth than such courts usually find. When advertisers sue each other under the Lanham Act, however, the court is obligated only to consider protecting them from each other. The proceeding is not required to address whether the public might need protection from both.

The arrival of Tylenol meant that Anacin had to compete against more than just aspirin brands. One of its responses was to claim that "Anacin reduces inflammation as Anacin relieves pain fast. These [referring to pictures of acetaminophen brands] do not." That's very tricky semantically, because consumers might see conveyed that the acetaminophens do not relieve pain as fast as Anacin. The latter is false. The claim would have been acceptable if it referred just to inflammation, but by being ambiguous, it was deceptive.

When Anacin's maker, American Home Products (AHP), decided to market its own acetaminophen brand, it named it Anacin-3. The name might have been confusing to consumers who knew Anacin to be principally aspirin, except that AHP had been hiding that fact for years. Despite its own trickiness, however, AHP soon challenged a similar trick by Johnson & Johnson. The J&J ads allegedly caused consumers to think, to Anacin-3's detriment, that Tylenol was different from other pain relievers. The court showed a lack of sympathy, however, saying: "The failure of consumers to appreciate that Anacin-3 is an acetaminophen product is the fault of no one but AHP. AHP's decision to give it a name so similar to that of its aspirin-caffeine product, Anacin, may be more to blame than the responsible AHP executives would care to admit."

Anacin-3 also tried to fight Tylenol's "hospitals trust" claim by advertising that hospitals "recommend acetaminophen, the aspirin-free pain reliever in Anacin-3, more than any other pain reliever." Hospitals did recommend acetaminophen. Anacin-3's ads were false, though, because their trickily worded reference to what hospitals did, which actually was to use Tylenol, implied that the hospitals recommended Anacin-3.

Ibuprofen has not refrained from such shenanigans. Consider this: "Advil contains ibuprofen, the same medicine that's in the prescription drug Motrin. But now it's available in nonprescription strength. It's been proven effective in relieving many types of pain. It's so effective that doctors have already prescribed it over 130 million times." That was yet another fascinating ambiguity from American Home Products, which seems bent on winning the gold medal in that category. The claim was found to invite consumers to think "it" was Advil. However, the references to effectiveness were true only for those few consumers who realized that "it" was Motrin.

Consider also the claim, "Like Tylenol, Advil doesn't upset my stomach." That was held to imply that Advil was equal in avoiding stomach upset, while in truth Tylenol was superior. The claim seems capable of suggesting that Tylenol does upset stomachs, because we could read it as implying "Like Tylenol does, Advil doesn't upset my stomach."

One of the most interesting charges made against any advertiser was an FTC complaint that Sterling Drug made mutually inconsistent claims. Sterling advertised Bayer to be as effective as any over-the-counter pain reliever while also advertising Vanquish as more effective than aspirin. It also claimed that Bayer would cause no more stomach upset than any other, and that Vanquish would cause less stomach upset than aspirin. Finally, it said Bayer was as effective for nervous tension headache as any other brand while also saying Cope was better for that than any other.

Without question the claims in each of those pairs logically contradicted each other. For that reason I personally have no trouble concluding that Sterling Drug knowingly committed three falsities. However, the FTC eventually dropped the charge on an incredibly weak argument. It was theoretically possible, the commission said, for any of the claims to be found supported inasmuch as the prosecutors failed to prove otherwise for each claim taken separately.

Meanwhile, the headache remedy advertisers have been no different from other advertisers in offering inadequate evidence to support their claims. Most of them introduced tests lacking the necessary scientific controls that we saw in discussing Aspercreme, such as placebos and blinding. Also, American Home Products offered tests on post-childbirth pain to support Anacin's superiority for headaches. As experts testified, that pain is caused by such different physiological processes that tests on it could establish nothing about headache pain. Bristol-Myers was similarly rebuffed for a study of arthritis sufferers, as was Sterling Drug for a study of potential stroke victims.

Some Anacin ads displayed technical graphs and chemical formulas to convince consumers of a claim. The FTC found such items to imply the existence of "authoritative medical opinion or scientific tests." There were none. Other headache ads falsely displayed scientific texts, medical reports, and white-coated technicians. Such symbols can be perfectly legitimate if they really stand for something. Of course if they do, the advertiser will probably describe the underlying support explicitly rather than letting it be implied.

One Anacin research study examined a formulation that combined aspirin and caffeine, but not in the same way that Anacin does. In other words, to support its claim that Anacin was effective, American Home Products tested something else. The FTC decided there was no certainty that Anacin would produce the same results. Cope was also tested in a formulation different from the one in which it was sold.

A survey showed doctors preferring Anacin two-to-one over the "leading extra strength analgesic." The FTC rejected the resulting Proof Implication because the survey used an unrepresentative group of doctors and reached only 10 percent of it. Also, the ads implied falsely that the survey showed doctors preferring Anacin over *any* nonprescription competitor. In another advertised survey, more doctors said they would prefer to take Bayer than various other brands to a desert island. They voted more for Bayer than for Tylenol, and they voted more for Bayer than for Extra-Strength Tylenol. However, they voted less for Bayer than for the two types of Tylenol combined. In other words, Bayer really lost. The survey was widely publicized, but escaped prosecution.

When a Sterling Drug study's statistical analysis revealed no difference between Cope and aspirin, the researchers switched to a different statistical method to get the results they wanted. A witness whom the FTC found credible said it was "a gross and obvious example of statistical manipulation, and . . . not acceptable scientific methodology." In a Bristol-Myers hospital study comparing Excedrin to aspirin, the re-

searchers did not choose patients randomly. They assigned more patients with severe initial pain to receive their brand, giving it an unfairly
greater opportunity to demonstrate relief.

In other research Bristol failed to screen out various types of
people. They included people who were nonresponsive to aspirin,
and people who at the same time were taking other drugs that might
have affected their response to the test drugs, and people who were
given no "washout period" to let the effects of previous aspirin use
wear away. All of these failures to exclude meant that the results
could have been due to factors other than the drugs that were presumably being compared.

This chapter gives a strong sense of how sellers compete with each
other. It's long been known that the best way to relieve a headache is to
create one. Here we have seen how the analgesics makers create them
not only for consumers but for their competition as well. The rule
seems to be: Do unto others as they would do unto you if they thought
of it first. Of course if they do think of it first, sue them.

It sure is a lot of work to claim you have a difference when you
really don't!

# PART 5

## THE OLD AND NEW VIEWS OF CONSUMER TRUSTING

*The regulator's reluctance to see falsity on the slippery slope is shown in this part to be directly related to the insistence on retaining an ancient view about consumers and trust. The regulators' assumption that consumers automatically distrust sellers in many situations is shown to derive from very old decisions about "puffery" claims. The contrasting argument that is then offered is based on the assumption that consumers do not distrust such advertising; in fact, consumers trust sellers generally because they must do so in order to participate in the marketplace. The regulators do not appreciate the extent to which consumers trust because they are not fully informed about the ways in which consumers respond to advertising, to products, and to sellers.*

*The assumption of consumer trust is the key assertion made in this book. It is the basis for the recommendations made in the final three parts.*

## 26
# PUFFERY: OPINION CLAIMS
# TO BE DISTRUSTED

I first became interested in advertising law upon hearing of puffery. The law's long-standing treatment of this type of claim accounts for the way the law today treats all the types of claims on the slippery slope. I'll take some time to describe puffery, and then show how it applies to the slope claims.

Puffery or puffing consists of exaggerated opinions, usually at the highest degree of exaggeration, which means superlatives, such as "the best" or "superior." You puff your product, blow it up, say it has the greatest qualities. It can be the best tasting, best looking, best lasting, best performing, or just plain best. The advertising textbook I was using in my university class told me that even though deceptive ads were illegal, puffing was okay. The puffers could realize they had no basis for claiming their brand was the best. They could even believe it wasn't. Yet they could still say it was the greatest in the world and no law would stop them.

That was nonsense, I felt, because deceptiveness is illegal and these claims certainly seemed deceptive. Our government simply would not approve of advertisers making unsupported claims, and doing so knowingly. There must be some explanation. Maybe the regulators had been so busy with more harmful claims that they hadn't gotten around to puffery's lies. I decided to visit the law school library to clear up the matter. An hour or two of investigation ought to satisfy my curiosity. Well, it did and it didn't.

What I found was that the law clearly says that puffery claims can be false and yet acceptable. Nothing tentative or wishy-washy about it; it's absolute. But that didn't satisfy my curiosity; I didn't want to leave the library without finding out why. Hours turned into days and then into months, and about four years later resulted in my book *The Great American Blow-Up*. The process was lengthy because every legal decision was based on an earlier decision. I had to keep going further back in history until I was blowing the dust off volumes left untouched for decades.

The trail of prior cases didn't go back just to the founding of the United States. It went deep into the English law from which American courts took their earliest precedents. In 1602, late in the reign of Queen Elizabeth I, a man felt cheated after buying something he'd been told was worth a certain amount. Unfortunately for this poor chap, the court said he had no recourse. What he thought was a false claim was merely what the decision innovatively called a "bare assertion." For more than two hundred years thereafter the law spoke of "naked" and "nude" and "bare" statements by sellers. They were claims that a thing had value when the speaker had no factual support for saying so. Naked meant fact-free; it meant you're on your own, Ms. or Mr. Consumer. The claim was what today we call an opinion.

As we saw in chapter 21, opinions differ from one party to another. A drink can taste lousy to you and great to me, and we're both right. It's subjective; you determine it for you and I determine it for me. What this came to mean in the law, with the help of the prevailing reasonable person standard, is that I *must* determine it for me. If I let you decide, I would risk having the assessment come out wrong, because only I am capable of making it.

By that reasoning, the man who claimed to be cheated was found in error himself for relying on the seller in formulating his own opinion. He had equal access, presumably, to all knowledge needed to make his evaluation. Thus it was up to him to do so independently. When he relied on the seller instead, he did so unjustifiably and so could blame no one but himself for the outcome. That was the start of why opinion claims, and other questionable facts and nonfacts, are legal today.

It was a rather thin start, because it did not ask whether the seller's behavior might have been improper. Another English case soon followed, though, in which the offended party charged the defendant not merely with falsity but with outright cheating—making a false claim while knowing it was false. The court quickly cleared up any doubt whether the listener deserved legal recourse because of the speaker's deliberate dishonesty. It said the deliberateness created no liability because the listener was irresponsible for relying on it. The basis was the same conclusion seen earlier that participants in the marketplace must rely on no one else's judgment in formulating their own.

The result for the marketplace was that even when sellers consciously intended to deceive, and did so successfully, they were not liable for buyers' losses. Buyers could check for themselves, and so they must, with the traditional reasonable person standard applying. The rule in that form crossed the ocean to the United States as though there were no revolution against England. The reasons for the American colonies' revolt of course included repression of speech, but in the English marketplace there wasn't much speech restriction to revolt against. As long as you were selling things, you could tell lies at great length.

U.S. courts soon adopted the same approach. In fact, they liked it so well that they gave it an extra twist to encourage falsity even more.

They did so by changing a step the English had taken to protect buyers against a small portion of sellers' opinion claims. The English courts had thought it only fair to grant an exception to the opinion rule where buyers had no opportunity to check for themselves. In most cases buyers could check merchandise personally, but occasionally they could not. For example, the item they were considering buying might be in transit at the moment. When buyers were disadvantaged in that way, the rule said, they would be legally justified in relying on the seller's opinion as a substitute for their own. It was only common sense, after all, to conclude that people can't form their own opinions about something they can't even look at.

In 1853, however, an American court took away that rule. The case was *Brown v. Castles*, in Massachusetts. The court's twist was to declare it "always having been understood, the world over" that sellers' statements of value deserved distrust, and that buyers therefore automatically disbelieved them. That blew away the earlier idea that you should be on your own as a consumer when you could decide for yourself. The transformed rule was that you must be on your own whether you can decide for yourself or not. Further, the court decided that all buyers do choose to be on their own when hearing valuations or opinions; they utterly ignore any such claims. Following the reasonable person standard, they do so even when they have no other source on which to rely.

Note that the court stated not only what buyers should do, but also what it thought they actually did do. Do you think all consumers utterly ignore sellers' opinions? Ask yourself: do you do that?

That judge in 1853 surely made an incorrect conclusion about what people really do. He did it seemingly out of the blue, with no basis. The earlier cases had decided what consumers ought to do, but he went completely beyond that precedent, drawing on his imagination and transforming it into a decision about what they do do. It was like practicing psychology without a diploma. In fact, it was practicing psychology before the invention of psychology. No wonder he got it wrong.

# 27

# WE NEED TO TRUST SELLERS, AND WE DO

More than a hundred years later the regulators still get it wrong some of the time when they fail to prohibit the puffery form of opinion claims. The Federal Trade Commission and the courts say they believe that ordinary consumers find such exaggeration obvious and so do not take such claims seriously. In fairness to the commission, it disagreed with that in its early years. It tried to attack puffery in the 1910s and 1920s, but was rebuffed by federal appellate courts. On the basis of precedents stemming from that 1853 case, the courts said puffery must be left untouched.

I have described such details of puffery's history at great length in *The Great American Blow-Up* and will not repeat the full explanation here. In brief, the FTC Act of 1914 gave the commission a mandate to define deceptiveness more broadly than before, going beyond the prior law when necessary. Many of its subsequent procedures and decisions, as seen in this book's first chapters, did exactly that. As advertisers well know, however, FTC decisions are subject to review and possible reversal by the U.S. circuit courts of appeal and the Supreme Court. Over the decades many advertisers have requested such reviews to challenge the commission's extensions of the law. In most cases the courts have confirmed the lawfulness of the FTC's actions.

At the same time, however, those appeals courts were regularly reconfirming puffery's legality in a line of cases that stemmed directly from the 1853 case, long before the FTC's creation in 1914. So when the FTC tried to apply its get-tough attitude to puffery, the courts decided not to depart from tradition in that area. They forced a continuation of the old precedent, declaring that all reasonable consumers must be, and are, distrustful. It was thus the courts, not the commission, who ruled that it's not necessary to look in the horse's mouth to make a decision involving puffery. In fact, no decision is even necessary, because it's already decided. The way consumers respond is already known.

These events occurred while the FTC was developing the ignorant person standard to replace the reasonable person standard. That created a contradiction, because the puffery rule does not reflect the newer standard. Reflecting the latter, the commission now interprets false factual claims as violations even though they would not deceive persons acting reasonably. Yet for puffery it maintains the old reasonable standard, deciding not only that reasonable consumers will disbelieve puffery, but also that no consumers will be unreasonable.

How do the regulators decide that? You'd think they would look to see how consumers respond to various opinion claims. Then they would identify the ones that people automatically disbelieve, and separate such puffery claims from presumably ordinary opinions. But that's not what they do. They look at the *form* of the opinion claim, to see whether it fits the definition of puffery. Is it a superlative, unqualified like "best" or "superior," or qualified, such as "best tasting" or "superior appearance" or "most comfortable"?

If so, then it's puffery, and the regulators simply assume the public will disbelieve it and not rely on it. They assume people will see it conveying nothing, either explicitly or impliedly. The regulators don't check to see what people actually do, or even think about checking. The horse keeps its mouth closed and it's still 1853.

Take Bayer's claim to be "the world's best aspirin." The FTC decided that such phrases "are merely puffing because the ad does not discuss any comparison of Bayer's quality." It's interesting to consider that the advertiser should want to fire its copywriter for ineffectiveness if such a phrase really failed to create a comparison to other brands. But the regulators never find out whether it failed or not; they insulate themselves from the facts by deciding without looking. They respond in a knee-jerk fashion to precedent, for which presumably someone drew all the necessary conclusions. They forget that those parties in the past also decided without looking.

Like all courts, advertising regulators must determine both matters of facts and matters of law. Although logically those should be separate determinations, they sometimes get mixed together because the law is authorized to determine facts "as a matter of law." There is often good reason for that, as when facts have been established so well in the past that it's appropriate to give them automatic recognition in the future. Nonetheless, the wisdom of doing so certainly can be questioned when a reasonable suspicion is raised that such a shortcut leads to faulty conclusions. In the case of puffery the appellate courts by legal presumption have wrongly imposed the last century's "facts" on this century's regulators.

How does this affect us all today? Let's say you're in the market for a new house, and a salesperson is showing you one right now. She says it gives more value for the given space and features, at the given price, than any other house on the market. She assures you she has seen them all, knows all the details about them, and is certain that such information proves the point to her complete satisfaction. You know you'll never have the time to look at all of the houses and information sheets, and even if you did you wouldn't want to go to all that effort. Also, you're being pressed to decide because other buyers may make offers soon. What do you do?

According to the law just cited, you do what all buyers do—you distrust completely the seller's evaluation (you can trust her for specific facts, but not for value statements). You decide you can base your opinion only on what you're personally able to see, whether it's a lot or even if it's only a little, and not at all on what she said. No matter how inadequate your own experience may be, you simply cannot trust that seller.

Is that the way consumers always act? Think now, wouldn't you be influenced just a teensy bit, or even a lot, by what that salesperson told you? Don't we in fact often conclude, when formulating our own opinion, that what the other party tells us is superior to what we ourselves are able to see? Despite a certain amount of distrust for real estate or other salespeople, we must admit that they are more knowledgeable about the product than we are. Obviously we don't always want to trust them entirely, but we certainly don't discount them down to rock bottom zero.

And sometimes we do trust them entirely. If I were buying a pair of socks about which the salesperson said "one size fits all," and if I knew the store had a policy of accepting returns, I don't see why I wouldn't feel justified in relying on that opinion. Indeed, whatever our finishing conclusion may be in dealing with a salesperson, doesn't our starting point usually consist more of trust than distrust? How else could we justify walking into a store manned by people we don't even know— that's trust right there. It's built into the system. We have to trust or we simply can't deal.

That may not be what we should do according to the law, but it's what we must do in order to participate, and it's what we *do* do. So instead of the law assuming distrust of opinion and valuation claims, it more properly should assume a mix. And within that mix I would say the primary element in most situations today is more likely trust than distrust.

An enlightening way to think about trust is to observe separately our feelings and our actions. While distrust characterizes our feelings, our actions are far more likely to reflect trust, and it's our actions that lead to the consequences, good or bad. Feelings we don't translate into action may produce mental satisfactions or dissatisfactions, but they don't result in purchases that we're glad or sorry we made. They simply don't create the problems discussed in this book. So let's not rely so heavily on the opinion polls that ask us whether we trust sellers, because they principally reflect feelings.

The advertisers may find it convenient to cite those polls as "proof" that consumers are skeptical and therefore need no legal protection. Legitimate proof, however, can come only from examining what we actually do rather than just what we think. We consumers accept many opinion statements in a trusting spirit as constituting claims of brand significance. That is, we see such statements to imply the existence of true underlying facts that make up a basis for such opinions. We then act on the opinions because we perceive the supporting facts as giving us a reason for relying.

The regulators don't seem to notice it, but after all, that's what it means to trust people. You assume they have a basis for what they're saying.

## 28

# MAKING UP OUR OWN MINDS, AND TRUSTING TOO

Of course the regulators should not pursue claims that people don't take seriously, and I'm sure people disbelieve puffs in some cases. But what makes the regulators assume they always do? The main reason is that the federal appellate courts continue to rely on the 1853 ruling that claims of a certain form will always be disbelieved—and, as mentioned earlier, the appellate courts have authority over the FTC and the federal trial courts that handle Lanham cases.

The FTC or trial courts have made no serious effort recently to challenge the appellate courts on the point. They are unwilling to fight precedent, even though they could make a good argument. They're probably unwilling to fight the advertisers, too. While technically an order to stop is made only against the specific advertiser named in a case, a prohibition of puffery would threaten all or most advertisers. That could result in serious pressures, probably through political channels, to bring back recognition of the ancient privilege.

So the regulators haven't done anything about puffery. But as long as they haven't, they're wrong. In fact, they're actually doing what the FTC stops advertisers from doing, which is to prohibit claims for which a reasonable basis is lacking (Reasonable Basis Implication, chap. 11). Despite enforcing that idea for factual claims, the commission and the Lanham courts are willing to draw a contrary conclusion about consumer response to puffery even though they have no basis for it.

There are other ironies. The opinion rule, which historically began with the requirement that consumers must check products for themselves, today lacks any requirement that the regulators must check consumers for themselves! Further, while consumers rely on sellers in part because they rely on the law to control the sellers, the law decides it doesn't need to control the sellers because it assumes that consumers know not to rely on the sellers.

Meanwhile, what do the advertisers think about whether consumers rely on puffery? Can we get any clue from the fact that they keep on using it?! Will advertisers run claims they think will automatically be disbelieved? Is it conceivable that a type of claim known not to work has been used anyway by countless advertisers countless times over the many decades that brand advertising has been done?

We've already seen reasons for arguing that consumers often rely on puffery. They do not always disbelieve and reject it. The support for saying so largely involves argument and logic, but a confirming body of experimental and survey evidence on consumer response shows that the automatic assumption regulators make about how people behave is right sometimes but also wrong sometimes. The evidence involves actually examining behavior, by showing people claims and seeing how they respond to them. It's a method far superior to simply sitting in an office and using old law books to determine how people act. Pardon my continuing to mention it, but didn't that go out with Francis Bacon?

Let's extend the discussion further to see if we can separate the conditions where disbelief of puffery is likely and not likely. The difference seems to be in whether or not consumers can make up their minds entirely on their own. Suppose a soft drink or beer says it's the "best tasting." Certainly we consumers, in keeping with what the early English courts believed, will recognize that decision as being our business alone. No one else can do that for us. We will decline to rely on the seller's opinion, because who cares what sellers tell us after we've taken a sip for ourselves! That's why there are brands that advertising couldn't save, such as Schlitz or New Coke.

Of course we have to buy a bottle to take that sip. One line of thinking says that even our first purchase should be protected by the law if the claim is deceptive and can harm us. We may never spend another nickel on that brand if we don't like it, but we have to risk the initial expense because we can't decide anything until we try. On those grounds, we should have a right to believe and rely, shouldn't we?

Well, it does seem that we might be hurt, but the damage will be limited to a small amount for many heavily advertised items. I wouldn't want to call the matter unimportant, but let's see if we can find a more significant reason for worrying about the effects of puffery. Such a reason may exist in the fact that claims about taste, or the attractions of sights, sounds, and the other senses, make up only one category of puffery.

An individual taste puff occurs when ads express a liking or valuation for something in a way that conveys nothing more than that the advertisers themselves, or the spokespersons representing them, have that opinion. They like this beer, or prefer that cola over another, or think this clothing line is the most attractive. They imply no basis for saying so other than their own minds.

Consumers seeing such a claim will naturally consider what their own opinion should be. Upon doing so, they probably realize that the claim has offered no basis for their own opinion because it hasn't involved them. They haven't been consulted and so couldn't possibly be represented by the advertiser. Not only is all the relevant evidence available inside their own minds, but no other relevant evidence could possibly exist elsewhere.

Those are taste puffs. With other types of puffery claims, however, we must base our individual opinions on more than just the advertisement, the advertised item, and our personal preferences. Consider the differences between these two claims: one is that "we prefer" or "I like" a brand of automobile tires; the other is that a brand of tires is "the best." The regulators say the latter is also protected puffery. That's a fundamental error, which they make by treating "best" the same as they treat the taste puffs.

Although some puffery involves looking only inside oneself, it's wrong to assume that all such opinions involve only that. I certainly cannot determine whether something is "best," which means to everyone, not just to myself, by looking only inside myself. I cannot accept or reject the "best tire" opinion for myself by acting on my own. I can do it only through knowledge that I cannot obtain from examining just the tires. While for individual tastes no one else can possibly decide, for a claim such as "best" there needs to be the realization that I cannot decide such a thing alone.

Of course, I am free to examine the tires myself. However, that opportunity exists only in a superficial way. I can have the tires before me and look at them. I can touch them, smell them, poke at them. I can put them on my car and drive them. I can drive other brands. I can do all those things, but when I am done I will not have examined those tires in the sense of determining whether they are the "best." I am not able and will never be able to do that by myself alone.

So let's correct that earlier statement—I am *not* free to examine the tires myself. What I need to see is hidden inside them, such as the ingredient mix, or perhaps can be seen only when they are in use rather than sitting in a showroom. Even then, I cannot see what needs to be seen because I do not know how to examine tires. I cannot recognize what I'm looking at. To do so I would need a considerable amount of expertise, as well as extensive testing facilities, which I do not have and cannot reasonably have.

It is nonsense to say I should go out and get that expertise and acquire that necessary equipment. Many consumers may be capable of being trained, in the sense that they would have the ability to absorb the training if they received it. The time and expense involved, though, make the idea utterly unreasonable. That's especially so when it would be required not just for automobile tires but for each of hundreds of products we regularly encounter in the marketplace. It's just not possible.

So we are in a bind. We can't determine by ourselves what tire brand is better than the others; we can't rely on ourselves. Yet we're expected by law to distrust the seller and refuse to rely on its assertion that its brand is the one. If you're among those consumers who believe that all claims are protected against deceptiveness, you can see how wrong you've been. You're on your own, madam or sir, because the law declines to help you at this point.

To whom are we left to turn? A transaction typically involves two parties, the seller and the buyer, but both of them are now eliminated as sources of aid. To the extent that the law is giving us any direction here, it seems to be forcing us toward reliance on some third party. Who might that be? I just finished reading an article on cellular phones in *Consumer Reports*—maybe a source like that can be a third party. Certainly it has expertise we don't have and does testing we can't do. It would seem to fill the bill. Newspapers and other mass media also give us consumer product information; in fact, more information seems to be available than ever before. Government sources also can be accessed, although not necessarily very easily.

Thus we *can* go beyond ourselves to some extent. Yet, while it's one thing to say that we have third parties out there to rely on, it's a different matter to suggest that we *must*. However good they may be, such sources are not always convenient and are often incomplete. It's likely that we won't get information on a specific brand we're interested in, or at least not on the specific information or model of that brand.

Furthermore, it's simply awkward to be compelled to drag a third party into the buying and selling process. Surely it would be better if transactions could be conducted solely by the two parties involved. Besides, isn't that what we actually do? We keep the transaction between ourselves and the seller, and because we can't rely entirely on ourselves we place some reliance on the seller.

All of this suggests that the proper interpretation of the old opinion rule is that I must be *responsible* for my own opinion, but not that I must make it by myself alone. If I am to act on the basis of an opinion I must rely on myself alone for my eventual decision as what opinion is appropriate—that's fine. However, I should not have to restrict my investigation of that question to nothing more than my personal knowledge of the product.

In addition to relying on my own resources to the extent I can, I should consider it normal and natural to go outside myself when I need help. When I do go outside I should consider it normal and natural to get help from, and rely on, the seller. After all, the seller is the party that asks for my trust by offering items for sale and by playing the role of an expert concerning those items.

So tell us, you regulators, why doesn't the law say that we can rely on sellers' opinions in the process of formulating our own?

**29**

# TRUSTING AND DISTRUSTING
# ALL OVER THE SLOPE

Have you been wondering why I've given puffery so much attention when it's only one of the types of claims lying on falsity's slippery slope? I've done so because the regulators appear to have handled all of those other types the same way. I say *appear* because the regulators have never recognized the idea of a slope as presented here. They have stated no rules about selected, minimal, and nonbrand facts. Yet they seem to assume rules, implicitly. I say that because their handling of all such categories seems to be consistent with the procedure they have stated explicitly for handling puffery.

Let's see how that works for selected facts, which in themselves are true and brand significant. As discussed in chapter 15, the regulators recognize that some selected facts make false implications through the facts the ads omit, the ones they leave unselected. The regulators, however, don't seem to recognize how generally this problem occurs. Selected facts all create the Sufficient Facts Implication, as if they accurately reflect the whole truth. They imply that full product information would convey the same brand significance and favorable purchasing decision.

Ads of course never identify selected facts as selected. If they did, they wouldn't produce the Implication. They would instead convey that they were providing only partial information. Let's not hold our breath, though, waiting for ads to tell us that they are leaving out many

facts that affect the purchasing decision. That would spoil the advertiser's intent, which is to have consumers perceive the selected fact as
though it gives the whole story.

Although the Sufficient Facts Implication will frequently be true,
sometimes it will be false. The selected fact may give consumers only a
minor degree of truth. That small sample may be contrary to the whole
truth, and may offer pipsqueak significance in comparison to what the
whole truth would provide. Recall the kitchen range ad (chap. 15),
which stated a selected claim giving a reason gas is superior. Consumers could also see implied that such reason accurately reflects the total
truth about gas ranges in comparison to electric ranges. By that, they
could see the ad implying that gas is superior overall. Such implication
when conveyed would be false for many consumers, because many
would find electricity superior overall upon considering the total truth.

That's what the regulators do not notice. They typically look only
to see whether the selected fact is itself misleading, for example, by
being improperly qualified. That could occur, for example, if gas burners turned down more quickly than electric burners only on some, but
not all, brands of ranges. In that case, the regulators could find that the
"turn-down" feature was described falsely. They are good at doing
that.

Meanwhile, they typically do not see the deceptiveness that any
and all selected facts may produce through the Sufficient Facts Implication. They typically do not recognize that ads often falsely imply
that the truth, the brand significance, and the purchasing decision
that the selected attribute indicates accurately reflect the truth, significance, and decision that the total of all of the brand's attributes would
indicate.

The regulators' silence on this matter suggests they assume that
consumers will automatically disbelieve such an implication, and refuse to rely on it for making a decision. Presumably consumers will
always see selected facts indicating nothing more than their specific
explicit content. They will always know to disbelieve any implication
that the selected fact says anything about the total truth. They will disbelieve that it conveys any overall brand significance or suggests any
overall buying decision. In other words, consumers will do with selected facts what the law presumes they do with puffery.

Of course I disagree with that. I think consumers typically respond
to selected facts as I think they do for puffery. I suggested earlier that
consumers often see implied that a true factual basis exists for puffery.
That could be a new implication to add to the list in chapter 11—the
Puffery Implication. For selected facts, then, I expect the same thing. I

believe consumers will often see the Sufficient Facts Implication, that is, they will see the ad asserting that the advertised claim is sufficient to represent the total of all claims that could be made.

The law's action toward selected facts is not the result of an explicit policy of the sort that has been stated for puffery. It is more a matter of no policy, because there have been no cases on this matter. Consequently we cannot say that the regulators have consciously applied the treatment of puffery to the treatment of selected facts. We can say, though, that the outcome is what it would be if the regulators had explicitly done that. The implicit rule for selected facts thus appears to reflect the legacy of the 1853 application to puffery statements. Reasonable consumers will not see the Sufficient Facts Implication, and no consumers will be unreasonable. There is thus, by law, no deceptiveness and no harm.

The same analysis applies to minimal facts, nonbrand facts, and puffery. They are all selected, too, and thus also produce the Sufficient Facts Implication. The law apparently seems satisfied to assume that minimal facts, just as selected facts, convey nothing more by implication. I would agree to that only for ads that identified the fact as minimal, although typically ads won't make that identification. Why would advertisers represent their minimal facts as anything other than highly significant!

Nonbrand facts also create the Sufficient Facts Implication, although only after doing something else first because, unlike selected and minimal facts, nonbrand facts explicitly describe not the brand but something other than the brand. To work, they must imply to consumers that they are about the brand; they must create the Brand Fact Implication. Such an implication cannot be true objectively, because nonbrand facts by definition do not describe the brand's physical, tangible qualities, its ingredients or performance.

When such implication is falsely implied, it may then in turn falsely imply the Sufficient Facts Implication. An example is the Vic Tanny claim from chapter 22 that you can "shape your life." That claim could be taken as being literally about some benefit provided by Vic Tanny, a brand fact. That fact in turn can be taken as constituting a sufficient fact for a favorable purchasing decision.

In some cases nonbrand facts will truthfully produce the Brand Fact Implication. That can happen, as discussed in chapter 23, when consumers feel subjectively that the relationship exists. In the Vic Tanny example, some consumers may be satisfied after using Vic Tanny's facilities that the service does indeed shape their lives. Given the poor quality of truth and brand significance existing objectively for that claim, I would not expect such a result with many persons. I expect, rather, that most consumers who accept the Brand Fact Implication upon seeing the advertising would reject it after they have personally experienced the service. However, the choice is theirs.

Advertisers may protest that they run nonbrand facts only to get attention or provide entertainment, not to state claims about the brand. I readily concede that such claims—for example, the popular lifestyle representations—can get attention and be entertaining. However, I would not so easily accept denials by advertisers that they intend such representations to make no claim about the advertised brand. The opportunities involved for creating brand significance are simply too great to be missed.

Brand Fact Implications and Sufficient Facts Implications are entirely pragmatic within the advertising context. I have no doubt that surveying of consumers will reveal their presence. The regulators, however, do not see these implications to exist, just as they do not see the Puffery Implication. Thus they appear to apply to selected facts, minimal facts, and nonbrand facts the same assumptions they make about puffery. They expect reasonable consumers to disbelieve that nonbrand facts say anything about the advertised brand, and to disbelieve that any of these claims provide sufficient truth and brand significance to be adequate for making purchasing decisions.

The richness of the law's ability to see implications appears clearly in the parade of the many types described in chapters 9, 10, and especially 11. That is a principal reason why I described those types at length. They show that the regulators know the process of identifying implications very well, and so can scarcely say the task is too difficult. The additional implications I have identified here seem to be made just as reasonably. To add them to the roster of advertising content would make an additional contribution to the proper identification of the messages that ads convey to consumers.

If the regulators would search for the implications that the slippery slope claims convey, they could easily identify them and examine them for possible falsity. Once the law looks, it is entirely capable of seeing. It is only the reluctance to look in various instances that impairs its vision.

In summary, the puffery rule isn't just a rule about puffery. Considering its impact, it has become a rule of the entire slippery slope. The rule is, according to the regulators, that the slope claims are innocent. You have to go all the way to the bottom to find deceptiveness; you won't find any on the way down. I suggest, oppositely, that there is considerable trouble for consumers on the slope—all the way down, not just at the bottom. And I say it is due to deceptiveness, regardless of whether the deceptiveness is legal.

In the chapters that follow I will further identify the problems consumers face, and then will move toward seeing what we can do about them.

## 30

# WHAT THE LAW DOESN'T SEE, AND THE PROBLEMS THAT RESULT

A free and open market is supposed to have buyers and sellers making transactions on the basis of full understanding of what each party is giving and getting. Yet we have been seeing that much of the "information" buyers get from sellers provides a false or an insufficiently truthful basis for their decisions. The law eases the problem by attacking what the regulators recognize as illegal deceptiveness. Although consumers benefit from that, they could benefit even more from prohibition of the additional deceptiveness, with its accompanying diminished truth and significance, that comes from the claims we are examining.

The deceptiveness the law doesn't recognize has been identified as the implied claims discussed in chapter 29. Although the law has recognized many types of implications, it seems to have barely scratched the surface in understanding this category of consumer response. It knows little of the implications conveyed by the facts and nonfacts that lie on the slippery slope. The law has poorly identified the process that leads people to see advertising as a conveyor of messages that other forms of communication do not convey.

To see the difference between advertising and other speech, imagine that a friend tells you he has a new car and likes it. You're impressed by what you hear, but you don't interpret the message to mean that your friend is promoting the car or that he will make any profit if you buy it. The statement is not an ad and your friend is not an advertiser, so you don't see him implying certain claims that the car maker's ads imply.

Because people see advertising as intending to sell, they interpret it as stating not merely persuasive claims but the strongest possible such claims that can be made for the item. When they see a brand advertised, they interpret the ad as claiming brand significance, differentiating the brand favorably and meaningfully from its competitors. Talk about pragmatic implications—we could hardly see a brand ad as intending anything else.

In most of our life experience, one thing doesn't imply another unless we see a link between them. Suppose we notice a man and a dog standing near each other on the street. Their nearness creates a kind of link, prompting us to consider an unstated fact, an implication, that the dog belongs to the man. However, we also notice there is no leash, and neither dog nor man acknowledges the other. The absence of those key facts suggests that the link we see may be mistaken. In the past we have seen such matters go either way, and the experience tells us we need more information. We can watch to see whether either man or dog copies the other's movements, or for some such sign that will maintain or destroy the nearness link. Eventually we will have an answer.

Advertising gives us the answer much sooner. At an early age we learn that for an ad to make the most favorable conceivable claim is quite natural. Anything else would be unnatural, and to say something negative would be inconceivable. The experience rarely varies; we seldom see ads doing other than wholeheartedly supporting the item advertised. Consumers thus have little uncertainty in their expectations about the purpose of an advertisement.

We could call the result the Advertising Expectations Implication. It means that simply to advertise an item at all is to imply that true and significant claims exist about it. Further, to advertise the claims on the slippery slope means to make the implications discussed in chapter 29. Other types of messages might not make the Sufficient Facts, or Brand Fact, or Puffery Implications, but advertisements do. Remember that all such implications are no more logically required than are the ones we saw in earlier chapters. As pragmatic implications, however, their only required relationship to logic is is that they make sense within the context of the nature of advertising, which is to sell.

While the regulators remain unacquainted with so much about that nature, it is unlikely that the advertisers are equally uninformed. They are experts who undoubtedly understand the implication process very well. They turn to the slippery slope because their search for significant claims leads them there. They use the slope claims because they work and are lawful.

If the claims work it must be because consumers accept them as an adequate basis for their buying decisions. Note the relationship which that produces between whether the slippery clope claims work and are deceptive. If they work, they are potentially deceptive and harmful even though they are lawful. If they are not potentially deceptive and harmful, it's because they have not worked.

Certainly some consumers will not see the implications of fact and significance that I have attributed to the slippery slope claims. However, a small number seeing them does not ruin the chance of regulatory action. Remember, the FTC criterion states that deceptiveness is in the public interest when it occurs for as few as 20 to 25 percent of consumers (chap. 2). Remember, too, that the advertisers probably won't keep the claims running unless they work for at least that proportion of consumers, or probably more.

Meanwhile, there is an extra problem for all consumers, both those deceived and those not. It is that other troublesome result of slippery slope claims—the diminishment of truth. Advertisers place consumers at risk by offering an unhelpfully small portion of the information they need. That problem occurs even for careful and skeptical consumers, because we are all deprived by what we do not get.

It's important to interpret marketplace outcomes in terms of the quality of truth they provide, rather than just discussing whether or not they are false. "Between falsehood and useless truth there is little difference," said Samuel Johnson. Consumers need not merely a lack of false claims in order to function but an abundance of true and significant claims. We do not get them from the slippery slope. From selected facts we get one good piece of information, while lacking all the others. From minimal facts we get one weak piece of information. From nonbrand facts and opinion claims we get no information, objectively. We get claims that are not harmful to us, the law says, but the law seems oblivious to the point that even if they are not directly harmful, they are indirectly so by being unhelpful.

We should all expect advertisers to be serving themselves, and there's nothing wrong with making a profit or otherwise tending to their self-interest. But should we excuse the advertisers for saying that what they do is acceptable simply because the law tells them it isn't false? Shouldn't we demand that they not think of their efforts as acceptable unless those claims are positively helpful? Should we be satisfied to know that the seller told us nothing at all rather than a harmful thing? That is hardly a satisfactory level of behavior for conducting sales transactions.

Hello, I'm a seller, and I'd like you to buy my goods even though I'm offering you no real reason for buying them. I'm giving you a reason for buying, of course, if I can get you to recognize it as such. But I'm not giving you a reason that's about the product. And that's okay, because I'm not being illegally deceptive; I'm doing good because I'm doing no harm.

What a standard! By avoiding deceptiveness the advertisers do nothing illegal, because diminishment of truth is not illegal. It's a gain to them, all right, but to pass that along as a gain to consumers is non-sense. Consumers are not merely ill served by the diminishment of truth; they may also be lulled by it. If they don't recognize what's missing, they are likely to misinterpret the available claims as adequate. Just as the advertisers are inclined to offer the best facts they can acquire, consumers in their need for information are inclined to accept the best facts they are offered. The result may work satisfactorily for the advertisers, but it's likely to be unfortunate for the public. The best available facts may sell, but they may not be very good.

Some consumers of course will recognize the diminishment of truth, and the falsity too. That's fine, but it won't be all of us, and even those of us who do won't get as much help as we need. It will leave us better able to assess the claims we do get, but the problem will remain of how to obtain the information we don't get. If we rely on the advertisers it's a problem, but when we don't rely on them, that's a problem, too.

It's remindful of the earlier point that we need to rely on sellers because they're such an important source. When the sellers let us down, the whole system lets us down because no other source has a comparable potential for helping us. When we need to trust but shouldn't, it's helpful to learn that we shouldn't. But it's not as much help as we deserve. Distrusting leaves a huge gap in our ability to make marketplace decisions, because it leaves a huge gap in our information supply. The only real solution is to be able to trust.

Consequently, the only real solution is to do something about the kind of deceptiveness that remains legal, and the consequent diminishment of truth which that deceptiveness produces.

# 31

# THE SUNOCO GASOLINE CASE

This story of a specific advertising case has a personal angle that the others didn't have. I participated in the case as an expert witness. The experience gave me some of the perspectives I have on how the law and the regulators work.

I mentioned the Sunoco case briefly in chapters 10 and 11 as illustrating the Demonstration and Halo Implications. In one ad Sunoco's maker, Sun Oil, showed an ordinary automobile pulling three railroad cars. In another ad the car pulled a U-Haul trailer up a ramp laid over a steep bank of seats in the Los Angeles Coliseum. The announcer's voice said it showed the power of a gasoline that was unusual in being "blended with the action of Sunoco 260 . . . the highest octane gasoline at any station anywhere. With 260 action the car and trailer go up the ramp just like that. You get that same 260 action at Sunoco."

Gas stations traditionally use different pumps for different grades of gasoline. Sunoco stations innovated for a time with a pump that gave a choice of grades by drawing gasoline from two separate underground tanks. One tank held a higher octane than any competitor sold; Sunoco called it 260. The other tank held 190, the lowest octane that any car on the road could use. The pump had a "custom blending" switch that let the operator dispense pure 260, pure 190, or various mixtures. Thus 200 was mostly 190 with a bit of 260, 240 was mostly 260 with some 190, and so forth. Most cars used 200, regular gasoline, which powered the cars shown in the ads.

Hardly any cars required undiluted 260, which no doubt explains why no competitors sold it. Nor did Sunoco make 260 primarily to sell it, at least not in its pure form. The purpose, rather, was to be able to claim that the blends to which the 260 tank contributed possessed what the ads called "260 action." The idea of 260 action was a farce, designed to make people think they were getting the advantages of the highest octane gasoline when they weren't. Any real advantage obtainable from 260 could exist only if it were undiluted, yet hardly any drivers bought it that way. When the "custom blending" pump mixed in various amounts of 190, consumers of course got a lower octane, a level that was available from competitors.

Suppose your bartender tells you he has the greatest Scotch in the world and is going to give you some "Scotch action." He thereupon pours you a shot having 10 percent of that brand and 90 percent of the world's lowest rated brand. What are your chances of recognizing the taste of that "greatest Scotch" when it comes in that form? They are the same as consumers had of benefiting from Sunoco 260 when their "260 action" blend was 90 percent 190.

The FTC charged Sunoco with claiming falsely that the blends called "260 action" would give users the highest octane benefits of any gasoline available. Other falsities it alleged were that 260 action would give more engine power than competitors, that it was the only gasoline enabling a car to operate at its maximum power, and that the ad demonstrations proved the power claims.

The commission conceded that none of these claims were made explicitly, so it charged they were implied. They included—see if you can recognize them—the Confusing Resemblance Implication, the

Halo Implication, and the Demonstration Implication. The principal sources of confusion were the phrases "260" and "260 action," which were so similar that consumers could easily equate them. If they did so, they would think that any "260 action" blend gave the benefits that 260 gave.

The next step was to imply that 260 gave cars greater power. That implication was aided by a false belief many consumers already held that more octane means more power. In truth, more octane gives more power only up to your car's sufficient octane level, and 260 exceeded that level for virtually all cars on the road. You could get the potential benefits of 260 by buying it in pure form at a much higher cost than for regular. If you did, though, in virtually all cases you would get no more power than other brands offered.

As to the demonstration, if the power claims were not true, the boxcar pull or the Coliseum climb certainly could not prove them. In fact, the ads couldn't have proved the claims even if they were true, among other reasons because the demonstration used only Sunoco and no other brand. (Put yourself in the place of a researcher and try to think of some other reasons!)

The FTC's main challenge in the case was to prove that the ad conveyed the false claims to consumers by implication. That's where I came in. The commission's attorney, Wallace Snyder, asked me to be an expert witness, a communication expert, on what claims consumers saw the ads to be sending. My basis would be my reasoning on how consumers perceive messages. I agreed to that, but Wally also accepted my suggestion that I buttress my reasoning with a survey of what consumers actually saw in the message. Just call me Francis Bacon Preston.

The FTC didn't easily accept the suggestion, because it was unaccustomed to introducing survey evidence of its own devising. Doing so wasn't unprecedented, but there was a reluctance for obvious reasons, principally the cost. Not many years later the commission would be spending a million dollars annually on such evidence, after having become convinced of its value. One reason it originally doubted the value of surveys was that the existence of communication experts was only beginning to be recognized. The commission had been using such witnesses as dermatologists if the challenged ad claim pertained to dermatology, or petroleum engineers if it pertained to gasoline. Just plain communication experts were something new.

Further, when the FTC first began using communication experts, it merely had them speculate from their general professional training and experience on what claims consumers would see an ad to be making. Everybody apparently assumed too casually that experts would simply present their credentials and have their testimony accepted at face value. Of course that didn't take into account cross-examination, which quickly became a barrier to such naive expectations. It's clear today that experts must have an excellent basis for saying that the claim in question was conveyed to consumers. It must be based on knowledge about the challenged claim in particular, rather than only about advertising in general.

I thought I could serve Wally Snyder and the FTC adequately with my reasoning on how consumers would respond to the Sunoco ads. I also thought, though, that the best procedure was to get responses to the challenged ads from consumers themselves. I'll admit I wasn't basing my judgment entirely on the abstract issue of the best way to carry out scientific inquiry. I was also thinking of how I would look on the witness stand. I was afraid the court could too easily reject sheer opinion. I would feel "naked" if I testified without a more substantial basis.

To my relief Snyder accepted my argument, probably in part because I also overcame the cost problem. I surveyed students in classes at my university at virtually no cost. That wasn't the best type of sample, but it was all the FTC could afford. Fortunately, a similar survey had been used successfully in a previous case. The professor doing that survey had testified convincingly that if an ad fooled college students to a certain degree, it would probably fool the general public even more. As it turned out, that argument worked just as well for me.

As we headed into the hearing before an FTC judge, we were both apprehensive. I was acting as an expert witness for the first time and Wally was introducing an expert for the first time. Early in the testimony our fears were realized. The first order of business was to get me accepted as an expert on what the ads communicated. The opposing attorney decided to try to block that acceptance. He would not have to cope with my opinions and my survey if he could convince the judge to forbid me from introducing them in the first place.

The tack taken by the attorney, John Harkins, of the Pepper, Hamilton & Sheetz law firm, was not merely to claim I was no communication expert. He also suggested to the judge that no such type of expert existed. I suddenly felt I was in danger, in a professional sense at least, of being declared a nonperson, of being granted no redeeming social value whatever. Probably I was overreacting, since a personal attack can be hard on a person. Still, FTC cases to that date had done little to confirm the existence of such expertise.

The attack came after Wally Snyder had introduced my degrees, my business and university positions past and present, and my record of published research. Harkins objected that the case was not made. He said Wally had not established me as experienced in the particular area of determining what claims ads communicate. Having introduced my accomplishments into the record, Wally wasn't sure what else he could do. He was nervous, I was nervous, the courtroom was hushed—and then suddenly the judge helped us out.

The judge told Wally he could ask me if any of my publications involved research in the area in which I intended to testify. Maybe it was because he was sympathetic to our position, or maybe he just felt it was his job to help that way—I don't know. But it was just what we needed, because I had done such research and realized it was probably the way to establish my expertise. I didn't know whether Wally realized it too, and he looked as though he wasn't sure what to do.

So I winked at him. He glanced up at me and I spontaneously gave a big wink with my left eye. I'm left-handed and, I guess, left-eyed, and that was the eye more shielded from John Harkins, who didn't see it. As I found out later, Wally was at the moment considering a basic rule in law: Don't ask a question if you don't know the answer. He had been thinking to himself that he didn't know the answer, but after the wink he did. He went ahead with the questions, I talked about my research, and the judge said I was now an expert. I presented my testimony, and the judge and eventually the whole commission ruled that the implications were conveyed and that the evidence I offered supported the finding. They ordered Sunoco not to convey such representations to consumers in the future.

It wasn't until later that I learned the wink was inappropriate behavior. I'm still not sure whether it was really improper or whether it was just that Harkins could have embarrassed us had he seen it. You know it now, John, but it's too late! Had you known then, I can imagine such problems as a quick line of questioning about whether Wally and I had a whole bunch of signals lined up. We didn't, but you could have raised the suspicion. I'll never know what you could have done, and I'm glad I didn't find out.

A lot was at stake, because consumer surveys soon became a staple way for the FTC to prove many of its charges about claims conveyed to consumers. For want of that wink the expert may have been lost. For want of the expert the testimony would have been lost. For want of the testimony the survey would have been lost. For want of the survey, later surveys may have been lost.

There may be an exaggeration in there somewhere. But still, I'm glad I winked.

# PART 6

## THE ADVERTISERS' VIEW OF THE PROBLEMS

*This part examines the way advertisers respond to issues of deceptiveness, diminishment of truth, harm to consumers, and the actions of regulators. They view very little that is not illegal as harmful. They do not control their behavior through ethics to degrees beyond the control the law exerts. Instead, they fight the legal definition of deceptiveness, hoping to reduce its coverage and thus its impact. They see the First Amendment's promise of freedom of expression as providing a vehicle for gaining such reductions. Their views are criticized here as shortsighted.*

# 32

# THE ADVERTISERS DON'T SEE
# THE PROBLEMS

I've been showing that many claims made to consumers are false or at least diminished in their truth, yet are not legally deceptive. I've also shown, in the stories of individual advertisers such as Sunoco, that the law is very good at detecting and prohibiting the kinds of claims—those at the bottom of the slippery slope—that it recognizes as deceptive. So I'm not saying the law is unconcerned with deceptiveness. It takes a strong stand against claims that are explicitly false or that produce the various types of false implications identified to date. Nonetheless, the claims on the slope remain beyond those categories, and consumers must continue to cope with them.

Before discussing solutions to these problems, I'm going to acknowledge the existence of some opinion that says there's no problem at all. To me, and I'm sure to many others, there undoubtedly is a problem. Nonetheless, I'm going to explore the point rather than take it for granted. Such contrary opinion comes of course from the advertisers, who are not impartial on the matter. They serve their own self-interest by avoiding increased regulation. Certain business sympathizers, including many economists as well as government officials who influence policies for regulating business conduct, share the advertisers' opinion.

One way for such parties to argue that no problem exists is to maintain that nothing is harmful except what's against the law. Anything that's not illegally deceptive must be completely harmless, and so presumably cannot be called unacceptable to society. By this tack, acceptableness becomes a matter of law to which no other viewpoint need be applied.

Such an approach lets the advertisers tell the world that they recognize the authority of the law. That's a smart thing for them to do. It helps them avoid such problems as legal liability and its accompanying unfavorable publicity. It creates a public relations bonus by suggesting a willingness to go along. It lets them retain the opportunity to make many claims that work with consumers, while leaving them free to ignore the various nonlaw viewpoints from which such claims appear unacceptable.

From society's viewpoint, however, the weakness of the advertisers' approach is precisely that it ignores those other viewpoints, which I will discuss here as representing the topic of ethics. When you are ethical, you follow rules of conduct based on moral principles. You do things you don't want to do, and avoid doing things you want to do. You make the choice that you believe is proper. While the law tells you what you must do and makes you do it, your ethics prompts you to do things even though you don't have to. You do them because of your beliefs about your obligation to society.

You can be ethical only when you have the option of being unethical. You can't choose to be ethical when you can't choose at all, so ethics begins only where the law ends. You are controlled involuntarily to a certain point by the law's identification of what's illegal. Beyond that point you control yourself voluntarily by your own identification of what's unethical.

The prospect of going beyond the law is what is missing from the approach I believe many advertisers take. They lean instead toward interpreting what's unethical as being basically no more than what's illegal. They tend to feel that what they should avoid doing is little or nothing more than what the law specifically directs them to avoid doing.

Such an approach means that ethics never really starts. The claims on the slippery slope are legal, and if they are legal they are what advertisers call ethical. Nothing is added; the law is the beginning and the end. Such a result is so useful to the advertisers that they seem not to notice how observers could interpret their approach as meaning, actually, that they have no ethics at all.

There is a reason advertisers might well equate ethics with legality. I don't mean a good reason, just an explanation. It is that the illegality of deceptiveness weighs so heavily on them. They feel quite put upon by it, because it interferes with their long-standing heritage of selling as an activity conducted freely, without restraints. That heritage developed in large part because selling historically was lawless in the sense of involving no restraints on what the seller said.

Of course sales transactions have always been restrained by what the consenting parties agree to, and that's not lawless—it's orderly and controlled. What the law controls, though, involves *what* the seller and buyer agree to rather than *how* they come to agree. The "how" part is the lawless part. The traditional rule of caveat emptor (buyer beware) specified that their negotiations included the seller's privilege to lie in a largely unrestrained way, for which a buyer's only recourse was to disbelieve and refuse to rely. Buyers who made the purchase bound themselves by having agreed to buy, while sellers who prompted the purchase were left unbound by the methods used to obtain that agreement.

Because I have discussed caveat emptor at length in *The Great Ameri-*

*can Blow-Up,* I will not do so here. Suffice it to say that today's explicit treatment of puffery and the parallel implicit treatment of other claims on the slippery slope are remnants of that old rule, showing that the law has never completely abandoned it. Of course what sellers may tell buyers today is no longer as utterly lawless as in the earliest days of caveat emptor. Nonetheless, marketplace speech remains lawless enough that the advertisers' experiences with deceptiveness restrictions are unpleasant for them. The rules give them the same sort of feeling you and I would get from encountering an unexpected speed bump on an interstate highway.

Deceptiveness restriction is tough for the sellers to swallow not only because it's tacked onto their restraint-free heritage, but because it isn't tacked onto the speech of other Americans. The First Amendment provides that there be no prohibition of deceptiveness for speech that is not commercial. That includes advertising that is noncommercial, such as for political candidates. Commercial activity, selling, is thus singled out as deserving a constraint not imposed on other activities.

In short, the commercial advertisers must face a law they once didn't have and that other speakers still don't have. That surely makes acceptance unpleasant and encourages a degree of indignation. Their reaction to this state of affairs recalls the old riddle about whether a cup is half full or half empty. While observers such as myself point out that the law's interpretation of deceptiveness excludes a lot, the advertisers tend more toward noticing how much it includes.

Given that, it's not surprising to find the advertisers reacting by saying, in effect, that if that's what society is going to stick us with, if the rules force us to endure all these prohibitions, then don't expect anything else of us. The regulators can get their pound of flesh, but that's all anybody's going to get. Whatever we're permitted to do after the law finishes with us, we'll do.

Thus the perception that the law is doing too much already transcends the urge to be ethical, the urge to do more than the law requires. As a result, advertising tends toward being not necessarily unethical but at least nonethical. Law is dominant; ethics is an absent or minor matter. The idea that harm can come from any deceptiveness the law has not recognized as illegal, or from diminishment of truth, is thus also a minor matter.

I do not claim that all advertisers hold this position. Certainly ethical behavior exists out there. Some advertisers voluntarily avoid slippery slope claims and make claims that give consumers better truth and product significance even though not contributing to brand significance. Still, any casual examination of ad content suggests that the average brand advertiser makes no great effort to avoid the slope or to emphasize claims that lie on the high ground above it.

I would be properly criticized in this context if I ignored the topic of ad industry self-regulation, which appears to involve acting ethically in the sense of volunteering to do something you don't have to do. Advertisers have their own apparatus, apart from the law, for investigating complaints and determining whether claims are acceptable. They do not bind themselves to accept such decisions, but their record of doing so voluntarily is very strong. That is admirable, and on the whole we are certainly better off with self-regulation than without it.

I feel, however, that the self-serving aspects of self-regulation considerably dilute its ethical aspect. For one thing, the process promises greater certainty of action than complaining to an FTC that cannot act specifically on behalf of given advertisers. It also lets the advertisers enter complaints against each other at far less cost than in Lanham Act cases. And, the self-regulation decisions that go against an advertiser prompt less coverage in the press than do FTC or Lanham prohibitions.

Further, and most significantly, participations by advertisers in self-regulation do not involve doing something more than what the law would do. It's more like doing what the law would do before the law gets around to it. That is not meaningless, but I would be far more impressed if self-regulation resulted in detecting general types of deceptiveness that the law has not detected. Self-regulation's results are helpful to the consuming public, but that's peripheral in the industry's eyes to the fact that it's helpful to its members. The advertisers are making no sacrifice; they are gaining more through self-regulation than they are giving up. That's why they do it, and that's fine. But it doesn't amount to the type of ethical action that clearly goes beyond what the law would eventually do.

My remarks on ethics or its lack, as with all observations made in this book, cover only the topic of claims made about commercial products or services. If a company protested that it had, say, voluntarily eliminated sexist images from its ads, I would say that is admirable and clearly indicates ethical behavior. However, the topic of the impact of ad content on women rather than on buying decisions is not the area I am discussing. That other area is important, but it would involve a different book from this one.

This chapter began by asking whether there is a problem over the falsity or diminished truth of the slippery slope claims. There certainly seems to be, because the lack of imposed controls over such claims is accompanied by a parallel lack of voluntary controls. The abandonment of ethics is inherently troublesome. That is so not only as a matter of general principles—meaning everybody should have an ethical outlook—but because the existence of advertising law does not render ethics unnecessary. While the law's short reach means there is much that ethics could do, the advertisers' response means there is much that is done by neither.

# 33

# HOW THEY TRY TO ESCAPE

We have seen that the advertisers tend to rule out any social force other than the law to control the marketplace. We shall now see that they also strive to fend off any action of the law beyond its current coverage. They want nothing but the law, and they want no more extensive law. In their long tradition of denial regarding deceptiveness, they routinely object to recognizing any new types of it. Although they probably wouldn't deny that they diminish truth, they would surely claim that the diminishment isn't illegal, which is correct. They would also deny that it causes trouble for anyone, which I feel is not correct.

Advertisers have been fighting expanded definitions of deceptiveness since the FTC's earliest cases. In 1919, when Sears protested that it hadn't deceived anyone, an appellate court confirmed the commission's right to find a violation without evidence of actual deception. The court let the FTC use the alternative evidence of a mere "capacity or tendency to injure consumers." That ruling turned Sears into a violator when it would otherwise have escaped.

Advertisers sought ways to deny a "capacity or tendency" to deceive, but they lost most of their deniability when the law defined the phenomenon as existing when a false claim was conveyed. For years the advertisers then shifted to arguing that the regulators should charge them with conveyance only for their explicit content. Implications shouldn't count, they said. They lost that argument, too.

Losing, of course, means to lawyers only that they fall back in military fashion to a position a little further to the rear. Then they dig another trench and fire away as before. In that way they've kept up their resistance to advertising regulation. They have refused to recognize each new type of implication, sometimes even after the law has identified it several times. With that stubbornness, it's easy to predict what they'll do in the future. They will fight recognition of the implications that I've described as produced by the slippery slope claims.

The ad industry's propensity to dispute deceptiveness findings has never been so well illustrated as in a research project commissioned by the American Association of Advertising Agencies. Researchers for the "Four A's" showed people thirty-second segments of television content, either ads or other programming. Then they asked the people whether each of several statements was true or false on the basis of what the segment had stated or implied.

People got 30 percent of the statements wrong. That approximate level of error was consistent with responses in other studies that examined television content and print content, and that examined different groups of people. The researchers interpreted the results as indicating normal miscomprehension. They concluded that human beings are prone to understand correctly only about 70 percent of the information they get.

The Four A's used that conclusion to imply a relationship between normal miscomprehension and deceptiveness. Suppose, they suggested, the regulators charged that an ad conveyed a false claim, but only 30 percent or fewer consumers saw the claim conveyed. If so, the result would represent no more than the normal level of miscomprehension by people, not illegal deceptiveness by the advertiser.

Given all that, the law should properly describe what happened as being the consumers' fault and not the advertiser's fault, and so should not prohibit the message. Only if the figure goes over 30 percent should the law hold the advertiser responsible. Even then, say, if the figure were 40 percent, regulators should regard the first 30 percent as miscomprehension and only the remaining 10 percent as deceptiveness. That line of argument would get rid of much deceptiveness, since the regulators currently accept figures below 30 percent as sufficient to reflect deceptiveness. Under this new analysis the law would excuse many claims that its traditional method would lead it to prohibit.

That thinking contained flaws. The trouble began with its argument that if consumer response to an ad was miscomprehension then it could not also be deceptiveness. In other words, if the mistake were the consumer's fault it could not be the advertiser's fault. That conclusion depended, though, on having the law interpret deceptiveness as the advertiser's fault, which the law doesn't do. Legally deceptiveness is a no-fault event, prohibitable even if it's not the advertiser's fault.

The advertiser can be completely innocent of intending to deceive, or of knowing of any deceptive impact, yet the regulators can still order the advertiser to stop the message. While that may seem a bit harsh on advertisers, it's a well-established custom. The law justifies it on the ground that prohibiting deceptiveness is important in serving the public interest. Also, the law restrains advertisers only to the extent of stopping the message. It imposes no punishment and does not brand the advertiser as a criminal.

The law's approach obviously disagrees with the suggestion of the Four A's that miscomprehension is typically present at the 30 percent level and nobody can do anything about it. The law assumes by contrast that miscomprehended claims that are also deceptive can be eliminated, and should be. Granted, there is some miscomprehension that advertisers can never eliminate. The amount, though, is probably much lower than 30 percent, perhaps more like 5 percent. The rest would be the sort that can easily be eliminated by revised wording. The law has frequently tried for such elimination by prohibiting advertisers from using certain claims unless they rewrite them to create a greater chance of being understood correctly.

Such substitution seems highly appropriate in the case of ambiguous messages. Take the statement, "I don't have no bananas." Some people will give those words the grammatically correct interpretation of being a double negative. By that, they will hear the speaker to be claiming to have bananas. Other people, though, will recognize the statement as common slang, and so will hear the opposite being claimed. In any event, the speaker can eliminate the ambiguity simply by saying either "I have bananas" or "I don't have any bananas."

In short, some speech produces considerable miscomprehension that it does not have to produce. Is advertising like that? Sure. We have seen how the name Aspercreme implied falsely that the product contained aspirin. Could the advertiser use a name that does not produce that implication? Of course. Do you think the advertiser used Aspercreme on purpose, anyway? Who doesn't!

The ad industry does not have a uniform approach toward dealing with such claims. On the one hand, its national organization complains that its members are getting blamed for innocent miscomprehension. On the other hand, some of those members regularly send the public messages deliberately designed to raise miscomprehension to high levels. If they are creating the miscomprehension in the first place, they are scarcely innocent of it when it happens. We saw such an effect with Sunoco's phrase "260 Action" (chap. 31). Eliminating that confusing usage could easily have prevented the false implication that the user of gasoline having a small percentage of 260 would get the advantages of using 260. The advertiser seems to have been willing to have that confusion occur.

We saw the same effect in chapter 25, with the various phrases used in headache remedy ads. Readers might review those phrases with an eye on how they produce miscomprehension. For example,

Anacin's claim to contain "the pain reliever doctors recommend most" implied falsely that the active ingredient was other than, and superior to, aspirin. Anacin's maker, American Home Products, could have communicated the truth with great ease by using the simple word *aspirin.*

That would assume, though, that the company had the slightest interest in avoiding such misunderstanding. With all such examples, the advertisers could easily have prevented most of the potential for miscomprehension. Any sympathy the regulators might show, then, toward excusing them for consumers' miscomprehension will disappear when the regulators see how so many of their claims actually invite misunderstanding.

Another problem with the Four A's miscomprehension project was that it recognized as accurate comprehension only those implications that followed logically from the explicit content. Remember, people saw thirty-second messages and then responded to a prepared set of statements. Some of them answered true for a statement that expressed an implication following logically. The researchers considered those persons to have answered correctly and to have comprehended the message. However, other times people answered true for a statement that expressed an implication not following logically from the explicit content. In those cases, the researchers said the people were incorrect; they miscomprehended.

The researchers' conclusions, of course, contradict the regulators' identification, discussed in earlier chapters, of numerous implications that explicit content prompts pragmatically rather than logically. For example, the Halo Implication involves first an explicit statement, E, that a brand is superior on one attribute. From that statement follows the implied statement, I, that the brand is superior on one or more other attributes, or superior overall. The statement does not follow logically, but it follows pragmatically. Thus those for whom such implied statements were true probably should have been interpreted in the Four A's research as having correctly comprehended. That is the interpretation the law makes.

The regulators see the problem to be that pragmatic implications are false, not that they are miscomprehended. Consumers do not miscomprehend the statement itself, but only its truth. Indeed, the reason they miscomprehend the truth is precisely *because* they correctly comprehend the E statement to imply the I statement, just as the advertiser no doubt expects they will.

If the Four A's research had not interpreted pragmatic implications as errors, the "normal" level of miscomprehension would have been well below 30 percent. If the research had also discounted miscomprehension that the advertisers could readily eliminate by clearer writing, the figure would be even lower. Certainly some errors are attributable to consumers as their own fault in miscomprehending, but not nearly so many.

Meanwhile, along with denying much of the role of deceptiveness, advertisers will deny that diminishment of truth causes any problems. They will say, correctly, that such diminishment is not against the law. More generally, being unhelpful or uncommunicative is not a violation. The regulators have no general power to force advertisers to make claims they are not already making.

In summary, the advertisers respond to the deceptiveness violation by arguing for its reduction or elimination. They respond to the diminishment of truth by seeing it as a privilege for themselves, and as a nonproblem for consumers.

# 34

# ADVERTISERS' FIRST AMENDMENT RIGHTS

I've been saying that advertisers take a dim view of ethics and have a low opinion of suggestions to expand the law. The would prefer instead to reduce the law's scope. It's unlikely that the miscomprehension argument can gain them that advantage. Many of them, however, may feel that a line of reasoning involving the First Amendment gives greater promise.

Let's read the First Amendment of the Constitution. *"Congress shall make no law* respecting an establishment of religion, or prohibiting the free exercise thereof; or *abridging the freedom of speech, or of the press;* or the right of the people peaceably to assemble, and to petition the Government for a redress of grievances." I have emphasized the portions relevant to our topic.

Despite the seeming definiteness of the phrasing, there have been various abridgements. "No law" does not literally mean no law, although it means not very much law. The abrigements include prohibiting deceptiveness in commercial speech. That restriction, based historically on English law predating the Constitution, seems to be so firmly adopted that there's little reason to think it will ever disappear.

Along with stopping deceptiveness, First Amendment interpretation traditionally held that regulators could control commercial speech in any other way they saw appropriate. Restrictions up to and including a complete ban on any type of advertising were acceptable. Such assumption existed implicitly in our law for many decades, and eventually the Supreme Court expressly stated it. The Court ruled in 1942 that "the Constitution imposes no . . . restraint on government as respects purely commercial advertising."

In the 1970s the rule began to change. The Supreme Court decided that some types of advertising regulation were not permissible. A key case involved a Virginia weekly's managing editor who published an advertisement offering to help women get abortions in New York. The ad and abortion itself were illegal in Virginia, but the advertised service was legal when performed in New York. The question the Supreme Court faced was whether nondeceptive information for a legal product or service was prohibitible. The Court said it was not and struck down Virginia's law.

The Court soon made a similar ruling about another Virginia law that let the state board of pharmacy stop druggists from advertising prescription drug prices. The Court also eliminated an Arizona law that kept lawyers from advertising. The result each time was to rule that the First Amendment gave advertising certain freedoms not previously granted to it. Congress or the states could continue to prohibit advertising that was deceptive or for illegal products. For other ads, however, the new rule was that prohibition was not permissible unless lawmakers clearly established a need for it.

The latter two cases cited were the ones in which Justice Rehnquist dissented (chap. 14). He said that allowing more and more freedom for advertising would sent the Court down a "slippery slope." It would lead eventually to more freedom for such messages than he could tolerate. He was, however, a minority of one on the point.

In all of these cases, the Supreme Court majority emphasized that the advertised information was of high public interest. To repress it would cause a shortage of knowledge that would seriously disadvantage people. The Court thus was reinterpreting the First Amendment to include a right by the people to receive useful information that other people wished to distribute. The Court said such information was no less important to society simply because it was commercial. That is a very flattering thing to say of an industry whose messages had traditionally been regarded as less valuable socially than the news content of the media.

Advertising people have tended to interpret these developments as indicating a trend in which their messages will gain more and more freedom. They might easily overdo their excitement about this, however. Before making too much of it, they should note that the cases cited did not involve typical selling situations. The ads before the Supreme Court emphasized product rather than brand information, involving facts having clear objective value.

It's hard to imagine that the Court would show similar enthusiasm for the more typical kinds of brand selling. Would it rush to protect, for example, Pepsi's right to offer Ray Charles's expression "uh-huh" as a reason for valuing Pepsi more than Coke? Not likely. Still, the ruling was an exciting development, within its limited application, for an industry that had previously learned to expect nothing whatever from the First Amendment. Suddenly there was something.

In subsequent cases the Supreme Court stated the rule more precisely. The law may regulate commercial speech that is not deceptive and not for an unlawful product only if a substantial government interest exists that the regulation will help to further. Also, the regulation must not be more restrictive than will achieve a reasonable fit with that interest. The law may still regulate commercial speech that is deceptive or for an unlawful product. A government interest in repressing that speech is generally assumed to exist, and regulation of that speech is generally assumed to achieve that interest. In the case of deceptiveness, however, the degree of regulation is restricted to fitting reasonably with what is necessary to eliminate the deceptiveness.

This new "commercial speech doctrine" gives advertisers more protection than before. In particular, it could mean that the Supreme Court would find proposed bans of nondeceptive cigarette or alcohol advertising to be unconstitutional. That could happen because such bans might not achieve the government interest in reducing smoking. Or the bans, if the law found them capable of reducing consumption, might be more restrictive than necessary to achieve that purpose.

What I find most significant about the new rule, however, is something other than its presumed guarantee of freedom. Actually, the new rule retains a great deal of the old restrictiveness, because many possible regulations could be fitted within the stated requirements. Besides, the new rule doesn't benefit most advertising anyway because there are not many ads that someone wants to block. Despite the very real issues about tobacco and alcohol, there is overall very little nondeceptive advertising for lawful products that any persons or governmental bodies have shown any interest in restricting.

Consequently, the whole affair is a nonissue for most advertisers because it simply won't affect them. Some of them *say* it's an issue because of the "domino effect," by which a ban for tobacco and alcohol today will mean bans for coffee, tea, and Coke tomorrow. I don't think they really believe that; they just use it as a way to argue.

What I find significant, meanwhile, about the commercial speech doctrine is that it gives the advertisers a *perception* that their freedom of speech will increase over time. The next chapter will discuss whether that is likely to happen.

## 35

# ADVERTISERS' FIRST AMENDMENT HOPES FOR ELIMINATING DECEPTIVENESS

When advertising's First Amendment freedoms emerged in the late 1970s, I was amused that some industry persons took it to mean they would get the fullest freedom of speech imaginable. Strangely, they translated the idea that advertising now had First Amendment rights into the idea that regulation, even for deceptiveness, might largely disappear.

Well, what's the harm in wishful thinking, even if so obviously incorrect! To cite the *Virginia Pharmacy* case, "The First Amendment, as we construe it today, does not prohibit the State from insuring that the stream of commercial information flow cleanly as well as freely." In that context, "cleanly" refers unmistakably to keeping out deceptiveness. No application of freedom of speech to advertising has ever said or implied otherwise.

Moreover, there could in fact be some harm in dreaming that deceptiveness might become legal. Such thoughts may be pushing advertisers unrealistically toward yearning for more freedom. To assess the prospects of that happening, let's take a close look at what it means, but also doesn't mean, for advertising to be protected by the First Amendment.

You would think that the instruction enacted, that Congress shall make "no law" abridging freedom of speech, would naturally mean no law concerning any kind of speech, even the deceptive kind. After all, the theory behind the idea would seem to apply to any speech. That theory was that if people hear everything from all sources and viewpoints, the will sort out the good from the bad. In *Areopagitica* Milton said poetically, "Let her and Falsehood grapple; who ever knew Truth put to the worse in a free and open encounter?"

Why, then, does the law prohibit deceptiveness in commercial speech? For one reason, the law under which the American colonists and their ancestors lived prior to the time of the Constitution had already identified commercial speech as different from other speech. What eventually became advertising law had its roots in the English regulation of personal sales transactions. Those rules developed not merely before the United States was created but even before Gutenberg turned the wine press into the printing press.

Still, could not this prior law have been canceled by the arrival of the First Amendment? Perhaps, but it wasn't. A major reason for not doing so was the consideration that commercial speech generally does not represent a "free and open encounter." Truth may indeed be "put to the worse" when one of the parties, the consumer, does not have equal access to the relevant information. Thus marketplace speech presumably is different from political speech, which was the principal kind the First Amendment's creators sought to protect. The Supreme Court has concluded that marketplace inequality exists and that it justifies banning deceptiveness by commercial speakers even though not by news reporters and commentators.

As Zechariah Chafee said for political speech, "Truth can be sifted from falsehood . . . if the government is vigorously and constantly cross-examined." The press as cross-examiner can be very effective in this way for covering political news and many other topics. It seems to be much less effective, though, when the object of investigation is the marketplace. To consumers' misfortune, the press receives most of its revenue from the advertisers. It thus may fail to scrutinize such parties with the enthusiasm it shows toward such activities as the president's behavior during Watergate.

The point is not that the encounter with truth never happens. Some scrutiny occurs, as in *Consumer Reports,* which quite notably runs no advertising. Also, many of the media that do run advertising commendably examine some consumer issues sometimes. However, such efforts are not enough to lift consumers routinely to a level of equality with sellers in their ability to assess truth and weed out falsity. If they were, I would not have a basis for writing this book.

News reporters describe events that they may not have personally witnessed, or on which they are not themselves experts. For that reason, it's accepted that they may sometimes misstate facts or make incorrect interpretations. Accordingly, the law typically excuses them for the deceptiveness their efforts sometimes produce. The greater good of conveying information that will usually be correct outweighs the harm of getting things wrong on occasion.

The seller of goods, meanwhile, as Justice Blackmun said in the *Virginia Pharmacy* decision, "seeks to disseminate information about a specific product or service that he himself provides and presumably knows more about than anyone else." The truth of commercial speech, therefore, is more easily verifiable by that speaker. As a result, the speaker must accept a higher degree of responsibility for insuring it not to be deceptive.

Another point Justice Blackman made is that commercial speech is more durable than the noncommercial kind. The concern is whether a ban on deceptiveness might "chill" future speech, creating a fear of prosecution that would cause a speaker not to speak. The ban on bad speech would thus amount in effect to a ban on much future good speech as well. Expert observers of the press are certain that such fear could repress reporters to an extent that much useful information would never reach the public. If that happened, the press would no longer play the "watchdog" role that society considers so important.

Commercial speech, on the other hand, is so central to the generating of profits that the Supreme Court feels a ban on deceptiveness will not chill it. The advertisers of Anacin or Tylenol, for example, presumably would never think of ceasing their ads entirely. They would keep on promoting what are, after all, perfectly good brands of a perfectly good product (even if not so superior as their false claims might make them seem). The law would eliminate their bad speech, and let their good speech remain.

The Court might have added that the penalty for deceptiveness is not likely to chill very much speech. If news reporters say something untrue about an individual, they and their employers can be at considerable risk, even though not for deceptiveness as such. They can be subject to other violations, such as libel if the falsity defames a person's reputation. Such charges can result in damages amounting to millions of dollars. In contrast, the deceptive advertiser usually must do no more than stop communicating the deception. That level of "threat" is scarcely likely to chill anyone into deciding to avoid sending a message.

A recent oddity is an argument by two lawyers that the First Amendment should protect, and thus allow to continue, deceptiveness created by implied claims. The reason they give is that advertisers face an "intolerable uncertainty" as to what implied claims the regulators may find. Since the regulators make such findings only after the fact, the advertisers presumably will be in the dark beforehand, with no way of knowing what to expect. As a result, they may decide to keep quiet rather than speak; regulation will chill their speech. The solution, the lawyers say, is to let implied claims go free, even when false and misleading, in order to "provide breathing room for legitimate commercial speech."

The problem with that argument is that those lawyers are wrong about the uncertainty. The types of implications I have identified, as listed at the end of chapter 11, are all easy for the advertisers to predict.

If a proposed new ad claim matches the explicit form of an already-known false implication, they may expect the implication to occur again. The advertisers can thereby avoid committing a violation, and stay out of trouble. They can also proceed with any explicit content not associated with false implications. Their "legitimate" speech will not be chilled.

The procedure will not work perfectly. There is always the possibility of new implications being identified. However, I think the list is similar to the Table of Elements in chemistry, which will always be open-ended but whose existing members probably represent the bulk of those that will ever be known. The law will find more in the future, of course, and in fact this book suggests some possibilities. However, any new implications will have the same structural characteristics as the existing ones, and thus will not be difficult to predict.

In summary, there is little reason to think the advertisers can use the First Amendment to eliminate the violation of deceptiveness. They are going to have to live with it.

## 36

# THE TRIUMPH CIGARETTE CASES

Cigarettes have been a declining product for years, but that doesn't stop individual brands from battling for their shares of the remaining business. Advertising often plays its role by using nonbrand images, such as the Virginia Slims woman or Joe Camel. It's also popular to make up real if questionable facts by obtaining consumer preference information. Surveyors ask consumers "Do you prefer Brand A or Brand B?" The results are published by the winner, who of course is usually the questionnaire's sponsor in the first place. The intent is to impress consumers by having them learn such facts as "80 percent of smokers surveyed chose Brand A."

I am going to treat consumer preference facts as real brand facts. Of course, they surely reflect nonbrand facts and opinions that consumers acquire from advertising. A famous example is consumers' preference for Marlboro because they relate the image of the Marlboro man to their own psychological or social characteristics. Such preference facts are also selected facts, because the ads using them typically omit mentioning the brand's actual qualities. Also, such facts will be "selected" only when the percentages are high; low results will never become ad claims.

We would all be wise to assume that the use of consumer preferences as claims probably means that the factual differences between a brand and its competitors are small or nonexistent. When the factual differences are great, advertisers will prefer to claim them directly rather than take the indirect route of referring to them through preferences. When you see an ad trumpeting a preference test, you can bet the advertiser is not confident about the brand's physical facts. It probably feels that such inherent features as ingredients, performance, and tangible benefits will not make a big impact.

Of course, when the factual differences between the brands are small or nonexistent, you might expect that the preference differences will be small, too. The percentages of people choosing A and B might be almost the same; many consumers might even say they prefer A and B equally if the testing method allows them to say that (as it should). Such results will disappoint the advertiser, and it might not publicize the survey.

That's not a big worry, however. A small objective factual difference will not necessarily prevent the advertiser from finding a large preference difference on the basis of subjective perceptions of the ad. If many people prefer A over B by even a small margin, the survey data will show an overall preference for A by a large margin.

The beauty of the trick is that the survey converts the nonfact claims into objective facts, those of preference. It produces a desired meaningfully positive objective differentiation that could never result from the physical facts per se. The problem, however, is that while preference victories may certainly be legitimate, they frequently occur because the preference measuring process has been improperly manipulated.

Consider this cigarette claim: "TRIUMPH BEATS MERIT. Triumph, at less than half the tar, preferred over Merit. In fact, an amazing 60% said 3 mg. Triumph tastes as good or better than 8 mg. Merit." Triumph's maker, Lorillard, obtained that result from a survey and accurately reported it in its ads. It did not, however, report the survey fully. In a classic illustration of selected facts and selected omissions, the ads did not say how Lorillard arrived at the 60 percent figure.

Consumers could deduce that the result came from summing the percentages of those calling Triumph better and those calling the two brands equal. However, consumers had no way of learning what those two separate percentage figures were. Upon learning them, the regulators saw that they contradicted the claim that Triumph had won. Thirty-six percent had preferred Triumph, while 24 percent said the two were equal. The rest of the story, of course, was that the remaining

40 percent preferred Merit. Combining 40 with 24 produced an even more "amazing" 64 percent who said that Merit tasted as good as or better than Triumph. Philip Morris's Merit was the real winner of Lorillard's survey.

Philip Morris sued Lorillard under the Lanham Act and won a prohibition of the false claims. Part of the case was the bizarre testimony of a witness for Lorillard. The case decision described John O'Toole as a "distinguished and obviously experienced president of a preeminent advertising agency." Mr. O'Toole's varied and longtime service to advertising has earned him high regard within the industry. This time, though, he served its reputation oddly by claiming that Triumph had won the contest despite the survey results.

Triumph established its win, O'Toole testified, by the fact that a brand with less than half as much tar, which is what produces taste, could do as well as Triumph did on a taste test. The judge gave a tongue-in-cheek acknowledgment of the proposition, saying that the advertising business apparently accepted "this subjective assumption." He concluded, however, that it "does not validate the misleading aspect of the ad."

There is a certain attractiveness, of course, to the idea that Triumph could do so well. It was surely the underdog in terms of taste, having only three-eighths the tar of Merit. Given that, it might have received zero percent preference from consumers. As the judge pointed out, though, the ad conveyed to consumers that Triumph won the survey. The ad implied that the win established that Triumph was a better-tasting cigarette. The claim illustrated the Proof Implication, and it was clearly false.

Ironically, Triumph might have created a true and significant claim by forthrightly describing how it came so close to winning with so little tar. The combination of being nearly as tasty while having less tar sounds like an appeal that could serve both smokers and Lorillard well. Lorillard, though, didn't think that was triumph enough.

Also suing Lorillard was R. J. Reynolds, for similar surveys comparing Triumph to its Winston Lights, Vantage, Salem, and Salem Lights brands. This time some of the comparisons truly showed higher scores for Triumph, so Reynolds had to use different arguments. It offered evidence of what smokers thought when they saw in Triumph's ads, or any cigarette ads, that one brand "beat" another or was "preferred" over the other. Typically smokers took the claim to mean that taste was the basis for the reported preference.

Reynolds argued that Triumph took advantage of this Ordinary Meaning Implication, and that it was false. The court agreed it was false, because the surveyors disclosed the tar levels of the competing cigarettes to people just before they smoked them and stated their preference. The tar information would have caused the smokers to make their judgments predominantly on the basis of tar to the exclusion of other attributes. The reported percentages, therefore, were not about taste. There was no support for the advertising implication that the survey findings were about taste or about overall preference.

To help prove that the surveyed smokers had responded to the tar difference specifically, Reynolds itself conducted two repetitions of the Lorillard surveys. It did them similarly except that in one survey it did not reveal the tar levels, and in the other it stated the tar levels in reverse, so that people thought Triumph had more tar. People preferred Triumph much less often in those two surveys. Clearly the tar difference had created the reported preference difference.

Triumph's ads also claimed that the surveys were "national" tests or studies. The court, though, accepted Reynolds's arguments that conducting the study in shopping malls across the nation gave the sample an urban bias. That and other factors made the survey nonprojectable to U.S. smokers overall. As a result, the phrase "National Taste Test Winner" had a total of three wrong claims in its four words. The test wasn't national, it wasn't about taste, and Triumph wasn't always the winner.

Advertisers use consumer preference facts frequently, and the law has discredited them a number of times. Another example involved a claim by Bristol-Myers that its Body on Tap shampoo got higher consumer ratings than several competitors. Vidal Sassoon sued because Bristol-Myers had, among other things, instructed the surveyed women to use Sassoon shampoo in a way contrary to Sassoon's instructions, thus biasing their preferences. The testing also had not truthfully studied what a high fashion model had said in the ad to be "over nine hundred women like me." While the model was clearly an adult, approximately one-third of the females surveyed were ages 13–18.

As Sassoon successfully argued, Bristol-Myers had operated on knowledge from previous surveys that Body on Tap appealed more successfully to teenagers than to adult women. Sassoon also established that while the ads implied that the surveyed women had compared the brands, none actually used more than one shampoo. Such testing produces scores that can compare competitors only indirectly. The court called it questionably valid because it made no actual comparisons and so did not obtain real comparison preferences as the ad claimed.

None of this discussion contradicts the fact that honest surveys can provide excellent consumer information. They can also give the advertisers legitimate selling points. The FTC put it this way in another case: "The existence of a 'survey' as support for a claim of superiority may well imply to many consumers a measure of precision and accuracy that they would be less willing to attribute to the same claim made without reference to any statistical support. We assume this is why advertisers wish to use surveys."

Indeed it is. Remember, though, that consumer preferences may derive from nonfacts and therefore convey little or nothing that is objectively brand significant. The advertiser first provides diminished truth and significance to many consumers. It then creates a vehicle, the survey, through which those consumers pass the same questionable values to the rest of us. Be wary!

# PART 7

# AN ALTERNATIVE VIEW THAT ADVERTISERS COULD TAKE

*The last three parts recommend solutions to the problems of deceptiveness through actions that could be taken by, respectively, the advertisers, the regulators, and consumers themselves. The advertisers come first, in this section, because the process starts with their claims. Should they not act, Part 8 states recommendations for legal action. Should neither advertisers nor regulators act, Part 9 advises consumers on steps they could take. This part also includes a final chapter on a particular deceptive advertising case, along with a chapter taking a look back at those various stories, to draw some conclusions about the actions of advertisers and regulators in such cases.*

# 37

## THE ADVERTISERS' PRINCIPAL
## MOTIVATION: AVOIDING COMPETITION

It's time to see what can be done about the slippery slope problems, starting with what the advertisers can do. In what follows, I am not going to place the blame entirely on them. I wouldn't pin a rose on the industry, but before finishing I will discuss the responsibilities of all involved parties, including the regulators and, yes, consumers too.

There's no doubt that the problem begins with the marketplace situation the advertisers face. The situation is that the public may buy most products and services from several suppliers, who thus compete against each other. Competition is admirable. Consumers benefit from it by escaping the higher prices and inattention to quality that can result from having only one source. Multiple sources ensure that the flow of goods will be plentiful and reliable. Certainly we would not want to throw out a system that serves us by allowing new participants to enter the marketplace freely to challenge those already there.

Nonetheless, while each brand is the apple of its owner's eye, the public's ability to join in such delight is dampened by the fact that many brands are objectively so similar to their competitors. The value of having a variety of choices is depressed even further by the fact that the various competitors collectively can manufacture more units than the public will buy without artificial stimulation.

None of that matters much to a public more concerned about product categories than about the fates of the individual brand makers. Such an orientation serves the public well, but the companies take a different view. Offering additional supply of an item that one's competitors already supply in sufficient quantity is not a happy situation. Nor is trying to match prices at low levels and quality at high levels, both of which eat heavily into profit. In other words, competition has its downside for the sellers. Taken to its extreme, it's a bummer for them.

The natural reaction of a competitor, then, is to ask how to stop being a competitor and start being a monopolist instead. The task might involve getting rid of competitors if that were possible, but it's typically not. So what it usually requires is to find a way to monopolize within the system, which means to tolerate the continuing existence of competitors yet manage to avoid competing with them.

That way, which we have already examined at length, is to create a brand. A brand is a monopoly; no one else can sell it. The result has been given the name of *monopolistic competition*. That term has a specialized meaning to economists, but I use it here simply to reflect the double nature of what is happening. Sellers are competing in selling the product generally, but not in selling those aspects of the product that represent their individual brands. They and only they can sell the public those aspects.

I once encountered what I took to be a corporate objection to giving this point a public airing. An executive from Parker Pen sat through a university class in which I described how advertisers were engaging in monopoly. Afterward he protested to me rather heatedly that the American system is competitive, and nobody should say otherwise. Monopoly is for communists; it's insulting to use the term to describe the American system.

So I said to him, "Russ, you sell Parker pens, right?" He said, "Right." I said, "Nobody else sells Parker pens, right?" He said, "Right." I said, "What if somebody else made pens and tried to sell them as Parker pens?" He said, "We'd stop them; we wouldn't allow it. We own the trademark." So then I said, "Okay, you have a monopoly on Parker pens—not on pens, but on the Parker kind, right?" He was too grumpy to agree right away, but eventually he grudgingly did. You really can't avoid the conclusion that if you're the only one allowed to do something, then you must have a monopoly on it.

Corporate America, of course, extols competition to the rooftops, and rightly so. When we have more than one maker of pens or toothpaste or whatever, we have competition and its consequent advantages. Nobody should say otherwise. But that doesn't change the point that a typical way for sellers to deal with competition is in fact to avoid it. They compete to the extent necessary, but they monopolize to the extent possible.

The desire to monopolize, however reasonable in certain ways, creates the root cause of the unfortunate treatment of truth and falsity we have been examining. It creates the pressure on sellers to give consumers reasons to buy a specific brand. That in turn translates into pressure to transmit true and brand significant claims, which leads further to using the best truth and significance that's available, be it very good or not.

Ask yourself: For what types of products do you see the weakest truth and significance? It's for those for which the brand significance, beyond the product significance, is objectively the least. In other words, it's for those brands that are the least different from the others. Monopolizing is the most difficult in that situation, so that's where the content of the advertising is most likely to go sliding down the slippery slope.

What brand advertising can accomplish, in the words of an *Advertising Age* columnist, is to "deflect attention from what brands are and onto what they *mean*. There may be no performance difference between Coke and Pepsi, but there is a difference between them. Coke is Mom and apple pie. Pepsi is the 15-year-old baby sitter and her boyfriend with the Camaro. . . . If you are skeptical of the ability of pure image advertising to persuade, may I suggest you look at Nike?"

The columnist was describing that ability as an advantage, which indeed it is to the seller who finds no other way to differentiate positively and meaningfully. However, he used the phrase "deflect attention from what brands are" apparently with no thought that society might be better off knowing exactly what brands are. To begin, they are each simply a version of a product made by one maker rather than another. Often that is all they are.

A seller, of course, cannot promote its brand as being just the product. The need to say more is urgent, so urgent that advertisers seem compelled to make what I think of as the Best Claim Assumption. Advertisers wish to promote their brands as being more than a product and maximally different from other brands. In doing so they seem to assume that they have the right to make the best claim they can lawfully make to entice the public to acquire that perception, using whatever distortion of objective truth and significance it takes.

The Best Claim Assumption has several steps. It begins with the fact that the seller has the right to sell, which is true and uncontroversial when a product is lawful. The next step is that the seller has the right to promote its own manufacture as being its particular brand rather than being just the product. That's no problem, either, since the process starts with simple identification: seller X is not selling just soap, it is selling X's soap.

The steps continue, however, with the assumption that the seller has a right to sell the brand as being more than merely its own separately identified version of the product. It has a right to sell the brand by maximally differentiating it positively and meaningfully from the product and from other brands. That is, it has a right to create brand significance.

Now we are moving into slippery territory, because of a possible gap between the selling claims and the factual realities. It is one thing to promote a brand as representing simply one's own manufacture of a product, because the claim is nothing more than that a company now makes what other companies have been making. The claim is virtually self-verified. It is quite another thing, however, to promote a brand as meaningfully and positively different from the product category, and from other brands. The first thing you must have to promote a brand difference is not the promotion—it's the difference. You can't promote what you don't have, or at least that's what many ordinary folks would assume.

The Best Claim Assumption, though, tends to ignore that problem by interpreting the right to differentiate one's brand as conferring the right to do so in whatever lawful way that the public can be given the message. It is a right that applies whether or not an objective difference really exists. In other words, you *don't* have to have a difference to promote a difference, not objectively. You needn't let the lack of a difference impede you from making the best lawful claim that will create the perception of a brand significance that isn't really there.

The pressure that advertising people feel to apply the Best Claim Assumption originates with the frustrations of those who hire them. Much advertising work results from the thwarting of the ordinary expectation that the task of making a brand different should be carried out by a company's production department. When the production people fail, surely often because the task is unreasonable in the first place, the company leaders reinterpret the problem as a matter of promotion.

An author some years ago gave the title "In the Courts of Power" to an article on advertising. The point was that ad people are only courtiers, never king. The stand near the seat of power, and use that power by delegation, but they don't have very much of their own. When their "king" tells them it's their responsibility to find the brand difference, they are likely to assume they had better get busy and do it, or else. From there it's only a small step to assuming they had better do it to the maximum degree; they should use the Best Claim.

So they do, despite it being a very distorting step. The result leads to an interesting comparison between brand advertising and other forms of human communication. Most ordinary communication reflects the natural expectation that we speak when we have something to say. If we have nothing to say, we don't open our mouths. What could be more sensible!

Nonetheless, for brand advertisers it goes differently. Brand advertisers have nothing to say, and therefore they speak louder and longer than if they did. The less there is to say, the more they advertise. They make up for having nothing to say by creating something to say within the speech itself. They don't merely promote the difference; they make it first and then promote it. No wonder claims can so poorly reflect their brands. The resulting distortions stem directly from the advertisers' need to avoid competition, to monopolize.

Consumers, of course, should reject that process as nonresponsive to their own needs. The public should attribute little value to brand differentiating that serves only the sellers' interests. The advertisers themselves should recognize that the slippery slope claims do them more harm than good. The next chapter suggests that they could accept that proposition and yet not give up the competition that they feel is necessary to their survival.

## 38

# DO ADVERTISERS NEED THE SLIPPERY SLOPE CLAIMS?

I can imagine receiving much objection to the tack I've been taking here. From experiences I've had with advertising people, including those responding to my previous book, I know that the favorite industry complaint has been forming on their lips for many chapters now. It goes like this: You want to get rid of the marketplace, Preston. Or maybe it goes: You want to get rid of the whole capitalist economic system.

You want to stop us from engaging in private enterprise, stop us from being able to sell our individual brands. You want to make us sell our brands as being nothing but the product, so that it looks as though there aren't any brands. You want to stop us from advertising at all, and reduce the market to one producer of each product. The American business enterprise will have to shrivel up and disappear before you feel satisfied!

Baloney! Some have taken such extreme positions in the past, prompting businesspeople to feel they must respond with their own extreme positions. Ralph Nader once gained such a reaction when he testified before a congressional committee about corporate practices. He listed one complaint after another until an exasperated member asked if he had anything good at all to say about business. He paused awhile and finally said he couldn't think of anything.

As much as I've admired most of what Nader has done, I think he hurt himself with that. He damaged his standing with an American public that the marketplace system has served well, even if serving itself well, too. The days of saying it's all bad have come and gone, and should not be missed. That doesn't mean it's all good, though. I've been describing the dark side of the nature of a competitive marketplace, based on how sellers manipulate it.

Let's emphasize the distinction, though, that while the troubles we are seeing in this book are a result of our competitive system, they are not a result of competition. Instead, they are a result of sellers' attempting to avoid the natural consequences of competing. Rather than implying any criticism of competition, my comments on their behavior really point toward the misfortune that can befall a system that loses sight of its intended ideal.

The goal, then, should be to see whether we can get rid of that bad aspect while keeping the good. What I'm asking here is simply this: Do you advertisers need to use the slippery slope claims to make the marketplace work, to sell your brands? I say that you don't. My point for the moment is not whether you should have the right to sell something as being more than what it is, as being different when it is not different. The point, rather, is that you do not *need* to do that. You do not need to engage in any such deceptiveness, whether recognized or unrecognized by the law, or in any diminishment of truth, to do brand selling.

You can do it without those things. You will still be able to avoid competition by creating monopoly aspects of your brand. It will be harder, of course, but it should be enough to create sales for any brand that has legitimate market value. It should certainly be enough to keep the system of selling brands alive and capable of making a profit for you as well as making a contribution to the rest of society.

In Finland recently a court prohibited a commercial showing a boy who was sad about moving to a new home until he saw a McDonald's there. The court said the ad "falsely leads people to believe that a Big Mac can replace friends and ease loneliness." The point I have to make about that claim is not that any suggestions I'm making here would outlaw it, because they might well not. The point, rather, is that the ruling does not in any way prevent McDonald's from selling the Finns what it really has to sell. An American advertiser's first thought no doubt will be that the Finnish court took away much content that is commonplace in the United States. That may be so, yet the court didn't take away anything that McDonald's really knows to be true about itself.

Without the slippery slope claims you advertisers will still be able to monopolize by promoting objectively real brand differences. If your brand lasts longer or tastes better to a majority of consumers than its competition, you will be able to say so. If your brand is objectively different in any way from other brands, you will be able to say so. Indeed, if a difference in your brand is subjectively rather than objectively perceived, but you can show factually that it gives a net perceived benefit to consumers, you will be able to say so.

If your brand has such differences, you should prefer to compete in a market that has no slippery slope claims. It would help consumers to know better how to identify the real thing. The brand with the real facts will be more likely to jump to the forefront of their minds and gain recognition and credit. The cream will rise to the top eventually, and if a better informed public will make that happen sooner, so much the better.

Of course, if my proposal would make it impossible for you to display any brand differences, it would disadvantage you. The question then would be whether you have any basis to complain. I feel that if you really believe in competition as the American way, you can't legitimately complain over being forced back into practicing it rather than being allowed to continue avoiding it.

Nor do I have much sympathy for the suggestion that my proposal is excessively harsh simply because advertising wouldn't look the same anymore. My students show this concern. Despite their young age they have come to appreciate advertising as it is, and it deprives them of a critical attitude. When I suggest in class that it might be helpful to stop using such things as puffery, there's always someone who remarks that advertising wouldn't be advertising anymore if it lacked all those things. People have a right to advertise, they say, and, they assume, the job simply can't be done without all the familiar methods.

I realize I must reject that point thoughtfully and carefully, because the suggestion is true in terms of the superficial look of ads. Without question the messages would be different if we removed many of their flamboyant features. They would be uncharacteristically subdued and even just plain dull in many cases. They would be less attractive, fun, and entertaining.

Students, and other consumers, too, often feel that removing such entertainment value of advertising would be unfair to the public. Certainly the messages are often entertaining, and that in itself is a contribution to society. Tell me this, though: would such a change mean that entertainment would cease being available to the American public? Good grief, we are up to our ears in it! With flocks of cable channels and magazine racks and video rental stores, I miss far more of the available content than I ever get around to seeing. Much of it could disappear overnight and I wouldn't even notice. If the ads disappeared, I would miss the information but I doubt I would miss anything else. Neither would the advertisers, really, because they don't entertain to entertain. They entertain to sell; they would miss the selling.

So I think the complaint overstates the potential loss. Removal of the excitement in ads would occur only where the ability truthfully to differentiate brands depended solely on claims from the slippery slope.

That will happen only for advertisers who look at their brand, *really* look at it, and find nothing truthful and brand significant to say about it. The proper rejoinder to advertisers who claim they would be in that situation is to tell them they haven't tried hard enough. That's a point made not by me but by various observers writing on the advertising business who have said there is *always* something to say about a brand. Those who can't find it probably should not be playing the game.

If they try but can't find real differences, or don't even try, maybe the capitalist competitive system has sent them a message that they don't belong. Doesn't a classic expression say that if you can't stand the heat you must get out of the kitchen? I can't recall its saying you have a right to have the heat turned down so you can stay.

I won't elaborate here on what ads might say about a brand, since many books and articles cover that so well. Briefly, it's a matter of taking a hard look at what you're selling, including related aspects like the manufacturing process, packaging, name, price, availability, and follow-up service such as repair facilities. More often than not there's something in that total context that your competitors don't have.

Moreover, inability to differentiate your brand doesn't necessarily mean you can't sell it. You could, for example, promote features of the product category that contrast it to other product categories. For example, Coca-Cola and Pepsi-Cola, even if unable to find differences that will leapfrog either of them out of the other's shadow, might nevertheless direct their efforts against other drinks to which cola users might be tempted to switch. The colas could compete against other soft drinks, bottled water, coffee, tea, and so on.

In short, to lack claims that are both true and objectively brand significant is not to come to the end of the road. The slippery slope claims make it easier to differentiate and sell a brand, no doubt about it. Still, advertising can differentiate brands without them, and can do brand selling even without successful differentiation. The result is that advertisers do not need the slippery slope claims. Knowing what to say would be harder without them, but not too hard. The loss would create no competitive disadvantage, at least no legitimate disadvantage, if the entire market dropped such claims. The playing field would stay level.

That won't stop advertisers from complaining about being unfairly impeded without the slope claims. None of them could put it better than my own student, Nick Davis. In response to my challenges about these issues, he wrote in a paper, "I am a strong opponent of advertising regulation. I feel it limits the consumer's right to information and denies the advertiser the right to educate the public sufficiently about the benefits of the product."

Nick probably felt he was disagreeing with me on that. In the case of legitimately informative claims, though, I feel he is quite right. I have no interest in blocking such claims. It's just that the slippery slope claims I've been emphasizing are not valuable as information. Many such claims offer weak or fake product benefits, and so educating the public about them is of no great value.

Advertisers who insist on their right to make such claims are thinking only of the disadvantage they imagine they would suffer without them. The disadvantage to consumers of continuing them, however, should also be part of a legitimate assessment. Selling is a desperate business. But nobody should forget that buying is, too.

**39**

# THE R. J. REYNOLDS CIGARETTE CASE

Remember riddles like, What time is it when the elephant sits on the fence? Here's another one: When is a cigarette company's ad not a cigarette ad?

Wouldn't it be nice if the answer were simple! We could just say, well, if the ad's not trying to sell cigarettes, if it's talking about something else, then it's not a cigarette ad. But you don't really think after 38 chapters that things will start getting easy, do you? There is always some messy detail. Here it's the possibility that the cigarette advertisement could be talking about something else and yet be selling cigarettes at the same time.

The advertiser could be describing, say, an art show it was sponsoring, or aid it was giving to a poverty-stricken or hurricane-damaged area. Things like that have nothing to do with cigarettes directly. Could they, though, enhance the image of the company and thereby help its sales? Some people will say that's too far-fetched to happen. Others will say it might happen, but only trivially. Some may say it will happen to a significant extent. All, however, will agree that the ad says nothing explicitly about cigarettes.

Let's see why it matters. It matters because the law bans deceptiveness from commercial but not from noncommercial speech (chap. 35). Suppose a cigarette company advertises falsely that it's giving money to a charitable cause. By speaking noncommercially, it may be as deceptive as it pleases without fear of a violation. The falsity may violate something else, but not the deceptiveness rule. We all have that First Amendment privilege in our noncommercial speech.

R. J. Reynolds tried to use the privilege in dealing with the FTC. A branch of RJR Nabisco, it's the second-largest cigarette maker, selling Winston, Salem, Camel, Vantage, More, Now, and other brands. In recent years the sales of these and all other cigarettes have been damaged by health concerns, against which their makers have fought back by denying the existence of evidence relating smoking to disease.

Reynolds contributed to that cause with a paid advertising comment, an "editorial ad," about a U.S. government research study called the Multiple Risk Factor Intervention Trial, MR FIT for short. The study examined 12,000 men who were high on three risk factors associated with heart disease: smoking, high blood pressure, and high cholesterol. The researchers arranged for medical treatment to lower those factors for half the men, but not for the other half. The finding, the ad said, was that the two groups did not have a significantly different number of heart disease deaths after ten years.

The ad described the study and then said, "We at R. J. Reynolds do not claim this study proves that smoking doesn't cause heart disease. But we do wish to make a point." The point was that although many scientists were continuing to believe that smoking causes disease, they should identify their beliefs as opinions rather than scientific facts. The question of the relationship's existence, Reynolds said, "remains an open one."

An FTC complaint charged that ad with falsely claiming to consumers that MR FIT "provides credible scientific evidence that smoking is not as hazardous as the public or the reader has been led to believe." Further, it charged the ad to claim falsely that MR FIT "tends to refute the theory that smoking causes coronary heart disease." The commission was considering writing an order to stop the claims.

Reynolds's first line of defense was not to deny the charges directly but to argue that the ad was immune from prosecution for deceptiveness. The company asked for dismissal because the ad was noncommercial and so not within the FTC's jurisdiction. Possibly the claims might be subject to some other charge, if false, such as libeling the government's researchers. That, however, would be irrelevant regarding an FTC complaint, because the commission has no enforcement powers over such other things.

Let's think about Reynold's defense. Its ad talked about the relationship of smoking to disease, a relationship that would tend to reduce cigarette sales for consumers who believed it to exist. The ad, however, was alleged by the FTC to claim that the relationship does not exist, which would, for consumers believing that, tend to maintain sales. If the relationship of smoking to disease, whatever it may be, affects sales, doesn't that make the ad commercial speech? How could anyone conceivably argue that the MR FIT ad would be equally as irrelevant to Reynolds's sales goals as an announcement about an art sponsorship that stated or implied absolutely nothing about cigarettes?

Someone did argue that. It was the FTC's administrative law judge, whose job was to conduct hearings and to write an initial decision that the FTC's five commissioners would consider when writing the final decision. The judge didn't give them an initial decision this time, though; in fact, he didn't even give the two sides a hearing. He decided instead to grant Reynolds's petition for dismissal on the ground that the ad was noncommercial.

The judge had reasons, as he must. They were not bad reasons, of themselves. He made the obvious points that the Mr. FIT ad did not name brands, discuss desirable attributes, or list prices or places for purchase. It contained no "express promotional language." The ad was "an editorial in format," meaning its use of columns of type, with no pictorial content, made it look more like an article than an advertisement. He felt it would be "easily understood by any reasonable reader as an op-ed type piece, not a cigarette ad."

For a while after his decision the cigarette promoters and other advertisers were dancing their "First Amendment boogie" in the streets. Their elation, though, lasted only until the commissioners ruled on the appropriateness of the judge's dismissal. The commissioners may agree or disagree, and in this case they disagreed. They sent the case back to the judge and ordered him to conduct a hearing and make an initial decision. He was to base his decision on the facts the hearing would bring out about whether the ad was commercial, and if commercial, whether it was deceptive.

The commissioners did not disagree with the judge over the superficial aspects of appearance that made the message look different from most commercial ads. Nonetheless, they found other aspects that they thought were characteristic of commercial speech. For example, the ad referred to a specific product and to a socially important attribute of that product. The message was paid-for advertising, typical of commercial speech. Most important, Reynolds's role as a seller of cigarettes made it reasonable to infer that it had a "direct, sales-related motive" for running the ad.

The commissioners did not decide that the speech was commercial. They decided only that they could not make that decision without a hearing. The hearing could produce evidence, they said, on such questions as Reynolds's purpose in running the ad, and what messages it intended to convey. Given Reynolds's assertion that it wanted only to affect public opinion, the hearing could determine whether the ad was likely to do nothing but that, rather than to affect buying demand.

The hearing never took place. Reynolds was apparently unwilling to open to public scrutiny the various documents needed to answer the indicated questions. Rather than defend itself, it chose to enter a voluntary agreement. In that consent order, the company agreed to be prohibited from claiming the MR FIT study was suitable for determining whether smoking causes heart disease. Also, it was prohibited from claiming that the study amounted to scientific evidence that smoking is less hazardous than the public previously believed, or that the study tended to refute the theory that smoking causes heart disease.

Reynolds also agreed that in any future mention of MR FIT it would make one of two disclosures: it would either acknowledge that men in the study who quit smoking had a significantly lower rate of heart disease death than men who kept smoking, or it would state that the study's results were consistent with previous studies showing that those who quit smoking enjoy a substantial decrease in heart disease death.

The agreement included Reynolds's continuing denial that the ad was commercial speech, although it waived the further right to argue the point. Should we believe the Reynolds people involved in preparing the ad had a conscious commercial purpose in running it? Of course we should.

# 40

# THE PROBLEM OF B_____

Let's look at still another problem the advertisers could avoid by sacrificing some of their freedom of speech. They value freedom for the way it helps them get away legally with falsity or diminishment of truth. However, they need to face the fact that they really don't get away with it other than legally. They pay a price for it that hurts.

The price is a name people call their ad claims. It's a sensitive term, and I have spent some time wondering how to handle it. It starts with B and ends with T and has two L's in the middle. It's a vulgarism that many people disapprove of. On the other hand it's quite commonplace now, and I have a serious reason for discussing it. So I'm going to do that, with apologies to those who feel I should not.

We could call this thing baloney. But why not just call it what it is— bullshit! I want to discuss it because I feel it is a socially important response to the falsity and diminished truth discussed in this book. It has an impact that makes a difference to sellers and consumers, which means to everyone. And there's so much of it in the world that it ought to rank in the list of chemical elements right up there with hydrogen and oxygen.

From examining my dictionary, I feel there has been too little appreciation of the way the public uses this popular term. While the reluctance is understandable, it is also unfortunate that the definition given is merely "nonsense, lies or exaggeration." That is much too little to say about such a fascinating and complex substance. It's a start, but once a thing's started it ought to be given a serious effort. I'll try to fill in the blanks, at least in regard to how the term is used in response to advertising. Readers may ponder for themselves the usage in other areas of modern conversation.

The dictionary definition's main problem is that it describes only the message, while saying nothing about how people respond to it. This difference between a "message definition" and a "response definition" is commonplace in examining communication terminology. We saw earlier how it works with the word *deceptiveness*. An ad is deceptive not simply for what it is, but also for the responses it causes in consumers' heads. Another example is that the law defines *puffery* in message terms as statements of evaluation or opinion, but also in response terms as statements that consumers understand they should neither believe nor rely on.

Similarly, the real meaning of bullshit is not just that it is untrue content. More importantly, it produces certain conclusions in consumers' minds about itself and especially about those who speak it. To say consumers see it as false is merely the first step. The next step involves what consumers see and think about the advertisers who transmit it.

The context is that consumers wish to make buying decisions. An advertiser sends a message suggesting that they buy something. They perceive the advertiser to be an expert, capable of giving them the information they need to decide about that item. On assessing the claim, however, they see that the advertiser hasn't delivered what they need. The ad gives them slippery slope claims, which many consumers will perceive as unusable for their purpose.

Some consumers will perceive the content to be usable, and the content will deceive them, as we've earlier discussed. They will think of the advertiser, mistakenly, as a teller of truth. They will have feelings of trust, and act in a trusting way. Relying on the ad content, they will make faulty purchasing decisions.

At present, though, we are considering the reactions of consumers who perceive the content to be unusable. Such consumers perceive the ad's content as false or as diminished truth. They therefore see the information as inadequate for obtaining the level of truth and significance they need. They see the advertiser as trying to produce belief of a claim while knowing of no basis for believing it, and thus having no faith that it is true. They see the advertiser as speaking insincerely in trying to get the public to rely on the claim when its own people would not do so.

The consumers also see that no other source of the needed information is available. Despite their feelings of distrust, they conclude they will have to act in a trusting way toward the advertiser in order to participate in the marketplace. They see no choice but to make their purchasing decision on such an unsatisfactory basis.

The consumers further interpret the advertiser as having known how to provide useful amounts of truth and significance, but to have knowingly chosen not to do so. They perceive the advertiser as being aware that it is leaving them in the lurch when it could have helped them, and as assuming it can get away with doing so without punishment. They perceive the advertiser to be correct about the latter, because they know of no way they can get it to stop.

When consumers have perceptions like that, what do you think they'll call the message? I think they'll call it bullshit. Remember, we are not discussing law here. We are not dealing with the protections of the courts, under which a statement can be called false only when it's laboriously proved to be so. The advertisers would like to keep the action on that legal plane, but they can't. We're talking perceptions. If consumers have them, then they do, and the advertisers' lawyers can't make them go away.

That's ironic for advertisers, because it means that those who live by the subjective perception also die by it. Advertisers achieve much brand significance because consumers are prone to accept subjective claims. But here they achieve considerable negative public relations by the same process. The First Amendment may protect the advertisers' right to speech that is not deceptive, but it does not protect the advertisers from having to endure consumers' assessment of that speech.

Not all kinds of false claims will be called bullshit. Authors of fiction will not be, despite their knowledge that what they write isn't true. Their fundamental falsity is well known and understood; there's no attempt to hide it. No reader of fiction perceives that the author is attempting to get anyone to accept the story literally. No application of the Advertising Expectations Implication, which may lead consumers to interpret ad messages as being insincerely claimed to be true, is made to fiction.

Let's look at some other kinds of falsity. Suppose somebody commits a shooting or burglary that dozens of onlookers observe, then denies it in court. Or, in the marketplace, suppose somebody makes an utterly false explicit claim from the bottom of the slippery slope, such as offering to sell land for building a home while knowing the land is underwater. Such persons aren't bullshitters, either. Well, some observers might use the term, but you can call those persons something much worse. You can call them plain old outright liars. You don't see them as believing they have a right to lie. Moreover, you can think of a way to stop them; you can prove their falsity.

Bullshit is something else. Its essence is that while you know it's false and you're sure the speaker knows it's false, you can find no way to stop it. It puts consumers in a miserable situation because they need to trust, yet the only party available for trusting is someone they feel doesn't deserve it. They go along because they have to, but they find it offensive to need to rely on someone that's untrustworthy. They do it, and then get their revenge by calling the advertisers that name. It's the only defense they have, the only way to fight back.

To call advertisers bullshitters is to perceive them as being liars, not merely about what they're claiming but about their own belief in what they're claiming. It's the perception by consumers, whether or not the law agrees, that the advertisers have no basis for their own belief in what they are claiming. The claim might even turn out eventually to be true, but the advertisers don't know that at the time. Consumers thus see them as insincere, willing to take a chance that what they're saying may be false.

Again, it's a matter of how consumers feel, of what they perceive to be the case. Whether their feeling can be formally proved in a court of law doesn't matter. The result is that just because bullshit escapes legal controls doesn't mean consumers can't prosecute. We can prosecute the advertisers in the court of public opinion. Any consumer can call a claim that name, and if enough other consumers call it that too, then as far as society is concerned, that's what it is.

When that's what it is, there's a serious loss of credibility for the advertisers. There's an old saying that names will never hurt you, but I think this is a name that does hurt. Polls show that people can earn low esteem for their actions. For example, the DDB Needham agency's annual Life Style Study of 1991 showed only 64 percent of consumers agreed with the statement, "Most people are honest."

Whether that's low per se, it was the lowest figure on that question since the survey began in 1975. The high was 76 percent in 1976. If the study had tested the statement "Most advertising is honest," it would surely have gotten a lower figure. It did use "Most big companies are just out for themselves," to which 79 percent agreed, up from 65 percent in the 1970s.

Other surveys over the years, by Gallup and other firms, have shown more direct disparagement of advertising. In a survey ranking ten types of citizens for credibility, advertising executives finished ninth, beating out only used car salesmen. They were less credible than, from first to eighth, clergy, doctors, police, TV news anchors, public school teachers, TV reporters, newspaper editors, and newspaper reporters. For those advertising people who provide information that is objectively important, as it often is when it stays off the slippery slope, it must be disappointing to rank last among categories that include several types of mass media personnel.

In another survey, only 17 percent saw advertising in 1990 as a source of information to help them decide what to buy. A similar statement in 1964 had gained agreement from 37 percent. Only 62 percent of the public found advertising to be at least fairly believable in 1990, down from 72 percent in 1987; 35 percent found it fairly or very unbelievable, up from 26 percent. Of advertising in the past four or five years 44 percent found it more deceptive; 43 percent said the same and only 13 percent said less.

Analyses by economists frequently deplore the costs that regulation imposes on business, the costs of restricting sellers from saying and doing whatever they please. Somehow the economists never seem to recognize how the ad business creates such costs itself, by using its freedom to reduce its public credibility. The economists have the professional ability to assess advertising effects such as the prices we pay, and the level of competition we get. But they don't know how to assess the impact of the revulsion we feel.

Probably they think that if we are objectively getting good prices, whether we realize it or not, we should just forget our other feelings. Presumably we should all just respond by being self-reliant. We should wade through the smell, holding our noses, dealing with people we wish we didn't have to deal with. Maybe someday the experts will care to search for a way to figure the costs of damaging the quality of life in that way.

One economist has complained that government does not properly appreciate advertising's contributions to society. He worried that the Clinton administration in its early days was gearing up to restrict the industry and thus hamper its ability to perform. It was one of many such articles I've seen over the years by advertising's supporters, most of whom fail to realize that this industry is its own worst enemy.

Don't they know that one of the best ways to influence the government is to create favorable public opinion! A public that likes advertising will display much more recognition and appreciation of its good points than a public that dislikes it. And when the public likes it, the government will, too. What the economists see as positive will no longer be obscured in government circles by what the public sees as negative.

As things stand, we consumers seem limited to two choices. We can believe the slippery slope claims and be deceived by them, or we can disbelieve them and think of the advertisers as lacking credibility. We can hate the advertisers because we have to trust them even though we feel distrustful. Why would an industry with such highly intelligent leaders want to endure that set of possibilities? Isn't there another alternative?

Just think, you advertisers. People may be seeing your slippery slope claims right now, and calling you bullshitters.

# 41

# A MORE REALISTIC ORIENTATION TO THE FIRST AMENDMENT

We saw in the previous section that advertisers think the First Amendment might extend their freedoms. What bothers me about such a hope is not simply that the evidence suggests it won't happen but that such dreaming interferes with our chances of getting advertisers to assess realistically the prospects of having more freedom.

Even more to the point, I am interested in the chances of getting advertisers to consider the advantages of having less freedom. Yes, I said *less*. The freedom they have is immense when one thinks of all societies of the world in all eras, past and present, yet all they can think of is wanting more. They might consider instead that their responsibilities regarding the types of claims this book is discussing might reasonably suggest the value of less freedom.

I am speaking of advantages to the advertisers from their own selfish viewpoint, as well as that of society's. I believe they would benefit their own causes by thinking more in terms of added constraints. Freedom of speech has prompted them to *hurt* themselves, and they could gain higher credibility by accepting less of it. They might opt instead for more regulation, and they might consider paying some real attention to ethics as well.

Let's look at some of the ways in which freedom of speech has encouraged advertisers to disadvantage themselves and society. It has meant, for example, that advertisers whose brands don't differ objectively from competing brands may make claims that their brands do differ. They exercise their First Amendment rights to create whatever claim it takes to turn false perceptions of differences into sales.

Freedom of speech has meant that advertisers may run ads mentioning only features on which they are superior. They may do so while omitting mention of features that make their brand inferior on an overall basis. By exercising their rights under the First Amendment, they prompt consumers to act on the basis of perceptions of superiority that are false.

Freedom of speech has meant that advertisers may make all kinds of social and psychological implied promises without having to stand behind them as promises. By exercising their rights under the First Amendment they give the public claims that the skeptical will reject as useless and the gullible will accept as true. Such claims thereby do a disservice to all.

Freedom of speech has meant that an advertiser may call a drink PowerMaster, thereby inviting the urban poor to buy a brand with a very high alcohol content. Such a product will if anything damage legitimate efforts to attain social or economic power. It certainly damaged the reputation of PowerMaster's maker, Heileman Brewing, and of the beer industry as a whole.

Freedom of speech has meant that advertisers may direct cigarette messages to children, as with Joe Camel. By exercising their rights under the First Amendment, they addict millions and doom them to disease and death.

Freedom of speech has meant that advertisers may state opinions for which they have absolutely no basis. They may state opinions they do not sincerely believe, or even sincerely disbelieve. They exercise their First Amendment right to convey claims that the law says consumers must know not to believe or rely upon. The advertisers would not convey them, of course, if they really thought consumers would respond to them that way.

Freedom of speech has meant that advertisers whose products would be a solution if there were only a problem, are free to invent the problem. When Mr. Lambert who invented Listerine also created the term "halitosis," many ad people admired his achievement. They wished they could have exercised their own First Amendment rights so successfully.

Freedom of speech has meant that advertisers may use facts that, although true, have little or no significance. They present them to the public as though they have infinite meaningfulness. I still remember where I was and what I was doing on the day Kennedy was shot, and also on the day when I learned that Oxydol has green crystals. Those were both a long time ago, but some things you just do not forget!

The world is awash in all kinds of questionable claims that freedom of speech makes possible. Any speech that's possible becomes reality in this field, despite that familiar declaration that with freedom should come responsibility. Maybe before the advertisers ask for more freedom, they could work to eliminate the harms done by the freedom they have. They could accept the responsibilities that ought reasonably to accompany their privileges.

Deceptiveness is lawful in journalism and other noncommercial public speech. Yet most people see advertising as more likely to be deceptive than journalism, and so give it lower credibility. Advertising has a higher standard, legally, yet the public perceives it as having a lower standard, probably because the public sees a greater discrepancy between advertising's rights and its responsibilities. Although advertising has fewer rights than journalism, people are likely to feel that the level of responsibility it shows in exercising those rights is even lower.

Something else the journalists have that advertisers don't have is a willingness to criticize within the field. Journalists regularly experience public bestowals upon themselves of "orchids and onions" or "laurels and darts," recognizing good or bad performance. Certainly those who get onioned or darted don't enjoy the attention. They know, though, that they can't escape because such attention goes with the territory.

Advertising people can escape, because they bestow upon one another mostly laurels and orchids. Few darts, few onions! Journalists, accustomed to criticizing public figures, take naturally to criticizing themselves as well. In advertising there is a deep distaste for doing that. While the journalists display loyalty to the profession and its standards by criticizing each other, the advertisers show their loyalty by criticizing very little apart from their ritual critiques of creativity.

Ad people probably feel that disapproval of specific problems strikes too closely to disapproval of the entire field. Criticism strengthens journalism, but it weakens advertising. Perhaps deep down they recognize that much criticism is justifiable, and that airing it in public would be too self-destructive.

Of course outsiders criticize the industry. Advertisers typically respond by referring to such persons as "self-appointed critics." I'll probably get that label before long. It's an attempted putdown that means something like, "Nobody asked you to speak up, so why don't you mind your own business!" What the industry doesn't realize about such activity is that advertising is everybody's business. Further, the way to avoid having self-appointed critics is to appoint some yourself. If a certain kind of commentary is going to happen and affect you, then be a leader in it.

While writing this chapter I read that the Association of National Advertisers held a panel discussion at its annual meeting on the topic of ethics, specifically, whether advertisers need to consider the ethics of such matters as targeting to low-income or less educated consumers. The amazing thing to me about that session is that the industry had not said yes to that question long ago.

The perceived vulnerability to criticism probably stems from the low level of responsibility advertisers show toward their First Amendment freedoms, largely because the claims on the slippery slope are legal under those freedoms. To advertisers, as I have pointed out, freedom of speech means the freedom to function on the slope.

Freedom is wonderful, yet the resulting falsity and diminishment of truth cry out for responsible legal or ethical treatment. Advertisers will have to continue feeling bad about criticism if they continue to let themselves be so vulnerable to it. Wouldn't you think they would want to consider that giving up the freedom of the slope might be one of the most daring and creative, and successful, steps of capitalist self-interest they have ever undertaken!

## 42

# LOOKING BACK AT THE CASES

In various chapters I have examined specific advertising cases, beginning with Sears in chapter 3. I want to sum up those cases here as showing advertising deceptiveness at its worst and the law at its best. There are more where those came from. For example, Warner-Lambert's decades of deceptive claims that Listerine would prevent or reduce the impact of colds and sore throats would have made a juicy chapter. The claim was so false (although highly brand significant, because no other mouthwashes used it) that the FTC made the company tell the public in further advertising that the product would not do those things.

Litton Industries claimed a survey to show that 76 percent of all technicians who service microwave ovens would recommend its brand over others to a friend. However, only technicians doing authorized service for Litton were surveyed. It was an obvious biasing factor, because if other technicians had been included the percentage would have been much lower.

Among recent "green" claims, the FTC and several states charged Mobil with falsely representing that its Hefty bags were biodegradable. True, they decompose if exposed to the elements, particularly sunlight, for a while and then will continue to decompose when buried in landfills. But if the bags go quickly into landfills, which is what usually happens, the process will never start at all.

General Electric advertised that its new incandescent light bulbs would eliminate pollution, save energy, and reduce costs because it designed them to replace ordinary bulbs of higher wattage. For example, a new 90-watt bulb would replace an old 100-watt model. The FTC and 32 states, however, said the claim implied falsely that we'd get the same light at greater efficiency. The truth was that our savings would come only from getting less light.

I'll stop the examples here, although those wishing to see many others may consult an article of mine in the references for this chapter. You may also read the trade press, such as *Advertising Age* or *The Wall Street Journal*, or even keep a close eye on your daily newspaper. More such examples will probably continue to appear in the future; however, if this book has any impact the number will eventually decline.

In summary, these various stories demonstrate that advertising frequently performs very poor public service. Furthermore, in my opinion the falsity discussed in those stories has typically been deliberate and knowing. Some FTC findings support me in saying so, as in the Sears and Thompson Medical decisions (chap. 3, 6), among others. In other cases evidence became public when seen accidentally, after the advertisers failed to keep it secret, as in the Volvo case (chap. 8).

Important to the assessment of advertiser credibility is that many of these cases demonstrate two levels of falsity. First, the advertisers make false claims, and second, they go into court and tell additional falsities in defending their false claims as true. By the latter I mean such things as Sears's tests using hotter water and longer wash cycles than consumers can get, and Kroger's and Lorillard's manipulations of surveys.

I believe the second level of falsity is typically just as deliberate and knowing and insincere as the first level. Those who present the phony tests and surveys are people who ought to know of their invalidity. It is

ingenuous to suppose that the expert researchers and attorneys involved are innocent parties who simply do not understand what they
are doing.

Consumers are unlikely to be aware of the second half of this two-
tiered system of deceptiveness. News announcements in the general
press tell of orders issued against advertisers, but they give little detail.
They tell of the first level of deceptiveness, but not of the second. Even
the trade press shows little inclination to publicize the latter. Consumers ought to learn about them, though, because they bear directly on
advertisers' trustworthiness.

The second level of falsity occurs in cases that go to court hearings,
where witnesses testify and introduce evidence. It is lawyers who conduct these activities, when presenting an advertiser's defense. The lawyers do what they do in large part because their profession orients itself
toward advocacy. That means winning. It is their job to get their advertiser client off the hook. To do that, they hire expert witnesses and
researchers to prepare testimony or conduct surveys or tests. It is now
the job of those researchers to win, too. According to their professional
obligations, researchers are supposed to orient themselves toward finding the truth, not toward winning. The attorneys won't use such people, though, unless their testimony and findings are compatible with
the attorney's needs.

When attorneys and researchers look to see what it will take to win,
they do wondrous things to the facts. They may observe, for example,
that the FTC intends to use a survey done by the advertiser as evidence
of what claims an ad conveys. They thereupon decide to criticize the
survey in court for improper methodology that renders it invalid for
finding facts. They hope the court will refuse to accept the survey as
evidence.

In doing this, the attorneys and researchers hope the court will not
notice that, until the present case came up, the advertiser routinely
used that survey method to determine conveyed claims and help decide ad content. It assumed the method to be valid. Now, however,
when a court may use those results against it, the advertiser suddenly
finds the method to be utterly inadequate for telling anybody anything
about its advertising.

Another accommodating attorney-researcher pair did an original
survey. The results revealed that the answer to a certain question was
damaging to their advertiser client's position. They thereupon ran a
second survey that was the same except for omitting that question. In
court, the researcher testified under the lawyer's guidance that the sec-

ond survey was more valid. Unfortunately for them, but fortunately for the truth, the court found the opposite.

Many such stunts have been tried; I have reported more than a hundred types of them. The FTC or federal courts typically catch and reject them, as they did the examples just given. The point, therefore, is not that the tricks always work. The point, rather, is that the tricks say terrible things about the credibility of advertisers, attorneys, and researchers. One would think such parties would want to avoid the criticism that is likely to come from publicizing these stories.

There seems little point in proposing that the lawyers be punished by the FTC or federal courts for such duplicity. The law includes penalties for frivolousness or perjury, but simply does not apply them in advertising cases. I am at a loss to know why not, except to observe that these cases involve civil rather than criminal law. In civil law the courts seem to be less sensitive about such problems. From the viewpoint of consumers and advertisers, though, these matters seem to be highly sensitive.

A sensible solution would be for advertisers to exercise their right to oversee the actions of the attorneys representing them. The usual procedure is to turn a case over to the lawyers and leave it up to them, which of course companies do because of the expertise involved. Still, anyone who hires lawyers and pays for their services has a right to direct their actions. The advertisers should retain control, especially in areas that go beyond sheer legal considerations.

The particular nonlegal consideration I have in mind would be the advertisers' knowledge of the damage that can happen. The advertisers must know that while they may not pay a price in court for their falsity and insincerity, they are subject to paying it in the court of public opinion. That should be enough to persuade them to adapt the old saying about war and generals to read that "advertising prosecutions are too important to be left to the lawyers."

Another part of the solution could be for industry organizations to help their members with cases. Usually the individual advertiser arranges for legal counsel entirely on its own. That custom eliminates any chance to benefit from the collective wisdom of experienced industry leadership that has much advice to give on how to pursue, and whether to pursue, a case in court. Advertising's national organizations do many things for the industry, such as lobbying against taxes or other restrictive laws. There's no reason why they couldn't help members with cases, too. They could readily give advice that would help eliminate both of the two tiers of deceptiveness.

To summarize, the cases I have described show advertisers at their worst and also show the law functioning at its best. We know from these events that the regulators display a high resolve toward eliminating deceptiveness as they know it. Now we need to get the regulators to identify the rest of the falsity that's out there and turn their high energy toward it.

# PART 8

# THE VIEW THAT REGULATORS COULD TAKE

*This part proposes a new conception of deceptiveness, incorporating the premise that consumer participation in the marketplace is grounded in trust rather than distrust. I propose (1) that the law recognize more types of implied claims than it does at present, and (2) that the concept of deceptiveness depend less on technical determinations of truth and falsity and more on whether consumers can rely on claims as trustworthy—the "reliance rule." Claims previously excused for a technical lack of falsity, even though greatly deficient in truth, would be prohibited if they adversely affected consumers who trusted them.*

# THE NEED FOR A LEGAL SOLUTION

The previous section showed how operating on the slippery slope makes problems for advertisers that they could choose to eliminate. They might well wish to avoid the slope claims in order to inject a greater role for ethics into their affairs, regain their public credibility, and avoid being called that nasty name. They don't need the slope claims, anyway, in order to achieve brand significance.

If I were sure those factors would convince the advertisers to stop, this book would now be over. However, I'm not at all confident of that. Some past thinking has stated naively that all that's needed to get advertisers to do "the right thing" is remind them of their role in society. The trouble with that strategy is that it isn't true that advertisers haven't thought of their role in society. They have.

When they think of it, however, they interpret it within the context of their position in the competitive market system, a system based on the pursuit of self-interest. It prompts the advertisers to see themselves as filling their social obligation essentially by making the sale. The system rewards them too little for their contribution to the overall society. It rewards primarily their personal gain, particularly on a short-term basis. It discourages them even from taking a long-term perspective on that personal gain.

Of course, if advertisers saw the slippery slope claims as hurting their chance for short-term gain, they would have a greater incentive to change. However, while they are aware of the survey results concerning their credibility (chap. 40), they are also aware that their immediate goal is not to make friends but to make sales. They're aware that they will achieve their goal of selling when people want to buy from them, whether those people like them or not.

Given that attitude, the distrust that's a problem for consumers isn't that much of a problem for advertisers. It's not a problem in the short run, that is. In the long run it's a disaster, but it's darn near impossible to get individual advertisers to think about that. The ad industry's national leaders do think about it, and attitudes would probably be different if they had any real influence.

Advertising's national organizations are far more sensitive to consumer welfare than they once were. In the early 1970s they objected every step of the way when the FTC increased its regulatory efforts. Today they support the general idea of regulation as a way of helping the field to maintain credibility. If those leaders controlled their members, they could effectively achieve a consensus on the matter of stopping questionable practices. No member of a group wants to quit a practice when it knows the others may keep doing it. But if the order came down from the top, they could all quit together and no one would suffer the inequality. That's only a dream, however, because the advertising industry's national leaders do not control their members.

Advertising is not a profession in which the national or state organizations create and enforce standards. It has no entrance standards of the sort found in other professions. Individual members go their own way as they please, and nobody can kick them out. The leadership may worry about the bad apples that spoil the bunch, but it cannot get the bad apples to *think* about the bunch.

It's an ironic fact that advertising's supporters support it by talking about its favorable aggregate effects, but its critics criticize it by focusing more on individual actions that they find objectionable. It would help a lot if the individual bad actors could be curtailed somehow, thus allowing the sun to shine on the good points. The way the business is organized, however, that's not likely to happen. Should things change and prove me wrong I will applaud the results, but I'm not holding my breath. Instead I'm going to suggest that we need to look elsewhere for a solution to the abuses of brand selling and the slippery slope claims.

That brings us to consider expanding regulation. With the lack of control within the advertising industry, the law would seem to be the principal hope. We might think that the self-regulation apparatus discussed earlier would be helpful, because industry members submit themselves to its decisions. However, such procedures go no further than the law goes, which produces nothing more than the status quo. Self-regulation will not change until the law changes.

There is a natural way that the law can change. The idea of conceiving advertising claims as being on a slope has been to emphasize that many problems of falsity and truth remain unregulated. The law concerns itself with the worst of these problems, the bottom of the slope. However, since the law may attack deceptiveness, and deceptiveness occurs everywhere on the slope, there is no question it may regulate the whole thing.

The issue is one of recognition, not of regulatory authority. The law can make the recognition, even though to date it hasn't. It has taken a strangely split view toward deceptiveness, recognizing some kinds and not others. We've seen one kind in the stories I've told every few chapters about specific advertising cases. The stance the regulators took in those cases indicates how strongly they can act toward claims lying at the bottom of the slippery slope. It's a distinct contrast to their inaction toward the claims we have found on the way down the slope.

Why did this split view develop? One reason could be that some kinds of deceptiveness are easy to recognize while others are harder, more subtle. That's a fair enough excuse for beginners, but the regulators have been in business for a long time and can be expected to develop sophistication. When the advertisers are smart enough to come up with new claims, the law must be smart enough to come up with new ways of coping. A certain lag time is understandable, but the slippery slope claims have been around for years.

Another reason for the split view could be that the recognized kinds of deceptiveness are capable of doing more harm. That's certainly a fair consideration, and I concede that the slope claims do less damage than certain blatant falsities. It's worse to claim that a product contains no alcohol or cholesterol, when it does, than to claim it will "shape your life" when it won't. Still, just because there are varying degrees of harm doesn't mean the lesser ones are not significant.

Another possible reason for the split view would occur if the recognized types of deceptiveness affect many more consumers than do the unrecognized types. That, however, seems not to be the case, because many slippery slope claims seem conveyable potentially to millions of consumers. Further, although no one has actually counted, it seems reasonable to suggest that the number of claims falling on the slippery slope is far greater than the number of recognized types of deceptive claims. The law may be giving such numbers too little consideration.

I get the impression from examining cases that when regulators choose what claims to pursue they attach more importance to the degree of harm per person than to the number of persons harmed. It's understandable, of course, that great harm per person, such as death or injury, will produce a tremendous degree of public concern. Lesser harms, such as paying more for a brand that's worth no more, will be of less perceived concern. Indeed, some of the harms mentioned in this book are no doubt rather difficult to pin down concretely. The harm caused by badly diminished truth in making purchasing decisions, although real enough to those experiencing it, is more subtle than death or injury, less likely to become the stuff of newspaper headlines.

The law's priorities may nonetheless be inappropriate, because great total harm can occur not only when there is a great amount per person, but also when a small amount per person is true for millions of persons. The law may be missing the latter point. While earlier we considered the subtlety involved in recognizing falsity, we are now considering the subtlety in recognizing harm. To me, the value of considering the slippery slope claims lies precisely in the fact that they affect many more consumers than does blatant falsity.

Let's look at more reasons for the law's split view. For one, the regulators disregard some types of deceptiveness when they look only at the message, and thereby fail to measure consumer response directly. This approach, as discussed earlier, reflects the puffery heritage, which seems to be a poor excuse.

Another reason could be that the regulators simply have political motives for wanting to cut business some slack. I get this feeling when I consider decisions such as the one involving Sterling Drug's superiority claims for more than one brand of the same product (chap. 25). Although it was obvious that all such claims simply couldn't be true, the FTC could not bring itself to say so.

Further, the regulators' tolerance of what we might call soft-core deception is no doubt due to the pressures placed on them. Besides the appellate court pressure discussed in chapter 27, there is also the difference between the activism of business and the passiveness of consumers. The advertisers press the puffery defense and other demands vigorously, while consumers make no similar demands. As a result, the law develops a relatively larger sympathy for sellers than it otherwise would. It becomes more prone to recognize the advantages of the slippery slope to sellers than to recognize the parallel disadvantages to consumers. It tends to equate the needs of society more strongly with the needs of sellers.

Consumers probably hurt themselves by going along passively with the inference that the law can't stop the slippery slope claims. They create a self-fulfilling prophecy, as follows. First, they feel nothing can be done, so they raise no outcry, following which the regulators feel more assured that they need do nothing, so they do nothing more, which makes consumers feel . . . and so on and on.

Those are the consumers who have come to recognize the law's split view and thereby concluded that distrust of advertising claims is appropriate. Other consumers trust the law and thus are likely to fail to recognize the split view. Naively they rely on the simplistic knowledge that "there's a law against deceptiveness." The fact that there often *is* a law that acts against relatively blatant falsity strengthens the traditional belief that "they couldn't say that if it wasn't true." To have consumers believe that statement makes the problem worse, because those who trust end up being betrayed.

These are the problems the regulators have created with their split view that leads them to prosecute some kinds of deceptiveness and not others. When the result leaves so much territory unpatrolled, it leaves the marketplace poorly policed. The good side, however, is that the split view provides the means for a legal solution. Eliminating the split would involve no more than simply recognizing all troublesome claims, to which the law as now constituted may then be applied. Such recognition would stop the deceptions and diminished truth of the slippery slope that so disadvantage consumers.

## 44

## THE BASIS FOR A LEGAL SOLUTION IN EXISTING LAW

Let's see the various steps the regulators could take to deal with the slippery slope. They could:

1. Look in the horse's mouth, that is, look directly at consumers' response to ads;

2. See the claims made, especially implied ones, that they haven't recognized before;

3. See that consumers need information, and so need to trust, and so do trust those claims;

4. See that many such claims do not merit trust;

5. Recognize existing legal developments that could support a requirement that all sellers' claims be trustworthy;

6. Create the requirement.

Previous chapters have argued at length that the law can and should carry out the first four of those points. This chapter and the next examine point 5, and chapter 46 takes up point 6.

What existing aspects of the law could justify a requirement that sellers must be trustworthy? Our look begins with a famous statement of the U.S. Supreme Court: "There is no duty resting upon a citizen to suspect the honesty of those with whom he transacts business." If such a statement really means what it says, we should be able to trust all sellers' claims. The exemption the slippery slope claims have been given from this lofty principle would not be tolerated.

From early times, moreover, the law has had some regulation, however limited, of the slope claims. English law entitled buyers to trust sellers when they had no other choice. As an English judge put it, "A seller is unquestionably liable . . . if he fraudulently misrepresent the quality of the thing sold to be other than it is in some particulars, which the buyer has not equal means with himself of knowing; or if he do so, in such a manner as to induce the buyer to forbear making the inquiries which . . . he would otherwise have made."

In other words, as seen in chapter 26, any buyer who could not inspect the goods, for example, when they were in transit in a ship at sea, was entitled to rely on the seller's description of them. The same would occur if the seller held the goods where they might be examined, but would not let the buyer see them.

A contemporary American expression of the English rule reads: "A statement of opinion as to facts not disclosed and not otherwise known to the recipient may, where it is reasonable to do so, be interpreted by him as an implied statement (a) that the facts known to the maker are not incompatible with his opinion; or (b) that he knows facts sufficient to justify him in forming it. . . ." Accompanying comment says that such an interpretation may be unreasonable if the speaker has an "adverse interest," such as a seller seeking a profit. In that case the buyer must make some allowance for exaggeration. But even then, the buyer may justifiably trust that the seller has "some basis of fact" and "knows of nothing which makes his opinion fantastic."

The proper interpretation of that rule could be, and I think it should be, that any knowledge of incompatible facts or lack of knowledge of justifying facts by sellers would make their opinions more exaggerated than buyers must make allowance for. If that were so, the rule would enable buyers to rely on opinions. In contrast, what the regulators seem to do with this rule in practice is to accept virtually all opinion claims as not overexaggerated. The regulators thus use the rule to excuse sellers of any responsibility for their opinions. The rule may superficially seem to give consumers the right to rely, but it really does not.

The underlying problem is the regulators' assumption seen earlier that consumers are able to examine advertised items themselves. Consumers must rely on no one but themselves, and so must disbelieve and refuse to rely on opinions expressed by sellers. The regulators assume from the 1853 precedent (chaps. 26–27) that consumers automatically distrust all such claims. If that were correct, then the sellers' incompatible knowledge or lack of justifying knowledge concerning their opinion claims could do no harm. Society consequently would not need to care whether such claims were false.

All of that, however, I feel is incorrect, for reasons discussed in chapter 28. Although we should rightfully be responsible for our opinions, we are not able to examine the goods by ourselves. We do not have "equal means of knowing" about advertised items just because they are in front of us, within our sight and touch. We are not able to make decisions by relying solely on our own personal resources.

Why would the advertisers work so hard to ply us with outside opinions if they believed that we all make up our own minds without such external influences? Their efforts reveal their conviction that consumers rely on such claims. The 1853 notion that consumers treat opinions as meaningless is an idea whose time should never have come, and should now be gone. The law should require sellers to honor opinions and the factual basis they imply. The law should also stop implicitly treating the other slippery slope claims in the way it treats opinion statements. It should require sellers to honor the implied truth of all such claims.

Our right as consumers to trust can be meaningful only when it includes trusting sellers, and that means all of their claims. Who other than the maker of a claim should know best whether there's a basis for relying on it? To invite us to rely on all sources *except* the sellers denies us too much of what we need. It's like getting a doughnut that's almost all hole.

Accordingly it does matter, contrary to the regulators' assumption, when sellers' claims are false. A requirement that all sellers' claims must be trustworthy would show a better understanding of how consumers really respond. The rules stated above, which help consumers very little as currently interpreted, could be interpreted to help them much more. The law should not exclude the slippery slope claims, because they are often the only ones the advertisers give us.

There is even more in existing American law that could help consumers. Another contemporary legal rule reads as follows:

> The recipient of a fraudulent misrepresentation which is one only as to the maker's opinion is justified in relying upon it in a transaction with the maker if the fact to which the opinion relates is material, and the maker:
>
> (a) purports to have special knowledge of the matter which the recipient does not have, or
>
> (b) stands in a fiduciary or other similar relation of trust and confidence of the recipient, or
>
> (c) has successfully endeavored to secure the confidence of the recipient, or
>
> (d) has some other special reason to expect that the recipient will rely on his opinion.

Sellers' opinion claims have been kept immune from this rule, too, in the past, on the ground that we're all supposed to treat sellers with suspicion. If we recognize consumer trust and treat it as legitimate behavior, however, the rule certainly makes important comments about sellers. Are they not people who purport to have special knowledge that consumers do not have? Do they not have a relationship of trust and confidence with consumers? Do they not successfully endeavor to secure such confidence? Isn't there a special reason to expect consumers will rely on them, namely, that sellers specifically urge consumers to do so? Certainly consumers' reliance on sellers is justifiable for these reaons, and thus consumers should be entitled to rely. The rule could reasonably be interpreted to provide additional strong support for assuring the trustworthiness of slippery slope claims.

A recent Supreme Court decision gives even more support for rethinking the treatment of opinion claims. The circumstances of the case were beyond the marketplace, but the principles seem applicable. A fight broke out during a high school wrestling match, injuring some athletes. Some observers felt that one of the coaches, Michael Milkovich, provoked the fight, but he denied it when testifying in a hearing. A newspaper columnist then wrote about his testimony that "a lesson was learned . . . by the student body. . . . It is simply this: If you get in a jam, lie your way out. . . . Anyone who attended the meet . . . knows in his heart that Milkovich . . . lied at the hearing after . . . having given his solemn oath to tell the truth."

Milkovich charged the paper with libel—damage to personal reputation by false representation. The paper defended by calling the statement exempt under the First Amendment for having the form of an opinion. Chief Justice Rehnquist's decision said, however, that such an exemption should not be automatic, because "expressions of 'opinion' may often imply an assertion of objective fact. . . . Simply couching . . . statements in terms of opinion does not dispel these implications. . . . [T]he statement 'In my opinion Jones is a liar,' can cause as much damage to reputation as the statement, 'Jones is a liar.' "

The key, Rehnquist said, lies in the implied facts. Opinions might imply no facts or imply only true ones, and thus be safe. However, they also might imply false and damaging facts, and if so, the speakers can no more avoid responsibility for such statements than if they stated them explicitly.

Isn't that how we should treat opinions in the marketplace! Under the libel law we don't hear any of that nonsense that the public will just automatically know to disbelieve what the newspaper said about Milkovich. We don't hear such idiocy as that each citizen will examine Milkovich's testimony independently, and will draw the proper conclusion on his or her own.

Yes, I realize Milkovich was not an object exchanged for money in a commercial transaction. The marketplace also differs in other ways from the area of public speech in which the newspaper operates. Observers might say, for example, that we must accept more of our own responsibility in assessing an advertised item than in assessing a wrestling coach. Presumably that's because we are not going to make so great a personal commitment toward Milkovich; we are not going to "buy" him.

Well, maybe we are, in a sense. When we recognize the similarities of the two situations on the matters of inability to examine and the consequent need to trust, the differences aren't really so great. Milkovich was in charge of our young sons whom he may have exposed to danger. Doesn't society make a big commitment toward public welfare when it hires such a person? Don't we then "buy" Milkovich in a vital social sense? Of course we do, and no one tells us we can't get help from the newspaper in assessing him because we must make up our minds and must refuse to rely on any outside source. Why, then, should we not also get help from sellers in making up our minds!

Additional indirect support for the right of consumers to rely comes from the commercial speech cases seen in chapter 34. The Supreme Court did not emphasize opinions in those cases, but it described commercial speech as having no less potential value to the public than noncommercial speech. It interpreted the First Amendment specifically to uphold the right of the public to receive messages that a commercial party wished to send. From there it's only a small jump of logic to suggest that if the Supreme Court encourages our right to receive commercial messages, then it should also intend to encourage our right to trust them. Imagine the Justices declaring, "We've gone to great lengths to get you this information, folks, but of course you mustn't use it because you know you can't trust it."

In summary, the existing law seen in this chapter goes a long way toward supporting the new regulation that I propose in chapter 46.

# 45

# AN ELABORATION ON THE MATTER OF ADVERSE INTEREST

The previous chapter briefly mentioned "adverse interest," which refers to the expectations the law says we must have about the meaning of certain speech. Some messages should prompt us to understand that those speaking to us do not have our best interests at heart. We must interpret those people as pursuing their own goals, and thus as taking actions that could be disadvantageous to anyone choosing to rely on them.

We would not be expected to apply that perception to a conversation among, for example, family members. It could be appropriate at times, but would not be typical. In other settings, though, such as having a seller speaker and consumer listener, the law thinks the adverse interest is routinely predictable from the elementary knowledge that it expects consumers reasonably to have about sellers.

The law expects a party who recognizes, or should recognize, an adverse interest to respond appropriately. In the marketplace, the consumer must expect the seller to try to make the sale on the most favorable terms. The consumer thus must anticipate that the advertiser may exaggerate the level of praise for the product or service beyond the factual basis that objectively exists for such claims. That's in contrast to listening to a speaker who has no evident special interest. Suppose you have friends who praise a product you are considering, but who will enjoy no personal gain if you buy it. There is no reason to expect that sort of speaker to exaggerate the factual basis.

With sellers, however, you may not rely on opinions to reflect the factual basis accurately. For opinions, and by analogy for the other slippery slope claims, an adverse interest clearly exists, and I do not dispute that consumers are likely to be well aware of it. Consumers surely know that the slippery slope claims are one-sided, and the side they work for is not theirs. Existing law thus obligates consumers, and I think fairly so, to maintain a questioning attitude toward the maker of such claims.

All of that works against my urgings that consumers should be able to rely on sellers' claims. I cannot deny the legitimacy of the idea of adverse interest, and so I cannot say the law is wrong in recognizing its existence. My position, however, is that the law is wrong in allowing that idea to be so dominating a factor in determining how the marketplace is regulated. Adverse interest is simply not all there is. Consumers' reliance interest is also a factor. While consumers see sellers as parties seeking deals on the best terms, they also just as reasonably see them as expert parties whom they must trust in order to make proper decisions.

However contradictory a set of perceptions of the seller that creates, it is nevertheless valid. Consumers know of sellers' adverse interests and distrust them on that basis. But they also know of the sellers' expertise and know it is impossible or at least burdensomely difficult to obtain that expertise elsewhere. On that basis consumers in fact do trust and rely on sellers.

Are consumers drawn equally toward the two orientations, half distrusting because of the sellers' adverse interest, half trusting because of their own reliance interest? I think not. Instead, I think consumers treat the reliance interest as the determining factor. Remember, consumers' distrust occurs with their feelings, their attitudes. They base their actions, meanwhile, on trust. It is, of course, their actions and not their attitudes that determine their ultimate welfare. In their actions trust prevails over distrust, and thus the reliance interest prevails over the adverse interest.

For that reason, the law should treat the reliance interest as a more determining factor than the adverse interest. That should not be overly difficult for the law to accept because, as shown in the previous chapter, there already exist such supporting legal ideas as the fiduciary relationship that lawyers have with clients. The problem is not that a reliance interest isn't already in the law. It's only that the regulators do not yet recognize the way it works between sellers and consumers.

## 46

# PROPOSALS FOR REGULATION

I make two proposals here for extending regulation. The first is an obvious one involving the messages conveyed by the slippery slope claims. It is simply that the regulators, by applying the analysis offered above, make the effort to recognize more implied claims than they have identified to date, particularly the Sufficient Facts, Brand Fact, and Puffery Implications (chap. 15, 29). Examining such claims for falsity would solve many of the problems consumers now have with the deceptiveness and inadequate truth of the slippery slope.

The task would involve no more than extending the regulators' traditional search for conveyed claims. It requires no new law, only the increased application of existing procedures. The regulators would simply be continuing a trend they have already demonstrated over the years, which is to show a steadily increasing sophistication in recognizing what advertising copywriters know and routinely apply about how consumers see claims conveyed.

Although that proposal could be powerful in its impact, the second proposal is potentially far more significant. While the first would simply extend business as usual, the second incorporates the ideas suggested in this book for new thinking on the nature of regulation. It would replace the outmoded beliefs about consumer behavior that have hampered the law for decades.

I have patterned the second proposal to reflect the existing FTC requirement that advertisers must have a reasonable basis for their factual claims. That requirement assumes the Reasonable Basis Implication (chap. 11), by which the commission sees all factual claims about the advertised item to imply to consumers that their maker has a valid reason for calling them true. The FTC calls that implication material, meaning consumers are more likely to base their purchasing decisions on claims that they think are so supported. The rule is not uniformly applied in the private suits brought under the Lanham Act, but my proposal includes the suggestion that it should be.

The proposal, then, is to expand the reasonable basis rule by requiring advertisers to have a reasonable basis for *using* their claims. That means not just for believing their claims to be true, but for relying on them. And that means virtually all claims. The only exceptions would be the obvious jokes and spoofs that have been excused traditionally, assuming they are truly obvious (recall the floating beer bottle spoof from chap. 5). All other claims would be included, which means more than just those covered by the current reasonable basis rule. It also means the slippery slope claims, including the nonfact claims that either are not factual or are not about the product.

This "reliance rule" would assume that advertisers imply to consumers that their own people have a reasonable basis, not merely for the truth of their conveyed claims, but also for the truthfulness of their own implied willingness to rely on those claims for making their own purchasing decisions. Regulators could reasonably assume that advertising conveys such a Reliance Implication simply from the fact that the advertiser uses the claim. Any party that invites consumers to trust, believe in, and rely on its claims should surely be willing to assert that it does the same.

The purpose, of course, is to hold advertisers responsible for honoring the trust that consumers place in them, reflecting the reliance interest identified in chapter 45. A trustworthy seller will not ask consumers to rely on a claim that its own people would reject. The idea that advertisers would insincerely make claims they disbelieved or had no basis for believing, and then would disavow them, refuse to rely on them, and decline to use them as a basis for their own purchasing decisions, is not acceptable.

To object to such a rule, advertisers would have to argue that they have a right to make claims for which they have no basis for reliance. That is a right they currently enjoy. Claims today that are not found factually false about the advertised item are excused from deceptiveness even when it is blatantly clear that their makers would in no way use them as a basis for purchasing. Advertisers invite consumers to use the claims as such a basis at the same time that they are thinking to themselves that they would not do that at all.

Claims that advertisers do not believe and do not rely on are called violations today only if they also misrepresent the advertised item. For example, the FTC found that Sears Roebuck's own personnel disbelieved their company's dishwasher claim (chap. 3). The commission also found, however, that the claim described the product falsely, and it prohibited the claim for the latter reason.

Regulators traditionally have been highly tolerant of sellers' insincere statements because they assume the insincerity misrepresents only perceptions of the seller itself and not of what the seller is selling. The law places little emphasis on whether speakers misrepresent themselves, owing to the presumption that consumers do not let such factors affect their buying decisions. The regulators assume that such claims are incapable of saying anything factual about the product, and therefore technically are not false with respect to the product. The claim presumably is not conveyed, or is not really about the product, or is an opinion incapable of being true or false. It means nothing.

That whole outlook should be changed, however, by the realization that consumers cannot examine advertised items themselves, and therefore need to trust others. The primary available others are the sellers, and consumers therefore do trust those sellers. When that happens, it definitely does matter to consumers when the sellers misrepresent themselves. Their claims affect buying decisions and so are material. The reliance rule, therefore, would provide that regulators could call claims illegally deceptive if the people who make them had no basis for believing them and relying on them for making buying decisions.

The advertisers should not be permitted to escape on the assumption that such a claim couldn't possibly be a reason for buying. Indeed, it's greatly incongruous for them to make that assertion after having spent many months and dollars telling the public precisely that it was a reason. The trick works, though. In hundreds of instances over the years the advertisers have been terrific at having their cake and eating it, too. A beer company, for example, claimed with immunity that its brand was "America's finest." While it told the public so at great length, it had to have known that it had no support for believing the claim, and probably in fact knew that it had support for disbelieving it.

The difference that the reliance rule would make, then, is that the criterion for deceptiveness would no longer be only the truth of the claim but also the truth of the seller's willingness to rely on it as a reason for buying. An advertiser could no longer escape simply through technical argument that a claim means nothing in a factual sense. To say it means nothing factually would now amount to conceding that there is no basis for relying on it.

That would give the advertiser a two-way problem. If it insisted that the claim meant nothing, it would fail to show a basis for reliance. If it conceded that the claim meant something, it would have to have a basis for why its own people would reasonably treat that something as a reason for buying. Either way, the advertiser would have to support the claim or give it up.

The reliance rule is designed to make the law concentrate on its real purpose, which is to prevent harm to consumers. What the law prohibits currently is not harm but deceptiveness. That can be acceptable as long as the deceptiveness is defined in terms of falsity that negatively affects purchasing decisions and thus does harm. Today, though, deceptiveness is defined more narrowly than that. It leaves a loophole through which advertisers may use claims from the slippery slope that technically are not false about the item but which nonetheless convey falsities about the item that negatively affect purchasing decisions.

If the reliance rule were used, the customary basis for deceptiveness would continue to be the explicit or implied falsity of a claim or the absence of a reasonable basis for the claim's truth. However, the basis would now also include the absence of a reasonable basis for the advertiser's reliance. Regulators would properly reveal advertisers' nonreliance, and would eliminate such insincere claims from the marketplace. The deceptiveness, diminished truth, and harm to consumers of the slippery slope would be acceptable no more.

## 47

# PROVING RELIANCE OR NONRELIANCE

This chapter is rather technical. I can't propose a new law without explaining how it would be carried out. The result is a discussion that is mainly for the professionals—the advertisers and the regulators. Other readers may feel free to bear the strain of the inside details, or else could skip on to the next chapter.

To prove a violation under the reliance requirement, the regulators' burden would be to show that the advertiser had no reasonable basis for its own reliance on the claim. Alternatively, it could be that the advertiser had or should have had a reasonable basis for nonreliance. The advertiser would defend by showing it had a reasonable basis for reliance, or by otherwise preventing the regulator from meeting its burden. As with the current reasonable basis rule, a company would not have to state the reliance basis in the advertising. It would merely have to possess the basis so that regulators could be shown it on request.

The rule would mean, just as it does with the current reasonable basis requirement, that the burden of proof technically is on the regulator. It would switch the burden to the advertiser in a practical sense, however, because the advertiser's failure to show a reasonable basis would open the door for the prosecution to conclude, perhaps arbitrarily, that it had none. Whether or not that is overly burdensome, that's how it's done under the current rules.

The claims for which the seller would need a basis would be those conveyed to consumers, including those I have identified as implied by the slippery slope claims. The reliance proposal thus incorporates my first proposal that all such implications be identified. There would always be the defense available of showing that implications ordinarily expected to be conveyed may be absent in specific instances because of additional information that consumers either already have or else get from the ad. For example, the advertiser might explicitly qualify a claim so as not to convey an implication. Such result, if demonstrated, would excuse the advertiser from making the implication and thus from having a basis for it.

Regarding the Sufficient Facts Implication, for example, an ad might say, "There are many reasons for choosing a car, and mileage is one of them. This may not be the factor you find most important, but if it is, you'll want to know that our brand excels on this feature. . . . (etc.)." Whether or not that exact wording would indicate that the diminished truth stands only for itself and not for the whole truth, certainly there is wording that could. If it succeeds, the advertiser would not convey the Sufficient Facts Implication and so would need no basis for it.

Recall the selected fact discussed in chapter 15 about the gas burner turning down faster than the electric burner. The advertiser would surely have no objective basis for calling that fact sufficient, because additional contrary facts exist about various advantages of electricity. However, the public undoubtedly knows many of those additional facts about electricity's benefits, and so is not likely to treat the burner claim as amounting to a sufficient basis for choosing gas. Probably an insignificant number of consumers would see that particular Sufficient Facts Implication conveyed.

That will happen with many products that are familiar; however, there are always new products that are unfamiliar. I recently pondered an ad for a laserdisc player claiming that the brand and its category give better color than videocassettes. That's probably true, but I wondered whether that means they have overall superiority. I have a suspicion that any further supporting facts, if available, would have been used in the advertising. After all, advertisers run selected facts because the unselected facts aren't so hot. I have heard, for example, that there aren't nearly as many laserdiscs available as there are cassettes. In general, then, it may be harder with unfamiliar or complex products for advertisers to defeat the regulators' charge that a Sufficient Facts Implication is conveyed.

What makes a reasonable basis for those claims found conveyed would depend on the total context of knowledge of the product category. It would be knowledge that a producer of a brand in that category has or ought reasonably to have. Included would be the advertiser's knowledge of reasons justifying its own people's reliance. Also important to include would be the justifiable absence of reasons that would indicate nonreliance. Appropriate reasons would include knowledge of facts about the advertised item that its seller either has or ought to have.

To be objective, such information would have to be subject to confirmation by independent parties having the same expertise that the advertiser should have. In practice the regulators would be unlikely to accept the assertions of sellers without such impartial outside support.

A subjective basis for reliance could exist even though an objective basis did not. It could happen, for example, if the Sufficient Facts, Brand Fact, or Puffery Implications appeared perceptually or psychologically true to the consumer. That means it would be true at the time of purchase, and would remain so to the consumer's satisfaction after the purchase. If the satisfaction offered were thus the satisfaction supplied, we would find subjective expectations borne out and the basis for reliance established. The confirming evidence would be that of consumers' perceptions.

It's always possible, of course, for consumers to become disillusioned if they are less satisfied with their purchase than the advertising led them to expect. Perhaps after using the advertised item the consumers found that the objective facts that supported their expectations were not true. If so, the satisfaction offered would not be the satisfaction supplied, and consumer harm would occur.

For that reason, surveys would not be valid if they obtained subjective perception information from consumers knowing the brand only as presented in the advertising, not experiencing it directly. The appropriate basis would have to come from surveys showing that consumers retain their subjective perceptions after seeing and using the brand. Usually the consumers would acquire such experience from buying, although a possible research alternative might be to have them experience the brand in a setting that reasonably simulates actual purchase and use.

With such appropriate consumer survey information, advertisers could demonstrate a subjective basis for reliance as an alternative to an objective basis. I personally feel consumers will often modify or eliminate their subjective satisfactions after they examine the advertised item. However, there is no denying that they might maintain such satisfactions, and so the proposal provides for that to be shown.

In summary, an advertiser must show a basis for its own reliance on its claims as a reason to buy. The claims include the Sufficient Facts, Brand Fact, and Puffery Implications and any other implied or explicit claims the advertising might make. The basis may be objective information satisfactory to parties having the expertise the advertiser has or ought to have. It may also be subjective consumer perception survey data that reveal more than just temporary satisfaction. There would also have to be an absence of any basis for rejecting reliance.

In the next chapter, we will see how the rule would apply for various specific claims.

**48**

# WHAT THE RELIANCE RULE WOULD ALLOW AND DISALLOW

The reliance rule is aimed at any claims that deceive about sellers' beliefs, but I have earlier said that slippery slope claims are not always deceptive. I will show here how some of them could stay in use, while some would be prohibited. The rule would allow all claims for which the advertiser could show either nonconveyance or a reasonable basis for reliance. It would disallow all nonjoking conveyed claims, either explicit statements or their conveyed implications, for which the advertiser could not show a basis for reliance.

The following, then, discusses the prospects for the advertisers of finding such a basis for the various slippery slope claims. To begin, for conveyed selected and minimal facts advertisers would need to have a basis for their own reliance on any conveyed Sufficient Facts Implication. As a reminder, that implication is that the claim reflects at least as much brand significance and as favorable a purchasing decision as the entire set of facts about the brand would indicate.

For selected facts, an advertiser might readily be able to cite additional facts that support the implication. For example, some suitably reliable independent source may have rated the brand as excellent in its product category. There may also be an absence of any facts to the contrary. If so, the value of the single aspect may be taken to reflect accurately the value that the total of all relevant information about the brand will convey. That would create the basis for the advertiser's reliance on it.

Such an example shows that omitting information is not automatically a problem. Truth is always diminished by omissions, but no harm is done if the diminished truth accurately reflects the whole truth. That may be so even when a negative fact is omitted, so long as it does not overcome the value of the selected fact. For example, when the first commercial firm began delivering letters or packages anywhere in the country by 10 A.M. the next morning, the price it charged was much higher than that of the U.S. Postal Service.

Surely it would surprise no one to imagine that the ads might have omitted such price information. Nonetheless, many consumers could benefit so much from this previously unavailable service that the price or any other negative factor would not have changed their buying decision. In that case the Sufficient Facts Implication would be confirmable. The basis would be subjective consumer perceptions showing that the buying decision was not more negative after people learned the negative price information.

Of course, the ad can omit negative aspects that would make consumers who learned about them less willing to buy. A car, for example, might truly give the advertised excellent mileage, but also give a seriously uncomfortable or dangerous ride. Upon learning the latter unadvertised facts, consumers might reject the implication that the mileage advantage supports a positive buying decision. Under the reliance rule, an advertiser who knew or should have known of such negative information would have no basis for its own reliance on the mileage advantage as sufficient to support buying.

The reliance basis for any conveyed Sufficient Facts Implication would be determined in the same way for minimal facts, nonbrand facts, and opinions because any of the slippery slope claims, standing alone, may act as selected facts. Any of them might imply truthfully or falsely to consumers that supporting facts exist and that no contradictory facts exist.

For minimal facts the Sufficient Facts Implication is even more likely than with selected facts to be false objectively, because we define minimal facts as having minimal brand significance objectively. However, an alternative subjective basis could exist. If an ad called a 31-speed blender an improvement over a current 30-speed model, the

Sufficient Facts Implication would be doomed objectively if expert testing could not detect that the new model performed significantly better than the old model. Still, the advertiser might provide a subjective basis for reliance if it could show that consumers believed the difference to be meaningful to them.

I suspect consumers often would not believe that, but the advertiser can give it a try. Minimal differences that mattered subjectively to consumers would thus be no problem under the reliance rule. The advertisers would need only to show that the perceptions are real. That means, we should recall from the previous chapter, that the perceptions must remain after consumers experience the brand and not merely after they have experienced the ad.

Let's turn to nonfact claims, including nonbrand facts and opinions. For conveyed nonbrand facts, advertisers would need a basis for both the Sufficient Facts and Brand Fact Implications. As a reminder, the latter involves the claim implying itself to be a fact about the advertised item (typically a brand). For conveyed opinion claims advertisers would need a basis for the Sufficient Facts and Puffery Implications. The latter involves the opinion implying to consumers that the advertiser has a factual basis for it consisting of true facts about the advertised item.

For nonfact claims the Sufficient Facts Implication is highly likely to be false objectively, because such claims are not even minimally factual about the brand. Advertisers might insist, however, that the implication would not be conveyed, precisely because the claims are nonfactual; that is, consumers would not see them as facts about the brand. However, I have argued earlier that nonbrand facts indeed imply to consumers that they are about the brand—the Brand Fact Implication.

Moreover, nonbrand facts often associate a brand with matters of strong motivational significance to consumers. Anyone who doubts that the typical nonbrand fact in the lifestyle category packs a lot of punch with consumers should recall the PowerMaster story (chap. 24). Nonbrand facts such as the PowerMaster name or the claim "You don't just shape your body, you shape your life" will probably imply the Brand Fact Implication and then the Sufficient Facts Implication.

Although I can't imagine the advertisers finding an objective basis for reliance on such implications, they might find, as with the other slippery slope claims, a subjective basis. In my opinion the relationship between a malt liquor and social power, or between an exercise club and "shaping your life," will seem less factually real, or not real at all, to most consumers after they experience the product or service in addition to experiencing the advertising. However, should the subjective

satisfactions remain strong for such claims, the advertiser could confirm them with survey evidence of subjective perceptions, and so have
a basis for reliance.

Opinions, our last category, imply to consumers that they have a
factual supporting basis—the Puffery Implication. The advertiser
must either reject the conveyance of that implication or else must
know of such supporting facts in order to have a basis for its reliance
on the opinion claim. That poses different levels of challenge because
there are different types of opinions. Suppose a celebrity such as Madonna says she prefers a certain brand of drink, or likes it best, always
chooses it, and so on. There should be little trouble in supporting
that, because the basis would be nothing more than her personal assertion, what I earlier called a taste puff. Alternatively, suppose that
Madonna, or just a voice or statement in the ad, says that "you'll"
prefer the brand. Again the basis would be one individual's assertion—your own.

On the other hand, suppose Madonna, or just the ad itself, says the
brand is the best. Finding a basis for that will be harder because "best"
implies the best overall. By appearing in a mass medium addressed to
millions of consumers, it implies that it means the best for consumers
generally. When a claim thus conveys that it's true for parties beyond
the advertiser and its endorsers, the basis must necessarily consist of
evidence about that wider group. The supporting evidence here, as
elsewhere, must be that persons to whom the ad attributes the opinion
really hold it.

A factually objective basis for an opinion claim might also be a consensus among experts in the given field, such as brewmasters judging
beer. Such judgments may sometimes require only observation by the
expert's eyes or ears, while other times it may require the use of instru-
ments or controlled tests. The requirement would vary by product category. For example, the basis for Bayer being "the world's best aspirin"
would require the controlled scientific testing we observed earlier for
headache remedies. A claim to be the "best movie" would imply a subjective basis that would require a consumer preference survey.

Some ads qualify a claim of "best," such as by saying "best ingredients" or "best tasting." A basis for the first of those could probably only
be objective. Consumers' opinions about ingredients should rightfully
be secondary to the opinions of experts. However, a basis for the taste
claim would appropriately be subjective, because for taste the consumers themselves should rightfully decide. A finding that the advertised
brand was picked as "best tasting" more often than its competitors
would provide a reliance basis.

Some opinion claims are so vague or fanciful as to be likely meaningless. The FTC has considered, for example, the description of a car as the "sexiest European." It decided the claim required no basis because it is nonfactual. The message conveyed to consumers is that the claim means nothing. The reliance rule, however, proposes that the advertiser may not offer the defense of meaninglessness, because that would mean the speaker could have no basis for the claim. The claim must be rejected because the advertiser has stated it insincerely and would not rely on it, and the consumer therefore cannot trust the advertiser. Advertisers who objected to that conclusion could defend the claim as meaningful instead, but then they would have to supply a basis for relying on the supporting facts that the claim implied to exist.

For any such opinion variations, neither the objective nor subjective basis is difficult to search for. The difficulty, rather, is that of having the search confirm that the basis exists for a particular brand. Obviously a basis can't exist for many brands, because only one can be superior by a given criterion. Remember, too, that sellers who have a fact basis will no doubt include it in the claim, rather than running the opinion unaccompanied.

In summary, the reliance rule will eliminate many slippery slope claims that existing law allows. It will also let continue any such claims for which the advertiser refutes conveyance or else shows a basis for reliance. A selected fact shown to have a basis would become a representative fact, and thus not deceptive. A minimal fact with a basis would no longer be minimal. A nonbrand fact or opinion with a basis would now essentially be equivalent to the true and significant brand facts making up that basis.

All such suitable claims would remain at the top of the slope—not slippery, not sliding, not deceptive. Claims would be either at the top or the bottom, and the troublesome area between, the slope, would no longer exist. The consumer would be able to trust a much greater proportion of advertisers' claims, and advertisers would be able to continue all claims that were trustworthy.

## 49

# SMART AND DUMB CONSUMERS
## AND THE RELIANCE RULE

One of the hottest disputes among those of us who discuss marketplace regulation involves whether consumers are generally smart and able to handle their own affairs, or generally poorly informed and unable to cope without outside help. Our answers to that question, you might assume, will determine our conclusions as to how much regulation society needs. We won't recommend much regulation if consumers are smart, but we'll ask for quite a bit if they are not.

How much do you want to bet, though, that the thinking process actually works the other way around? That is, the debaters have an advance interest in a certain degree of regulation, and then make the assumption about consumer competence that supports that interest! Of course, then the conclusions about consumers would merely be an excuse for the desired level of regulation, rather than a genuine justification for it.

I can't be certain which way the process works, but I have noticed that the disputants tend to argue their positions without presenting much evidence; they don't look in the horse's mouth. Also, most of them claim that the public is predominantly smart or predominantly dumb. That's probably not a conclusion that would always result if impartial observers examined consumers with no predetermined finding in mind.

Because I propose an increase in regulation, readers may interpret me as advocating the supporting conclusion that consumers are predominantly dumb. Actually, though, I think the marketplace has both smart and dumb consumers, each in proportions large enough to be significant for public policy considerations. I identify them, in the context of this book, as consumers who distrust (smartly) or trust (dumbly) the slippery slope claims. Readers will recall (from chap. 40 and elsewhere) that some consumers will trust while others will distrust those claims.

The fact that there are so many claims being advertised that smart consumers would distrust certainly suggests that the advertisers believe there is a substantial proportion of trusting citizens. The existence of any claim of course implies that the advertiser thinks a substantial number will rely on it, and when there are distrustworthy claims the obvious implication is that the advertisers think many consumers will trust them. I doubt that the advertisers are wrong very often about this, because it's the precise area, after all, in which they are experts. If they think a claim will be trusted, and the regulators think it will not be trusted, I will bet on the advertisers every time.

In a further disagreement with those leaning toward extremes, I reject the position that only the dumb, trusting consumers need outside help in coping with advertisers' claims. I think the smart, distrusting consumers need help, too, and therefore the existence of a substantial number of them does not mean that the marketplace needs little or no regulation. I oppose the idea that public policy should concern itself with determining which kind of consumer is predominant and adapting regulatory measures to the needs of that group only. Rather, we should adapt regulation to the needs of both groups.

Suppose two consumers, one trusting and one distrusting, are exposed to a slippery slope claim that, although not deceptive under current law, is a claim on which its maker would not rely. Suppose the trusting consumer relies on the claim and makes a resulting inappropriate buying decision, while the distrusting consumer refuses to rely on it and is not affected by it. The proposed Reliance Rule, unlike existing regulation, will help the trusting consumer by prohibiting that claim. Is there any role, though, that such a new rule will play for the distrusting consumer?

Conventional wisdom says that the smart consumers, the distrusters, don't need the proposed or even the existing regulation because their own distrust does all they need to prevent slippery slope claims from adversely affecting them. In disagreement with that conventional wisdom, I observe that smart consumers are also poorly served by slippery slope claims with respect to the quality of the information they need for the buying decisions they want to make.

Of course a distruster is better off than a truster in knowing what claims to reject, but the distruster is nonetheless left unfulfilled in getting the expertise it needs from the advertiser. As earlier argued, every consumer needs information from outside sources, and the best of those sources is the maker itself. The dumb consumers may not know that, but surely the smart ones do. These same smart consumers who distrust the distrustworthy claims are also the ones who best know that self-reliance is not enough, that reliance on outsiders therefore is necessary, and that the maker of the product is an expert on it and therefore an excellent source of information about it.

In short, much of what it means to be a smart consumer surely involves wanting, indeed demanding, to be able to rely on the advertiser. The Reliance Rule offers both the trust-prone and the distrust-prone precisely that opportunity. Under it, consumers would be able to rely on advertising by having claims be permitted only when the advertiser is able to vouch in advance for their reliability.

Granted, forcing advertisers to make only reliable claims will not necessarily result in useful information as long as there is the alternative of making no claims at all. Certainly the latter could happen, yet when an advertiser makes no claims it sacrifices the opportunity to sell. A company must compete to survive, and if it were prohibited from making claims that merit distrust, and therefore had to choose between trustworthy ones or none at all, I expect that many trustworthy claims would result.

Economists, tending to see market behavior as traditionally rational, are prone to say that the market automatically takes care of consumers' information needs. I believe that under current conditions it does not. Brand advertisers who lack objective advantages to promote will not emphasize making trustworthy claims as long as the distrustworthy kind are permitted, because the latter tend to convey much more brand significance than the former. Advertisers will use the distrustworthy kind to sell to the trusting consumers, and the distrusters will not be served.

If the market consisted entirely or predominantly of distrusting consumers, such smart people would have to be treated as such. Advertisers would not use distrustworthy claims because they would not work, and the market would indeed police itself. It's different, though, when a substantial body of trusters are present, because then the distrusters will get less attention. I'm arguing, then, that while the welfare of the trusting and otherwise dumb consumers calls for regulation, the welfare of the smart ones does, too, *as long as* there are a significant number of the dumb ones around and *as long as* distrustworthy claims are permitted by law.

If we could eliminate the dumb consumers, then the smart ones would receive the respect of the advertisers and all would be well, but what are the chances of that happening? I don't think we can eliminate the dumb consumers, because most of us, including myself, are in that category much of the time. By "dumb" I don't mean just people having low IQs, but rather any of us who simply lack the level of expert information that is required to make the buying decision that's right for our needs. With so many products today containing complex technology or long lists of ingredients, the chances are great that all of us are dumb more often than we are smart, at least when we have our first confrontation with a new product and a new set of claims about it.

The only strategy remaining, then, in order to serve us when we exercise our smartness by seeking trustworthy and reliable claims, is to eliminate the advertisers' use of distrustworthy claims. The Reliance Rule, by doing that, promises to serve us when we are acting smartly just as much as when we are acting dumbly.

# PART 9

## THE VIEW THAT
## CONSUMERS COULD TAKE

*This final part advises consumers on actions they could take if neither the advertisers nor regulators eliminate the slippery slope problems. Such advice is not offered as the ideal resolution; rather, advertiser action would be most desirable, and legal action next most. However, if consumers are left to fend for themselves, they can participate in the marketplace far more effectively through more informed and aware interpretations of advertising. If perceptions of products are what consumers base their behavior on, then the most important thing they can know is that they are fully able to monitor and control those perceptions.*

# 50

# THE PROSPECTS OF CONSUMERS
# HELPING THEMSELVES

Earlier I said the law could act if the advertisers don't. Now it seems necessary to say that if the law doesn't act either, consumers may have no source of help beyond themselves. And, even if they do get help, consumers will always be wise to aid themselves to the extent possible.

I hope I am not too cynical about the law. It usually gets where it needs to go, but it can take very long in doing so. I am sure the reliance rule is an idea whose time has come, but the way time works with regulators is about the way geologists see it working with glaciers. That's especially so at a time like the present when government budgets are squeezed. Because the enforcement of the law is a separate matter from its substance, my proposals could be affected by budgetary weakness. Agencies such as the FTC and state consumer protection offices will not happily expand what they need to cover, no matter how appropriate the expansion may be, should they fear that resources for doing the added work will not be forthcoming.

So let's see what consumers ought to know and do about sledding down the slippery slope on their own. I'll make some suggestions I think are useful, although first I'll cite some past ones I feel are not. One of the cries of consumerism I recall from the 1960s and 1970s was that consumers should simply distrust sellers. Another was that consumer education was the answer. Some advocates carried these suggestions to rather great lengths, for example, in airing the idea of distrust as virtually an absolute. Consumers should distrust advertising so completely that they shouldn't even look at it. Then they should educate themselves from other sources, and they would have what they need.

I think distrust and education are both useful, but not sufficiently to be relied upon to those extremes. I'll talk below about the role each can play. For the moment, though, my point is that consumers can't use these methods to obtain their minimum daily requirements of ability to cope with sellers.

In assessing the value of distrusting sellers we should first recall that we can do so readily only as a matter of attitude, not of action. When we act with utter distrust we stop acting; we paralyze ourselves. We can no longer participate in the marketplace. That's no solution, as we can easily tell by watching what consumers do—they keep on buying. Realistically, what other option do we all have? Moreover, we cannot distrust sellers even as a matter of attitude, not absolutely. If we did that, we'd never have enough information on which to base our trustful actions. If we're going to act, we must be able to believe *some* sources, *some* information. Further, much advertising is trustworthy. We shouldn't reject the whole category outrightly.

There's also a problem with educating ourselves about sellers and the marketplace. If we use education in conjunction with distrusting, meaning as a substitute for trusting sellers, we limit our options too much. Sure, alternative sources of product information are available, but the seller is the primary one. To have to exclude the seller as an outside source is simply an unreasonable act of exclusion. Education can be best only when it uses all sources, including learning how to interpret what we get from sellers. We should learn to use trustworthy independent sources, by all means, but also to recognize and use the kinds of advertising claims that merit trust.

Even that, you understand, is not ideal. The only thing I consider ideal is to be able to trust all claims. However, I will speak further in the next chapter about education in learning to discriminate among ads. That's a skill we will need if the advertisers and regulators fail to arrange for us to be able to trust. Under such unfortunate conditions we will all have a continuing need to cope with claims to the best degree we can. We not only should do that, but should recognize an obligation to take care of ourselves to the extent we can. As Ronald Reagan said at the 1992 Republican convention, "You cannot help men permanently by doing for them what they could and should do for themselves."

While the viewpoints I express in this book are not easily reconcilable with those of such a political conservative, I really have no trouble agreeing with that statement. Where I disagree is in identifying what people can and cannot do for themselves. Regarding the advertising claims that are my topic, I believe consumers can separate the trustworthy from the untrustworthy to a far lesser degree than the representativeness of business believe.

Consider whether a consumer can tell that a claim is true or false, just by looking at the ad. Some apologists for advertising will say that if we look carefully, we can tell. Suppose, though, that it's an ad saying a brand of paint covers more area than others. If that's false, how can we tell for ourselves, Mr. Reagan? We often can't do that on our own; we can't undiminish the diminished truth. The only thing education will do about that is make us aware that there are things of which we're not aware. For that reason I think the idea of consumers helping themselves as a sole or even primary solution to their problems is no good. It simply won't work. Education that tells us what to check for is of no avail regarding checks we can't make.

However, there are things we can examine about the truth and falsity of claims, and we should not miss the opportunity to detect as many of those as we can. Consequently, in this final section I urge that we should all do so. Each of us will function best in the marketplace by acquiring and using knowledge of claims and of products to the greatest possible extent. The knowledge is out there today, much more than it used to be.

When I first began teaching about advertising and other mass media topics in 1963 consumers had few sources of information on such matters. There were always the trade publications, such as *Advertising Age,* but the general public typically never saw them. The daily newspapers and consumer magazines had little to say. Today, by contrast, we have considerable coverage in types of media that many people see. For most of us, the primary source is our own local daily paper. Media such as *The New York Times, The Wall Street Journal,* several newsmagazines, and certain cable channels also cover business extensively.

From such sources we can expand our awareness of how the media work. We can do it much more so than in, for example, the early days of television when people were far more naive about such things. I recall in the 1950s visiting an aunt and uncle in their small town where we watched Jackie Gleason on an evening that turned out to be his birthday. We learned that when the cast interrupted the Great One's chatter by swarming onto the set, bearing the appropriate cake and song and good wishes. A moment later my uncle exclaimed, "Look, he's got a tear in his eye; they surprised him completely."

So they did, I thought at the time. It wasn't until considerably later that I realized that TV programs had time constraints and couldn't very well have had surprises not written into the script well in advance. How naive we all were! Gleason must have had all the time he wanted to plan how big a tear it would be and how far it would run down his cheek—the one toward the camera, of course.

Today we routinely hear a lot of the "inside" stuff. Our local press has stories about topics such as what companies will be running new ads on the upcoming Super Bowl. We learn that some advertisers were luckier than others by getting ad slots early in the game, avoiding the possibility of lopsided scoring that would make much of the audience tune out well before the end. The media tell us many more such things about advertising than they once did.

I don't mean to imply that we can ever learn all we need to know. That's particularly so when we must learn more about products than merely how they are represented in ads. In the next chapter, though, we will see that there are definite steps consumers can take with resources available to all.

# 51

# WHAT CONSUMERS CAN DO

The most important thing consumers can do is to eye advertising content more knowingly. Although we often can't test for the truth of ad claims, we can usually identify their types and so assess their likely validity. That, of course, is why I have identified such things as the process of implying claims beyond those explicitly stated, the nature of the specific implications we are likely to draw, and the slippery slope claims.

Along with using these tools we can observe our own behavior, especially in realizing how our habits of perception play a role in what we notice the claims to be saying. That is, while the presence of the explicit content is scarcely in doubt, we should recognize that any implied claims are products in part of our own subjective perception. They are there if we choose to see them being there, but we also may choose not to see them. For example, when you see a statement in an ad for a brand, are you prone to accept it unquestioningly as saying something significant about the brand? There's a natural human tendency to see such a proposition, because, like all the other implications we have discussed, it's pragmatically logical. However, it's also often incorrect.

We need to remember that it's always our own choice, not the advertiser's. We have the option of keeping such mental processes from happening automatically, and we should exercise that option. If we recognize that a claim is of a certain sort, we can make a judgment about it. We can realize, for example, that a nonbrand fact or opinion has no brand significance objectively. We can take that into account in forming our subjective perception. That doesn't mean we can't accept such claims subjectively, but only that we may choose to do so realistically. We can keep an eye on the factual limitations and make up our own minds about what we are willing to accept subjectively.

A story about image advertising quoted a whiskey marketing executive as saying, "Everything we do is to create a friend of Jack Daniel's. Our customers are emotionally involved with the brand." You should ask yourself: do you want to involve yourself emotionally with Jack Daniel's? Thousands do it every year to the extent of visiting the old-time, down-home distillery in little Lynchburg, Tennessee. If you'd like to be one of them, that's fine, but just try to make sure it's your own decision. Don't let Jack Daniel's make it for you. Don't agree passively to be a friend of the company; make sure you want it to be a friend of yours. And, base your choice on an understanding that none of such involvement means anything about the whiskey itself.

While you're examining your thinking processes, consider whether what the ad has told you amounts to sufficient information for buying. We need to know and appreciate what's missing just as much as what's there. I know a chap who visited the Daniel distillery, but he drinks no whiskey but Jim Beam. What he learned about Lynchburg was enough to get him to visit the site, but not enough to get him to use its product. Why not! You can keep these things separate in your mind.

If you ever tell kids about these matters, use a figure such as Tony the Tiger as an example. Suggest that they consider whether they have their own reasons for liking such an image. Adults may be wrong in thinking that kids have trouble understanding these things. If we talk to them, they will grasp the point. It would be ever so much better to start doing so at a young age, as soon as they start being exposed to ads.

Moving to opinion claims, remind yourself that there ought to be facts supporting them. You can't tell what those facts are, or whether they really exist, by looking at the ad. You can remember, though, that companies are likely to consider factual support for an opinion more valuable than the opinion itself. In other words, they'll run the underlying fact if they have it; if they're not running it, you can reasonably conclude they don't have it.

In the process of assessing claims you will frequently find, at least until present-day customs change, that you ought to distrust. Although we should never have to adopt distrust as our basic orientation, it can play a role in moderation. We will function best by appropriately distrusting sellers as a short-term, although never a permanent or long-term, solution.

What I've been saying boils down to our need to be active, not passive. The next time you feel like doing nothing, remember the following words from that master manipulator Machiavelli, "One who deceives will always find those who allow themselves to be deceived." Another famous essayist, Montaigne, added this: "Easily does the world deceive itself in things it desireth or fain would come to pass."

Everything suggested so far involves an individual's own actions. We also need to make our views known to others. We need to tell each other when claims seem false or too diminished in truth. We need to make sure the advertisers hear it, too. We should fuss; we should be indignant. We should call the advertisers phonies, or bullshitters, or harassers, when we think that's what they are. If they deserve embarrassment, they should get it. We should not allow our own silence to be one of the reasons why things stay the same. The law's makers and enforcers may knuckle down to industry pressure, as they have in the past. Consumers don't have to knuckle down, though, and if we stand firm the law will eventually firm up, too. The industry complains to legislators, but we can complain even louder; we can outshout them.

We can air the absurdities rather than just forgetting them. Remember the bread seller that defined a serving as three-quarters of a slice. Does it strike you as odd that we live in a society where nobody's ever had a serving of bread? Shouldn't it strike you as even odder that we live in a society that seems not to care whether such things make sense?

Some things like that may seem too little to bother with, yet the result of our saying nothing about them is that we keep getting more of the same. A passivity that breeds little problems carries us on to bigger problems. We are incredibly tolerant. Ours is a society of persuaders, which means it's also a society of those who tolerate persuasion. The sellers act as though they exist to manipulate and not be manipulated. The consumers act as though they exist to be manipulated without manipulating back.

When California's consumer regulators charged Sears with making unneeded auto repairs, Sears's business in the next several months dropped 20 percent in California and 15 percent nationwide. If you think that means consumers were giving the company what it deserved, think again—aren't those figures rather low? Sears's customers could have gone to other repair shops, but most often kept going back to Sears as though nothing had happened. There's a whole lot of trusting going on.

We consumers who do complain don't extend our comments beyond our immediate contacts very often. We do some complaining about retailers with whom we have dealt personally, but we are far less likely to complain about advertising. That's probably because the retailers are present in our hometowns, while the advertisers are elsewhere. We often don't know where they are; we never meet anybody from the producers and promoters of the goods and services we buy.

Consumers aren't a group; we aren't organized. Perhaps it's understandable that we often operate separately, since participating in the marketplace is an individual thing. Organizing joint action takes time, and it's not marketplace time; it's more like engaging in politics. Still, consumers should be aware that such activity can amplify our voices many degrees. When we take the time, it pays off.

I opened this discussion by saying that helping ourselves is an alternative we can pursue if the advertisers or the regulators do nothing. Notice, though, that it's also a way of getting those parties to *start* doing something. If we don't act they may or may not act, but if we do act, they'll have to.

To sum it up, we need to tell the sellers that we're the buyers, we're running the show. All the money you advertisers make comes from us. If you offer us brand values, you'll have to earn them. Give us the things that really matter to us. Give us the products, and the information about those products. You give us those things, and *we* will make our decisions.

# 52

# A FINAL PERSPECTIVE

After all I have said, readers may be surprised to hear that I like advertising. Nevertheless! I admire it as a masterful method of communicating, a highly developed human capability for sending messages effectively and efficiently. The effectiveness in is the ability to establish a message clearly in people's minds. Advertising easily excels other communication forms in that way, at least when the advertiser chooses to achieve that goal. The efficiency is in the ability to reach millions of people at a tiny cost per person reached. There is great potential value to society in these characteristics.

I also like many of advertising's uses. I object here only to its deceptiveness. Granted, deceptiveness can occur in any of advertising's uses, and anywhere it occurs I oppose it. However, it occurs largely in only one use, the selling of brands as distinctive versions of a product. Deceptiveness happens often in brand selling simply because brands in many product categories have no natural physical differences. The resulting desire to make up differences is what prompts deceptiveness and is the primary engine that runs it. Because the problem does not occur nearly so much in other uses of advertising, I am left free to admire those other uses generally. They, and the phenomenon of advertising itself, should not be tarred with the same brush.

I observed in the Introduction that falsity affects all phases of our lives, not just advertising. NBC News dramatically confirmed this recently when it rigged a false demonstration of a General Motors truck catching fire when struck by another vehicle. That journalistic event was highly similar to the advertising event arranged by Volvo (chap. 8). And of course falsity also occurs widely beyond the marketplace. While I have no specific recommendations for coping with those other aspects of falsity, I suspect that some of the same factors, such as a strong expectation that a speaker can get away with it, may often apply.

After my previous writings, several defenders of advertising told me I should recognize that falsity is a natural part of our lives. We tell little white lies, for example, about a relative's or friend's necktie or dress or hair style because we don't want to say what we think. This does no harm, they said, and in fact it does quite a bit of good. I'm not sure I agree it does no harm. People might suffer severe embarrassment by going public with a personal style after someone close to them failed to issue the appropriate caution. When we deal with falsity, any falsity, we take chances.

I concede, of course, that it's relatively easier to tolerate false statements when we're sure that people will not use them for making decisions that will seriously affect their welfare. That would mean, though, that even if I tolerated little white lies I would still not be tolerating advertising claims. Such claims do typically have serious impact on people's welfare.

Advertising's defenders will continue to insist that it makes a difference that falsity comes in degrees. If the lesser degrees are often acceptable in life generally, why shouldn't that be so for advertising as well? It's a clever argument from the defenders' view, I must admit. It smoothly justifies what I earlier called the regulators' "split view" of deceptiveness. I used that phrase in chapter 43 to point out that the law recognizes some deceptive claims and not others. Of course, it's the claims of lesser degree, the slippery slope claims, that it doesn't recognize.

It's interesting to note, by the way, that the FTC formulates its tolerance of little falsities somewhat indirectly. It has declared stoutly that deceptiveness "never offers increased efficiency or other countervailing benefits." In other words, when it finds it, it stomps on it. My problem with the commission, then, is not that it coddles any of the falsity it recognizes. My problem is that there's a lot it doesn't recognize.

Isn't such nonrecognition appropriate, the advertisers would say, because it accurately reflects life as we currently live it? I hope my readers will join me in saying no, it's not appropriate. It may be an accurate reflection, but that doesn't make it acceptable. Just because people tolerate falsity in the sense of not complaining loudly about it doesn't mean it's okay. It doesn't even mean necessarily that the public even really thinks it's okay. I've already devoted much space to explaining the damage that's done in the marketplace by tolerating little falsities. Certainly both advertisers and consumers would benefit if they stopped accepting them.

Whether lesser degrees of falsity are acceptable outside the marketplace, in life generally, is a very significant additional question. It reaches, however, well beyond my relatively narrow expertise. Indeed, it involves the mastery of the most broad and weighty topics known to human beings, such as philosophy and religion. In that formidable context, most of us must limit ourselves to whatever narrow personal perspective our meager experience gives us. Mine is that falsity easily reaches a level where it is harmful to us. It is prone to weigh us down, to impede us from achieving the constantly improving society that the human race so badly needs.

I realize I might never be able to shake the argument that some minor types of falsity are okay. Still, I would like to see us reduce our tolerance to far less than what currently exists. I write these words at the time of a new presidential administration, when hopes are raised for new levels of quality in our lives. It is also a time when our society is paying the price of a gradual falling of standards. We are experiencing lower levels of educational and economic achievement, and higher levels of cheating and violence.

It is not the time to defend any level of falsity as tolerable simply because it's accepted. It is not the time to interpret that tolerance as an opportunity to make self-serving claims. It is the time to see a way to serve society by creating a standard of personal and corporate credibility under which all advertisers, regulators, and consumers should want to live.

*REFERENCES*

*INDEX*

# REFERENCES

Most of the analysis in this book is previously unpublished. However, much of the underlying research has been published under my name. In what follows I first list my own publications. Then I cite sources on a chapter-by-chapter basis. In the latter, references to my work are labeled Preston 1, Preston 2, and so on, reflecting the numbers attached in the first list. Some chapters have no references.

Citations to case decisions use shortened forms, such as 95 FTC 406. That means volume 95 of Federal Trade Commission Decisions, beginning at page 406. Other abbreviations used include:

U.S.       United States Supreme Court Reporter
S. Ct.     Supreme Court Reports
F.2d       Federal Reporter, 2d Series
F. Supp.   Federal Supplement

Unless cited otherwise, all factual content of cases discussed is taken entirely from such reports.

## *Preston List*

1. "A Role for Consumer Belief in FTC and Lanham Act Deceptiveness Cases." Co-author Jef I. Richards. *American Business Law Journal,* vol. 31, no. 1, 1993.

2. "The Scandalous Record of Avoidable Errors in Expert Evidence Offered in FTC and Lanham Act Deceptiveness Cases." *Journal of Public Policy and Marketing,* no. 2, 1992.

3. "Proving and Disproving Materiality of Deceptive Advertising Claims." Co-author Jef I. Richards. *Journal of Public Policy and Marketing,* no. 2, 1992.

4. "Relating Research on Deceptiveness Law to Ethics in Advertising," chapter in N. Smith and J. Quelch, eds. *Ethics in Marketing.* Homewood, Ill., Irwin, 1993.

5. "The Definition of Deceptiveness in Advertising and Other Commercial Speech." *Catholic University Law Review,* no. 4, 1990.

6. "False or Deceptive Advertising under the Lanham Act: Analysis of Factual Findings and Types of Evidence." *Trademark Reporter,* July–August 1989.

7. "The FTC's Identification of Implications as Constituting Deceptive Advertising." *University of Cincinnati Law Review,* no. 4, 1989.

8. "Consumer Miscomprehension and Deceptive Advertising: A Response to Professor Craswell." Co-author Jef I. Richards. *Boston University Law Review, Mar.,* no. 2, 1988.

9. "Description and Analysis of FTC Order Provisions Resulting from

References in Advertising to Tests or Surveys." *Pepperdine Law Review,* no. 2, 1987.

10. "Extrinsic Evidence in Federal Trade Commission Deceptiveness Cases." *Columbia Business Law Review,* no. 2, 1987.

11. "Quantitative Research: A Dispute Resolution Process for FTC Advertising Regulation." Co-author Jef I. Richards. *Oklahoma Law Review,* no. 4, 1987.

12. "Data-free at the FTC? How the Federal Trade Commission Decides Whether Extrinsic Evidence of Deceptiveness is Required." *American Business Law Journal,* Fall 1986.

13. "Consumer Miscomprehension as a Challenge to FTC Prosecutions of Deceptive Advertising." Co-author Jef I. Richards. *John Marshall Law Review,* Spring 1986.

14. "Research on Deceptive Advertising: Commentary." Chap. 13 of *Information Processing Research in Advertising.* Richard A. Harris, ed. Hillsdale, N.J.: Erlbaum, 1983.

15. "The Potential Impact of Research on Advertising Law: The Case of Puffery." Co-author Herbert J. Rotfeld. *Journal of Advertising Research,* Apr. 1981.

16. "Enhancing the Flow of Information in the Marketplace: From Caveat Emptor to *Virginia Pharmacy* and Beyond at the Federal Trade Commission." Co-author Dee Pridgen. *Georgia Law Review,* Summer 1980.

17. "The Federal Trade Commission's Use of Evidence to Determine Deception." Co-author Michael T. Brandt. *Journal of Marketing,* Jan. 1977.

18. *The Great America Blow-Up: Puffery in Advertising and Selling.* Madison: University of Wisconsin Press, 1975.

19. "Advertising: More Than Meets the Eye?" Co-author Steven E. Scharbach. *Journal of Advertising Research,* Jun. 1971.

20. "Logic and Illogic in the Advertising Process." *Journalism Quarterly,* Summer 1967.

## References by Chapters

**Chapter 1**—For the general procedures of advertising regulation, see these sources: Ross Petty, *The Impact of Advertising Law on Business and Public Policy* Westport, Ct.: Quorum Books (1992); Martha Rogers, "Advertising Self-Regulation in the 1980s: A Review," *Current Issues and Research in Advertising 1990* 13 (1991); Jef I. Richards, *Deceptive Advertising: Behavioral Study of a Legal Concept* (Hillsdale, N.J.: Erlbaum, 1990); Preston 1, 5, 6, 18 (chap. 9).

For statements by FTC commissioners: James Miller, *Policy Statement on Deception,* letter of Oct. 14, 1983, reprinted in the case of Cliffdale, 103 FTC 110, at 174 (1984); Patricia Bailey and Michael Pertschuk, *Analysis of the Law of Deception,* letter of Feb. 28, 1984, reprinted in *Antitrust and Trade Regulation Reporter* 46, no. 1154 (1984).

See also these reference works that are updated regularly: *Trade Regula-*

*tion Reporter; Antitrust and Trade Regulation Reporter;* Council of Better Business Bureaus, *Do's and Don't's in Advertising Copy;* Kenneth Plevan and Miriam Siroky, *Advertising Compliance Handbook* (New York: Practicing Law Institute); George E. Rosden and Peter E. Rosden, *The Law of Advertising,* 3 vol. (New York: Matthew Bender); Stephanie W. Kanwit, *Federal Trade Commission,* 2 vol. (Colorado Springs: Shepard's); Dee Pridgen, *Consumer Protection and the Law* (New York: Clark Boardman).

*Advertising Law Anthology* (Arlington: International Library) is a series of annual volumes published since 1974 that reprints most law review articles about advertising.

For the issue of whether the regulators do, or should, consider whether ad claims are believed rather than just conveyed: Preston 1.

**Chapter 2**—Preston 18 (chap. 10), also references listed above for chapter 1. Encyclopedia decision by Justice Black: *FTC v. Standard Education Society,* 302 U.S. 112, 116 (1937), 58 S. Ct. 113 (1937). Clairol case: *Gelb,* 33 FTC 1450 (1941), affirmed by appellate court, *Gelb v. FTC,* 144 F.2d 580 (1944).

**Chapter 3**—Sears, Roebuck, 95 FTC 406 (1980).

**Chapter 4**—For general background: Paul LaRue, "FTC Expertise: A Legend Examined," *Antitrust Bulletin,* Spring 1971. The senator from 1914, Senator Newlands, was quoted by LaRue from 51 Congressional Record 11083 (1914). For statement by the "law-trained" commissioner: Robert Pitofsky, "Beyond Nader: Consumer Protection and the Regulation of Advertising," 90 Harvard Law Review 661, at 678 (1977). For background on implications: Preston 7.

**Chapter 5**—The beer ad was for Miller Genuine Draft, on network programming in 1990. The computer ad: Commodore Business Machines, 105 FTC 230 (1985). Bacon's story is quoted from Norman Munn, *Psychology,* 4th ed. (Boston: Houghton Mifflin, 1961). The Supreme Court case was *FTC v. Colgate:* see references for chapter 8. For summary of cases allowing FTC to look at nothing but the ad, and its realization of the problems with that: Preston 12.

**Chapter 6**—*Thompson Medical Co.,* 104 FTC 648, 835 (1984), affirmed by appellate court, *Thompson Medical Co. v. FTC,* 791 F.2d 189 (1986). Data on Thompson's spending for various brands come from a summary of 1991 data, "100 Leading National Advertisers," *Advertising Age,* Sep. 23, 1992. A summary of 1992 data, same title, *Advertising Age,* Sep. 29, 1993, shows Slim-Fast Foods listed separately as 94th largest and Thompson no longer in the top one hundred.

**Chapter 7**—For the "commission's exact rule": *Thompson Medical Company,* 104 FTC at 789. See also statement by Miller, cited above for chapter 1. The Lanham Act rule was stated in *American Brands v. R. J. Reynolds,* 413 F. Supp. 1352, 1356–57 (1976). See also Preston 6 (pp. 526–28), 12. For FTC's increased use of survey evidence: Preston 17. Statement quoted from the Anacin case was made in the appellate decision: *American Home Products v. FTC,* 695 F.2d 681, 689 (including footnote 13) (1982). The *Consumer Reports*

item was in its regular feature "Selling It," but unfortunately I cannot re-
trieve the issue and date. The Efficin case: *Adria Laboratories*, 103 FTC 512
(1984).

**Chapter 8**—*Advertising Age* headline and story, including Dan White's observations: Nov. 12, 1990, 1. FTC's 1991 orders against Volvo and its ad agency,
Scali, McCabe, Sloves, will eventually be published in FTC Decisions and
are available now in unpublished form from the Public Reference Branch,
FTC, Washington, DC 20580.

The Colgate case: 59 FTC 1452 (1961), sent back for modification, *Colgate
v. FTC*, 310 F.2d 89 (1962), modified by FTC, 62 FTC 1269 (1963), sent back
again, *Colgate v. FTC*, 326 F.2d 517 (1963), modification affirmed, *FTC v.
Colgate*, 380 U.S. 374, 85 S. Ct. 1035 (1965).

Other cases: *Campbell Soup*, 77 FTC 664 (1970). *Libbey-Owens-Ford*, 63
FTC 746 (1963), affirmed on appeal, 352 F.2d 415 (1965). *Carter Products*, 60
FTC 782 (1962), modified on appeal, 323 F.2d 523 (1963), modified, 63 FTC
1651 (1963). *Borden*, 78 FTC 686 (1971). *Mattel*, 79 FTC 667 (1971), modified,
104 FTC 555 (1984). *Topper*, 79 FTC 681 (1971). *Rhodes Pharmacal*, 78 FTC 680
(1971). Alcoa Wrap case: *Aluminum Company of America*, 58 FTC 265 (1961).

**Chapter 9**—Preston 6, 7. Baggies case: *Colgate*, 77 FTC 150 (1970).

**Chapter 10**—Preston 6, 7. Baggies case: see references for chapter 9. The FTC
activity that leads to more than just stopping the claim comes under its
§13(b) authority; see Robert D. Paul, "The FTC's Increased Reliance on Section 13(b) in Court Litigation," *Antitrust Law Journal* 57 (1988): 141. Black
Flag case: *American Home Products*, 81 FTC 579 (1972). Sunoco case: *Sun Oil*,
84 FTC 247 (1974); see more details in chapter 31. Ford case: *Ford Motor*, 84
FTC 729 (1974), affirmed on appeal, 547 F.2d 954 (1976). Chevron case: *Standard Oil of California*, 84 FTC 1401 (1974), modified on appeal, *Standard Oil v.
FTC* 577 F.2d 653 (1978), modified, 95 FTC 866 (1980); see more details in
chapter 12.

**Chapter 11**—All cases discussed here are cited in Preston 6, 7: refer to section
headings naming the various types of implications. There are also more re-
cent cases; for example, weight control advertisers charged with false En-
dorsement Implications in the 1990s include Michael S. Levey and Positive
Response Marketing, National Media Corp. and Media Arts International,
Synchronal Corp., Fleetwood Manufacturing, Spanish Telemarketing, and
Slender You. These cases will eventually be published in FTC Decisions.
They are available now in unpublished form from the Public Reference
Branch, FTC, Washington, DC 20580.

**Chapter 12**—FTC's 1991 order against Kraft Foods will eventually be published
in FTC Decisions. It is available now in unpublished form from the Public
Reference Branch, FTC, Washington, DC 20580. Affirmed on appeal, *Kraft
v. FTC*, 970 F.2d 311 (1992). For materiality: Preston 3, 5. For Chevron case
see references for chapter 10.

**Chapter 14**—*Virginia State Board of Pharmacy v. Virginia Citizens' Consumers Council*, 425 U.S. 748, 96 S. Ct. 1817 (1976). *Bates and O'Steen v. Arizona*, 433 U.S.
350, 97 S. Ct. 2691 (1977).

**Chapter 15**—For rule on deceptiveness of omissions, see *International Harvester,* 104 FTC 949, at 1056–58 (1984). *Firestone Tire,* 81 FTC 398 (1972), affirmed on appeal, 481 F.2d 246 (1973). Advertising man cited: Peter Geer, "Those Fourteen Words," pamphlet published by American Association of Advertising Agencies (1970).

**Chapter 16**—*Kroger,* 98 FTC 639 (1981), modified, 100 FTC 573 (1982).

**Chapter 19**—FTC's orders involving Money Money Money, Inc., and Wayne Phillips, 1990, TV Inc. (Vince Inneo program), 1990, C C Pollen Company (also Inneo), 1992, and Twin Star Productions, 1990, will eventually be published in FTC Decisions. They are available now in unpublished form from the Public Reference Branch, FTC, Washington, DC 20580. BluBlockers case ("Consumer Challenge"): *JS&A Group,* 111 FTC 522 (1989).

**Chapter 23**—Readers should consult library listings for numerous books on applying psychological and social motivations in advertising. For articles, see the various indexes in the social sciences. Some of the most useful research publications include *Journal of Advertising, Journal of Advertising Research, Journal of Marketing, Journal of Marketing Research, Journal of Consumer Research, Journal of Consumer Affairs,* and *Journal of Public Policy and Marketing.* For article in *The New Yorker:* Bill McKibben, "Reflections (Television)," Mar. 9, 1992, 40.

**Chapter 24**—The PowerMaster story ("A PowerMistake . . . ," *Advertising Age,* Dec. 23/30, 1991, 12) reported the magazine's annual picks for Product of the Year and said PowerMaster was the only such product never to have been actually placed on the market. For Abrams and Neuborne quotes: "Panel Delves into Ad Ethics," *Advertising Age,* Oct. 19, 1992, 53. For "Cool Colt": "Critics Shoot at New Colt 45 Campaign," *Wall Street Journal,* Feb. 17, 1993, B1. For "Run 'N Gun": "Run 'N Gun, a New Converse Sneaker, Kicks Up Fears it May Promote Violence," *Wall Street Journal,* Feb. 8, 1993, B7.

**Chapter 25**—FTC cases: Anacin, *American Home Products,* 98 FTC 136 (1981), modified on appeal, 695 F.2d 681 (1982), modified, 101 FTC 698 (1983), modified, 103 FTC 57 (1984), modified, 103 FTC 528 (1984); Bufferin, Excedrin, *Bristol-Myers,* 102 FTC 21 (1983), affirmed on appeal, 738 F.2d 554 (1984); Bayer, Cope, Midol, *Sterling Drug,* 102 FTC 395 (1983), affirmed on appeal, 741 F.2d 1146 (1984).

Lanham Act cases: Anacin, Tylenol, *American Home Products v. Johnson & Johnson,* 436 F. Supp. 785 (1977), affirmed on appeal, 577 F.2d 160 (1978); Maximum Strength Anacin, *McNeilab v. American Home Products,* 501 F. Supp. 517 (1980); Advil, Motrin, *Upjohn v. American Home Products,* 598 F. Supp. 550 (1984); Tylenol, Anacin-3, *American Home Products v. Johnson & Johnson,* 654 F. Supp. 568, 586 (1987); Tylenol, Advil, *McNeilab v. American Home Products,* 675 F. Supp. 819 (1987), affirmed on appeal, 848 F.2d 34 (1988).

For an overall look at headache remedy advertising: Charles Mann and Mark Plummer, *The Aspirin Wars: Money, Medicine, and 100 Years of Rampant Competition* (New York: Knopf, 1991).

**Chapter 26**—For case from 1602: *Harvey v. Young,* 80 English Reports 15. Next

English case: *Baily v. Merrell,* 79 English Reports 331, 81 English Reports 81 (1615). English case stating the exception for buyers who could not check for themselves: *Vernon v. Keys,* 104 English Reports 246 (1810). *Brown v. Castles,* 11 Cush. (Mass.) 348 (1853). For more detail on these and other early puffery cases, see Preston 18 (chap. 7).

**Chapter 27**—For cases and background: Preston 18 (chap. 11), Preston 7 (sec. XX). Bayer case: *Sterling Drug,* 102 FTC 395, 752 (1983).

**Chapter 28**—For evidence that consumers treat puffery as meaningful, i.e., they do not always distrust it: Preston 15. On cellular phones: "Phones to Go," *Consumer Reports,* Jan. 1993, p. 9.

**Chapter 30**—For the ways that people perceive advertising differently from other types of messages: Preston 19, 20. Samuel Johnson is quoted from *The Idler* (London: Harrison, 1787).

**Chapter 31**—Sunoco case: *Sun Oil,* 84 FTC 247 (1974).

**Chapter 32**—For details on advertising's selling heritage, the caveat emptor rule: Preston 18. For industry self-regulation: M. Rogers, "Adv. Self-regulation in the 1980s: A Review," *Current Issues and Research in Advertising* (1991); Jean Boddewyn, "Adv. Self-Regulation: True Purpose and Limits," *Journal of Advertising,* no. 2 (1989); G. Miracle and T. Nevett, *Voluntary Regulation of Advertising: A Comparative Analysis of the United Kingdom and the United States* (Lexington: University of Kentucky Press, 1987).

**Chapter 33**—*Sears, Roebuck v. FTC,* 258 F.307 (1919). For later cases contesting implications: Preston 7. For Four A's research: Jacob Jacoby, Wayne D. Hoyer, and David A. Sheluga, *Miscomprehension of Televised Communication* (New York: American Association of Advertising Agencies, 1980); Jacob Jacoby and Wayne D. Hoyer, *The Comprehension/Miscomprehension of Print Communication* (Hillsdale, N.J.: Erlbaum, 1987). Later work by the same authors suggests that the proper miscomprehension level may be lower than 30 percent: Jacoby & Hoyer, "The Miscomprehension of Mass-Media Advertising Claims," *Journal of Advertising Research,* Jun.–Jul. 1990, 9. See also comments on miscomprehension in Preston 8, 13, 14. Anacin case: *American Home Products,* see references to chapter 25.

**Chapter 34**—1942 case: *Valentine v. Chrestenson,* 316 U.S. 52. 1970s cases: abortion, *Bigelow v. Virginia,* 421 U.S. 809 (1975); drug prices, *Virginia State Board of Pharmacy v. Virginia Citizens' Consumers Council,* 425 U.S. 748, 96 S. Ct. 1817 (1976); lawyer ads, *Bates and Van O'Steen v. Arizona,* 433 U.S. 350, 97 S. Ct. 2691 (1977). Cases stating rule for regulation of commercial speech: *Central Hudson Gas & Electric v. Public Service Commission of New York,* 447 U.S. 530 (1980); *Board of Trustees of SUNY v. Fox,* 109 S. Ct. 3028 (1989). Cases differentiating commercial from noncommercial speech: *Bolder v. Youngs Drug Products,* 463 U.S. 60 (1983); *R. J. Reynolds,* 111 FTC 539 (1988). For story of FTC's efforts, parallel to those of the Supreme Court, to create increased levels of information in advertising: Preston 16.

**Chapter 35**—*Virginia Pharmacy:* see references for chaps. 14, 34. Zechariah Chafee, *Free Speech in the United States* (Cambridge: Harvard University

Press, 1946). Argument by two lawyers: Richard Schmidt and Robert Burns, "Proof or Consequences: False Advertising and the Doctrine of Commercial Speech," *University of Cincinnati Law Rev.* 56 (1988): 1273.

**Chapter 36**—Merit case against Triumph: *Philip Morris v. Loew's Theaters* (Lorillard), 511 F. Supp. 855 (1980). Other brands against Triumph: *R. J. Reynolds v. Loew's Theaters,* 511 F. Supp. 867 (1980). Shampoo case: *Vidal Sassoon v. Bristol-Myers,* 661 F.2d 272 (1981). FTC quote on surveys: Litton, 97 FTC 1 (1981).

**Chapter 37**—Interpreting brands as monopolies: Edward Chamberlin, *The Theory of Monopolistic Competition* (Cambridge: Harvard University Press, 1962). The columnist: Bob Garfield, "Ad Review," *Advertising Age,* Sep. 21, 1992, 48. Advertisers as courtiers: Ian Lewis, "In the Courts of Power," a chapter in Peter Berger, ed., *The Human Shape of Work* (New York: Macmillan, 1964).

**Chapter 38**—On Ralph Nader's singlemindedness, see Charles McCarry, *Citizen Nader,* (New York: Signet, 1972). The Finland story is from the McKibben article (see references for chap. 23). For discussions of what ads might say about brands, look for library listings under "advertising."

**Chapter 39**—*R. J. Reynolds,* 111 FTC 539 (1988). The later consent order, in 1989, will eventually be published in FTC Decisions. It is available now in unpublished form from the Public Reference Branch, FTC, Washington, DC 20580.

**Chapter 40**—My dictionary: *The Random House Dictionary of the English Language,* unabridged, 2d ed., 1987. DDB Needham's Life Style Study: Winski, "Who We Are, How We Live, What We Think," *Advertising Age,* Jan. 20, 1992, 16. Other surveys: Survey conducted by Media Opinion Research, Minneapolis, for American Society of Newspaper Editors, 1985; survey conducted by Opinion Research Corp., reported in "Ad Credibility Gap Growing, Study Says," *Milwaukee Sentinel,* Feb. 27, 1990, D4. Article by economist: John Calfee, "Here We Go Again; Ads under Fire," *Advertising Age,* Mar. 15, 1993, 24.

**Chapter 41**—PowerMaster: see references for chapter 24. Old Joe Camel: "Poll Shows Camel Ads Are Effective with Kids," *Advertising Age,* Apr. 27, 1992, 12. An excellent example of journalism criticism is the "Darts and Laurels" column appearing regularly in *Columbia Journalism Review.* ANA panel on ethics: "Panel Delves into Ad Ethics," *Advertising Age,* Oct. 19, 1992, 53.

**Chapter 42**—Listerine case: Warner-Lambert, 86 FTC 1398 (1975), modified on appeal, 562 F.2d 749 (1977), modified, 92 FTC 191 (1978). Microwave oven case: Litton Industries, 97 FTC 1 (1981), modified on appeal, 676 F.2d 364 (1982), modified, 100 FTC 457 (1982). FTC's orders involving Mobil, 1992, and General Electric, 1993, will eventually be published in FTC Decisions. They are available now in unpublished form from the Public Reference Branch, FTC, Washington, DC 20580. For details on additional deceptiveness cases, and on the "two levels of falsity" and many instances of them: Preston 2; see also Preston 4, 6, 9, 10, 11.

**Chapter 43**—Activities of advertising's national organizations can be tracked in the trade press, particularly *Advertising Age*. The principal organizations are the American Advertising Federation, American Association of Advertising Agencies, and Association of National Advertisers.

**Chapter 44**—The Supreme Court statement was by Justice Black in the encyclopedia case: see references for chapter 2. The English judge's statement was in *Vernon v. Keys*, 104 *English Reports* 246 (1810); see also references for chapter 26. The "contemporary legal expression" is from sec. 539, *Restatement of Torts (Second)*. "Another contemporary legal rule" is from the same source's sec. 542; it is paraphrased to simplify reading. The wrestling coach's case: *Milkovich v. Lorain Journal* 110 S. Ct. 2695 (1991).

**Chapter 45**—See reference to "adverse interest" in the text of chapter 44.

**Chapter 46**—For FTC's reasonable basis requirement, see statements by Miller and by Bailey and Pertschuk, cited in references to chapter 1; see also FTC Policy Statement Regarding Advertising Substantiation, 48 *Federal Register* 10471 (1983), reprinted in *Thompson Medical*, 104 FTC 648, at 839 (1984). For the Reasonable Basis Implication: Preston 7. For materiality: see same statements by Miller and by Bailey and Pertschuk, also Preston 3, 5. Materiality is also discussed in chapter 12. "America's finest" was Andeker beer, years ago.

**Chapter 48**—Bayer claim: *Sterling Drug*, 102 FTC 395, at 752 (1983). For "sexiest European": *Bristol-Myers*, 102 FTC 21, at 321 (1982).

**Chapter 50**—Reagan cited his convention statement to Abraham Lincoln, one of several statements often attributed incorrectly to Lincoln although actually written by William J. H. Boetcker: see Martin D. Tullai, "More Memorable Words of Wisdom Lincoln Never Said," for the *Baltimore Sun*, as located on Nexus in *Minneapolis Star-Tribune*, Aug. 30, 1992, 23A.

**Chapter 51**—For Jack Daniel's advertising: "Jack Daniel's Pours to Loyal Fans," *USA Today*, Aug. 5, 1992, 5B. Machiavelli quote is from *The Prince XVIII*. Montaigne quote is from *Essays II*. For Sears's auto repair case: Gregory Patterson, "Sears Will Pay $15 Million, Settling Cases," *Wall Street Journal*, Sep. 3, 1992, A4.

**Chapter 52**—For NBC News's false demonstration: "How GM One-upped an Embarrassed NBC on Staged News Event," *Wall Street Journal*, Feb. 11, 1993, A1. For FTC position on deceptiveness: International Harvester, 104 FTC 949, 1056 (1984).

# INDEX

A. B. Dick Company, 56
Abrams, Floyd, 93
Adria Laboratories, 32
Adverse interest, 180, 183–85
Advertisers: disrespect of, for law,
41; proposed obligations for, 119,
165–68; unaware of certain problems, 127–31; positions on ethics
and law of, compared, 127–31;
hopes of, to minimize deceptiveness, 131, 138–41; First Amendment rights of, 135–41, 165–68;
need of, to avoid competition,
149–54; not needing slippery
slope, 153–57; lacking privilege to
avoid competition, 155; subject to
charges of bullshit, 160–65; insincerity of, 163, 166, 171, 187, 195;
and credibility problems, 164–68,
171; contrasted with journalists,
167; vulnerability of, to criticism,
167–68; perceived social role of,
175; relationship of, to national organizations, 175–76; non-
professional status of, 176. *See also*
Self-regulation in ad industry
*Advertising Age,* 33, 151, 169, 203
Advertising Expectations Implication, 118, 162
Advertising law: procedural elements of, for stopping deceptiveness, 9–16; examples of inability
of, to stop deceptiveness, 64, 73,
94, 114–20, 168–72; compared to
advertising ethics, 127–31; coverage of deceptiveness, possibility
for expanding, 176–79, 185–88;
split view of, on deceptiveness,
176–79, 208; prevents deceptiveness but not harm, 188. *See also*
Reliance on sellers
Advil claim, 98

*Areopagitica,* 138
Alcoa wrap case, 36
American Association of Advertising
Agencies' miscomprehension
study, 132–35
American Gas Association, 61–62
American Home Products, 32, 97–
99, 134
Anacin cases, 32, 43, 94–100, 134
Aspercreme case, 22–27, 32–33, 43,
95, 99, 133
Association of National Advertisers,
168

Bacon, Francis, 22, 110, 122
Baggies case, 38–40
*Bates v. Arizona,* 60, 136
Bayer cases, 94–100, 107, 194
Beer (floating bottle) ad, 20–21
Belief, of slippery slope claims by
consumers. *See* Distrust; Trust
Belief of claims, 10–12
Beneficial loan case, 44
Best Claim Assumption, 151–52. *See
also* Branding, Advertisers' need for
Better Business Bureaus, Council of,
National Advertising Division, as
regulator. See Self-regulation in ad
industry
Black, Hugo, Justice, 15
Black Flag ad, 41
Blackmun, Justice, 139, 140
Blublockers sunglasses case, 75–76
Body on Tap shampoo case, 144
Borden, 34
Brand Fact Implication, 115–16, 118,
185, 190, 191, 193
Branding: advertisers' need for, 55–
59, 81, 149–53; advertisers' lack of
need for, 154–57; consumers' lack
of need for, 57, 79; as cause of fal-
sity, 58–60, 151–52, 207